LITERARY
NORTH CAROLINA

A Historical Survey, Revised and Enlarged

by

Richard Walser

assisted by E. T. Malone, Jr.

Raleigh

Division of Archives and History
North Carolina Department of Cultural Resources

1986

DEPARTMENT OF CULTURAL RESOURCES
Patric Dorsey
Secretary

DIVISION OF ARCHIVES AND HISTORY
William S. Price, Jr.
Director
Suellen Hoy
Assistant Director

NORTH CAROLINA HISTORICAL COMMISSION
Dan G. Moody
Chairman
T. Harry Gatton
Vice-Chairman

Jerrold L. Brooks
Betty L. Burton
Mrs. Frank A. Daniels, Jr.

C. W. Everett, Jr.
Mary Faye Brumby Hull
H. G. Jones
Gertrude S. Carraway
Honorary

Percy E. Murray
William S. Powell
Lala Carr Steelman

To the Memory of
Zeb Vance Walser
(1863-1940)

Contents

Illustrations

Foreword

In 1970 the Historical Publications Section of the then State Department of Archives and History issued Richard Walser's *Literary North Carolina*. The book was the first study to survey all of North Carolina's literature and literary figures from the earliest explorers to the present day. Over the years the book has become a staple in history and English courses devoted to the study of North Carolina. This revised and enlarged edition updates the first publication by incorporating new scholarship, by detailing the rise to national prominence of numerous Tar Heel writers in the 1970s and 1980s, and by including new chapters and appendixes.

The first edition was completely revised through the joint efforts of Mr. Walser, professor emeritus of English at North Carolina State University, and E. T. Malone, Jr., of the staff of the Historical Publications Section. Mr. Malone made a complete revision of the chapter entitled "Contemporary Poets," wrote the new chapter entitled "Publishers of Books and Periodicals," prepared the appendixes and index, and drew six illustrations. Mr. Walser has added a new chapter on science fiction and mysteries.

For suggestions, information, and obscure materials, the authors wish to thank Alice Cotten, Russ Garwood, Joe Haas, Bob Hersh, Damon D. Hickey, Jeffrey T. Hicks, Thomas McGowan, Walter E. Myers, Benjie Nau, Kep Parrish, and Gene Warren. The Historical Publications Section acknowledges with appreciation the assistance of the North Carolina Collection, University of North Carolina Library, Chapel Hill, in providing various illustrations. Robert M. Topkins edited the manuscript and saw it through press; Stephena K. Williams prepared the manuscript for typesetting on a microcomputer; and Lisa D. Bailey assisted with the proofreading.

Jeffrey J. Crow
Historical Publications Administrator

June, 1986

I

THE EXPLORERS

In a broad sense, literature comprises all writing about everything, even the school compositions that a student carefully composes for his teacher to read. In a narrow sense, literature is made up of only those productions that outlive the occasions and times for which they were written.

If these premises are accepted, last month's newspapers, which are not apt ever to receive any further attention except by scholars bent on research, are not strictly literature. But the letters, reports, and books of explorers and historians who wrote centuries ago are literature most certainly. They are still being read today. So are hundreds of later works of history, biography, travel, humor, and especially books of drama, fiction, and poetry. The last three types, even more than the publications of the early explorers or, for instance, of the more recent biographers, will be discussed in the following chapters devoted to the most enduring, most remembered, and most typical, though not always necessarily the best, literary efforts about North Carolina or by North Carolinians.

It was the explorers who were first upon the scene; and thus the history of literature in North Carolina began in 1524—only thirty-two years after Columbus's first voyage—when the Italian sea captain Giovanni da Verrazzano sent his employer, King Francis I of France, a letter about a coastline where his sailors had gone ashore. Verrazzano's document, like other accounts written in an age when men's imaginations were lively and when hearsay was recorded as fact,

is as zestful as a modern adventure story. European travelers had keen ears for the music of the land and keen eyes to note the unusual and amazing. For a couple of centuries after Verrazzano, Europeans who came to this realm, afterward called North Carolina, wrote home to France and Spain and England about all those things they believed the folks back there would like to know.

Giovanni da Verrazzano

Verrazzano was searching for a northwest passage when, in the spring of 1524, he made a landing in the Cape Fear vicinity and met with friendly natives. The country, he wrote, had a "good and wholesome air, temperate, between hot and cold; no vehement winds do blow in those regions." On up the coast, probably near Cape Lookout, one of his crew was dashed upon the beach while trying to swim ashore after falling from his boat. Indians rescued the semiconscious fellow, built a fire, and took off his clothes to dry them out. It is no wonder the astonished man thought he was about to be roasted for an Indian luncheon. But soon he recovered and was allowed to return to his boat. A third trip ashore was made in the vicinity of Currituck, where a little native boy was kidnapped for transportation to France. Verrazzano was pleased with what he observed, especially with the grapevines so like those in his native Italy. "We found also roses, violets, lilies, and many sorts of herbs, and sweet and odiferous flowers different from ours," he reported. This first European visitor was indeed most complimentary to the coastal country of future North Carolina. He then sailed north to discover New York harbor.

Experiences of the second explorer were not so happy as those of the first. In July, 1526, a Spaniard named Lucas Vásquez de Ayllón, with a commission as captain general and governor of Terra Firma, set out with five hundred men and "eighty or ninety very good horses" to populate the mainland. Ayllón's large flagship and three smaller vessels were accompanied by a brigantine and a small *gabarra*, or tender. His men, most of whom had lived in the West Indies, were "well fitted out with supplies and things that seemed necessary for the journey." Ayllón's expedition was the first to arrive on North Carolina soil with the purpose of establishing a colony, but it was haunted by ill fortune from the beginning. At the entrance of the Rio Jordan (presumably the Cape Fear River) the flagship sank with all its supplies. Next, in a desperate escape from the hated Spanish, the native guides and interpreters fled inland. An exciting but confused account of all this was told to the historian Gonzalo Fernández de Oviedo, alias y Valdés, by eyewitnesses Friar Antonio Montesino and others. Oviedo's book relates that the colonists were "unhappy with the land" and stayed only a few

Ayllón's landing

days before sailing westward to the Gualdape River (probably at present-day Georgetown, South Carolina). The *Historia* continues with Ayllón's death, a subsequent mutiny, and the eventual failure of the expedition.

Hernando de Soto's gold-seeking trek through the mountains of North Carolina in 1540 was reported by several historians, one of whom was Garcilaso de la Vega, noted as the first writer to be born in the Western Hemisphere. Garcilaso, an Inca from Peru, got his information from two men in the de Soto expedition, one of whom was an anonymous member of the campaign known simply as the Gentleman of Elvas. At Guaxule (in the western tip of the state) an Indian chieftain, "accompanied by five hundred noblemen," met the Spaniards. The natives, "adorned with large feather headdresses and rich robes of different skins," welcomed de Soto "with very courteous words, spoken with the most lordly semblance," then escorted him to their town of three hundred dwellings. The king's house "was situated on a high hill and was surrounded by a walk that six men could pass along abreast." After four days, de Soto's party moved toward the west. It had found no gold.

Another Spanish explorer, Captain Juan Pardo, wrote a brief account of a trek in 1566 from Florida into the Appalachian

Oviedo, *Historia General* (Madrid, 1853)

foothills (of North Carolina), his object being not to find gold but to spread among the natives the Catholic faith and the sovereignty of the Spanish monarch. For fifteen days he remained at the village of the sachem Juado, where "a large number of Indians and chiefs . . . were brought under the power of His Holiness and His Majesty." There Pardo built a fort, leaving Sergeant Boyano "and some soldiers, with their provisions of gunpowder, rope, bullets, and corn to eat." Pardo later retrieved his men at the garrison and returned to Florida.

The most impressive documents of sixteenth-century North Carolina literature were written by Sir Walter Raleigh's adventurers at Roanoke Island. In 1584 Captain Arthur Barlowe, after reporting on the flora and the fauna and describing in some detail his encounter with the natives, wrote, in the language of England at the time of Elizabeth I, "The soile is the most plentifull, sweete, fruitfull, and wholsome of all the world." Concerning the colonists who arrived the following year is Governor Ralph Lane's long discourse, which again commends the site but explains why the colony failed and why the men returned to England in 1586 aboard the ships of the famous privateer Sir Francis Drake. For the little known about the "Lost Colony" of 1587, there is Governor John White's narrative, which tells, among other matters, of the baptizing of the friendly Indian Manteo and the birth of Virginia Dare. The 1590 report of White's search for the English settlers is also part of the series.

The most valuable production, however, at least from a literary point of view, is Thomas Hariot's *A briefe and true report of the new found land of Virginia* (London, 1588), the first book about the New World written in English by one who had lived there. Hariot, who had been a member of Sir Walter's household and had tutored his master in "the mathematical sciences," was twenty-five when he arrived with the Lane colony of 1585. Among other responsibilities, it was his duty to study the Indians and make a survey of the natural resources of the region. Hariot's report, published two years after his return to England, is divided into three sections: the "merchantable commodities," or those products which could be sold profitably in England; the commodities that would provide "victuall and sustenance of mans life" in the New World; and "the nature and manners of the people" (that is, the Indians). Hariot's little book, of which only six copies are extant, is a delectable treatise. Not unlike later reports by adventurers written to their sponsors back in Europe, it set the pattern for the "promotional" literature of the next two centuries. The Roanoke Island area is highly praised, of course, but it is Hariot's scientific precision, phrased in the graceful style of Elizabethan English, that makes it superior to other accounts.

Trinity College, Oxford, England

Thomas Hariot

Perhaps Hariot's most famous passage concerns an herb "called by the inhabitants vppówac," but even then generally known as tobacco. The natives believed, he wrote, that it had curative powers, that "it purgeth superfluous fleame & other grosse humors, openeth all the pores & passages of the body . . .

wherby their bodies are notably per-
serued in health." At other times, "being
in a storme vppon the waters, to pacifie
their gods," the natives "cast some vp
into the aire and into the water." The
colonists, too, "vsed to suck it after their
maner, as also since our returne, & haue
found manie rare and wonderfull experiments of the vertues thereof."

Except for occasional explorers like
John Pory, who wrote about the Chowan
River region after visiting it in 1622, few
travelers had much to say about North
Carolina for almost a century. *The Dis-
coveries of John Lederer . . . To the West
of Carolina* (1672), written by a German
and translated from Latin, has puzzled
many geographers. Lederer mentions a
large lake in the west (near present-day
Charlotte) and a "barren Sandy desert"
toward the east. In any case, Lederer
thought the Indian women "handsome"
and remarked on the hardiness of the
men, one of whom, "strangely infatuated
with illusions of the devil," could "stand
bare-foot upon burning coals for near an
hour, and then recovering his senses, leap
out of the fire without hurt, or signe of
any."

The high-water mark of exploration
literature, not only in North Carolina but
in all America as well, is *A New Voyage
to Carolina* (1709), a sprightly and charming book by adventurer and surveyor
John Lawson. Often erroneously titled
History of North Carolina, it is not a history at all, but a survey, written in the
Thomas Hariot vein, describing the flora
and fauna of the area, relating the customs and manners of the Indians, and, in
Lawson's case, narrating a journey he
made across the colony in 1701. Lawson,
a Londoner, had a sense of humor that
enlivens almost every page he wrote and
makes his book a delight to read. Like the
work of Hariot and others, the *Voyage*
was frankly intended to encourage more
financial support for the colony and to
attract settlers to it.

"The Inhabitants of *Carolina*," he
assured his readers, "thro' the Richness of
the Soil, live an easy and pleasant Life."

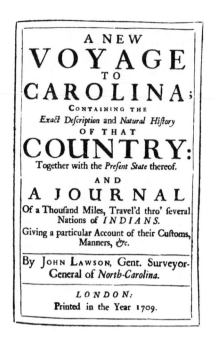

A NEW
VOYAGE
TO
CAROLINA;
CONTAINING THE
Exact Description and *Natural History*
OF THAT
COUNTRY:
Together with the *Present State* thereof.
AND
A JOURNAL
Of a Thousand Miles, Travel'd thro' several
Nations of *INDIANS*.
Giving a particular Account of their Customs,
Manners, &c.

By JOHN LAWSON, Gent. Surveyor-
General of *North-Carolina*.

LONDON:
Printed in the Year 1709.

There is "Plenty of Fish, Wild-Fowl,
Venison, and the other Conveniencies
which this Summer-Country naturally
furnishes" to induce "a great many Families to leave the more Northerly Plantations, and sit down under one of the
mildest Governments in the World."
Those born there "are a straight, clean-
limb'd People" whose girls "marry very
young; some at Thirteen or Fourteen;
and She that stays till Twenty, is reckon'd
a stale Maid. . . . The Women are very
fruitful; most Houses being full of Little
Ones. It has been observ'd, that Women
long marry'd, and without Children, in
other Places, have remov'd to *Carolina*,
and become joyful Mothers." Almost
never, even in passages treating personal
or unpleasant subjects, is Lawson without wit. "The *Indian* Children are much
addicted to eat Dirt," he wrote, "and so
are some of the Christians. But roast a Bat
on a Skewer, then pull the Skin off, and
make the Child that eats Dirt, eat the
roasted Rearmouse [bat]; and he will
never eat Dirt again. This is held as an
infallible Remedy." One imagines that it
most certainly would be.

Among later visitors was that sophisticated wag, William Byrd of Virginia,

whose *History of the Dividing Line* has some acid comments about his forays into North Carolina in 1728 when he served as one of the commissioners to oversee the surveying of the boundary between the two colonies. Byrd writes of the "Indolent Wretches" of "Lubberland" (his term for North Carolina), who "devour so much Swine's flesh, that it fills them full of gross Humours." Byrd's uncomplimentary remarks were later offset by some glowing pages in his *A Journey to the Land of Eden* (1783), about his holdings in present-day Rockingham County.

II

LITERARY FIRSTS

In early North Carolina, the writing of books was almost wholly confined to works by travelers and explorers. Only such books and imported volumes serving some practical, everyday purpose were thought to be of any value. When a small public library was established about 1700 by the Reverend Thomas Bray for St. Thomas Parish (with Bath the eventual site), the 176 books brought from England were, as would be expected, mostly about religion. Only one volume of this set has survived, Gabriel Towerson's *Explication to the Catechism*, published in London in 1685. Though the hardworking colonist generally owned only one book, the Bible, the prosperous planter might have on his shelf a modest collection of poetry and drama.

To name a particular literary product as a "first" is hazardous—for new evidence is always a possibility—but it is interesting, even so, to investigate the record as presently documented.

Poetry made a humble start in 1698 when Henry White, a prominent Quaker in Perquimans Precinct, wrote a long untitled religious poem about "the fall of man" and his "restoration by Jesus Christ." The poem remained undiscovered for almost three hundred years. Representative of its primitive spelling and style are the following lines:

and all things answered well in swet harmonee
the will of god was trewly then obeaid
and all things in the power that god had maid
untell the serpent the sutelest of all
that god had maid both great and small
begone to temt the woman as wee see
to eat the frute of the forbeden tree
and tould her it would make her wise
to understand in opening of her eise

and she shuld be as god to knowe
the good and evell here belowe
thuse she obeayed and wente from god
and did procure the allinated Rode
of his displeseur because of sin
which did involve mankind ther in
for adam did obeay his wife
and soe he lost his enasent life. . . .

In 1737 an anonymous rhymster from North Carolina sent some untitled heroic couplets to the editor of the *South Carolina Gazette* in Charleston. "As blustering Winds disturb the calmest Sea," he began, so do "Tyrants drive the People to Extreams." It is well to notice that in this early poem was expressed a feeling of North Carolinians throughout the centuries—a feeling of hatred for despots.

The making of poems is frequently resorted to when man's emotions are aroused. For instance, with the coming of the Moravians to their Wachovia settlement in 1753, the Reverend Adam Grube composed a song to mark the occasion: "We hold arrival love feast here in Carolina land, / A company of Bretheren true, a little pilgrim band. . . ." And in 1759 Royal Governor Arthur Dobbs, in order to celebrate the victory of the English over the French at Quebec, proclaimed a day of thanksgiving and himself wrote a patriotic hymn to be sung on that day throughout the province. About the same time, a Philadelphian, Thomas Godfrey, moved to Wilmington and, among other literary productions, wrote poetry about the coastal country. A characteristic selection is "Piece [Verse] upon Masonborough," in which he describes a grove on the banks of a sound near Wilmington that was peopled with "Nymphs and Swains" and pastoral ladies like Myra

6

Morning Star (Wilmington)

St. James Churchyard, Wilmington

and Chloe. In 1774 a Scotsman named John Macrae arrived in the Cape Fear region and soon thereafter wrote a Gaelic lullaby ("Duanag Altrium") in honor of his daughter. Here is a line with its translation: "Gur h-ann an America 'tha sinn an dràsd" (In America now are we).

The first nonlegal book written and published in North Carolina was *A Collection of Many Christian Experiences,*

A

COLLECTION

OF MANY

Chriſtian Experiences, Sentences,

AND SEVERAL

Places of Scripture Improved:

ALSO,

Some ſhort and plain Directions and Prayers for ſick Perſons; with ſerious Advice to Perſons who have been ſick, to be by them peruſed and put in Practice as ſoon as they are recovered; and a Thanksgiving for Recovery.

To which is added,

Morning and Evening Prayers for Families and Children, Directions for the Lord's-Day, and ſome Cautions againſt Indecencies in Time of Divine Service, &c.

Collected and Compoſed for the Spiritual Good of his Pariſhioners, and others.

By C. H. Miſſionary to the Honourable Society for the Propagation of the Goſpel in Foreign Parts, and Rector of St. Paul's Pariſh, in North-Carolina.

O! how ſweet are thy Words unto my Taſte, yea ſweeter than Honey to my Mouth, Pſal. cxix. 103. I am well pleaſed that the Lord hath heard the Voice of my Prayer, that he hath inclined his Ear unto me; therefore will I call upon him as long as I live, Pſal. cxvi. 12.

NEWBERN:

Printed by JAMES DAVIS, M,DCC,LIII.

Sentences, and Several Places of Scripture Improved (1753), by Clement Hall, a native of England and at that time a missionary in northeastern North Carolina. A lively beginning it was. Hall's little book is full of sensible religious advice intended for his parishioners, advice often mere paraphrases from the Bible. Many of the other aphorisms were made up by Hall himself. "It is much easier to talk like a Saint than to be one," Hall opined. There are scores of similar pithy statements.

Another religious book, the first sermon printed in North Carolina, was a *Sermon, Preached in Christ-Church, in Newbern, in North-Carolina . . . Before the Ancient and Honourable Society of Free and Accepted Masons* (1756), by Michael Smith, a "scandalous" missionary of the Church of England who had come up from South Carolina to escape censure. His theme was the difference between deceitful friends and the uncompromising love of brothers as exhibited by the Masonic order. Four years later his poem "On the Reduction of Guadaloupe" appeared in the *South Carolina Gazette.*

The political troubles with England energized any number of North Carolinians possessing a talent for poetry. During the War of the Regulation, Rednap Howell, a schoolmaster at Deep River, wrote a number of balladlike poems satirizing the haughty British officials and tax collectors. The stinging words of his contemptuous songs were often sung by the oppressed people whenever they gathered to protest the unfair decisions of their overlords. Later, during the Revolution, at least two governors of North Carolina were known to compose patriotic poems. Governor Thomas Burke, a one-eyed, excitable Irishman whose complete lyrics were finally collected in *Poems* (1961), alternately exclaimed against the tyranny of Great Britain and dashed off rhymed love notes to the ladies. Governor Alexander Martin poetically honored the fallen American heroes. It was an age when prominent

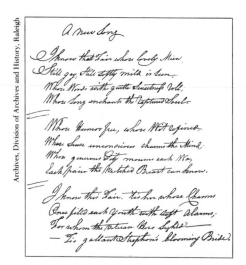

A new Song

I know that Fair whose lovely Mien
Still gay, still softly mild is seen;
Whose Words with gentle Sweetness roll,
Whose Song enchants the raptured Soul

Whose Humor free, whose Wit refined,
Whose Sense unconscious charms the Mind;
Whose generous Pity mourns each Woe,
Each Pain the wretched Breast can know.

I know this Fair, 'tis her whose Charms
Once filled each Youth with soft Alarms;
For whom the return Hero Sighed —
— 'Tis gallant Stephen's blooming Bride.

Thomas Burke's poem "A New Song"

A

COLLECTION

OF VARIOUS

PIECES OF POETRY,

CHIEFLY PATRIOTIC.

PUBLISHED AT THE EARNEST REQUEST OF A NUMBER OF GOOD
CITIZENS FOR THE IMPROVEMENT OF PATRIO-
TIC MINDS.

BY JAMES GAY,
Of Iredell County, N. C.

May truth and freedom still prevail,
O'er all the powers of Earth and Hell;
May Independence be renow'd,
Columbia's lands with glory crown'd;
May union, peace and love combine,
Then will our land in lustre shine,
And foreign nations wond'ring stand,
Not daring to invade our land,

RALEIGH:

Printed by Wm. Boylan.

1810.

men in public life thought it quite appropriate to write poems as well as to make laws and fight wars.

A love for country also inspired a work that can, more or less definitely, be labeled the first North Carolina book of poems. *A Collection of Various Pieces of Poetry, Chiefly Patriotic* (1810), by James Gay of Iredell County, is a strange little book of forty-two pages containing a poetic autobiography in the form of a dialogue, to which are added a number of Fourth of July poems that were read at Statesville as part of the holiday celebrations there. A few of the selections are in Scottish dialect, which Gay knew well. Gay had arrived in America in 1765 and six years later settled permanently in North Carolina. He participated in the Revolutionary War, then returned to Iredell, where he became a well-to-do and respected citizen. His book, published when Gay was sixty-six, has some uneven lines, but no one can doubt their sincerity:

> God save the constitution
> And all good wholesome federal laws;
> I hope each true American
> Will firmly stand to the old cause. . . .

No dramatic writing was composed in the colony until 1759, when Thomas Godfrey came down from Philadelphia to work as a mercantile agent in the Cape Fear country. In addition to poetry, he continued the writing of a play he had started in Pennsylvania. When completed, *The Prince of Parthia* was sent north and, when acted on the stage in 1767, was acclaimed the first American play to be produced by professional actors. It was not a success, however. The play, filled with long, dull speeches in blank verse, takes place in ancient Persia and is abundantly supplied with villainies, poisonings, and murders.

The honor of writing the first play by a native North Carolinian with a North Carolina subject goes to Lemuel Sawyer of Camden County, whose *Blackbeard* (1824) is a far more endearing work than *The Prince of Parthia*. Sawyer, an eccentric fellow on many scores, managed through political skulduggery to be elected a representative in Congress for many terms. *Blackbeard* is not about the famous buccaneer; rather, it deals with people who were Sawyer's close acquaintances. In Currituck County are four stupid country fellows eager to find the pirate's buried treasure. They fall for the cock-and-bull story of some sharp talkers

BLACKBEARD.

A Comedy, in Four Acts.

FOUNDED ON FACT.

BY LEMUEL SAWYER.

WASHINGTON:

PRINTED BY DAVIS AND FORCE (FRANKLIN'S HEAD)
PENNSYLVANIA AVENUE.

1824.

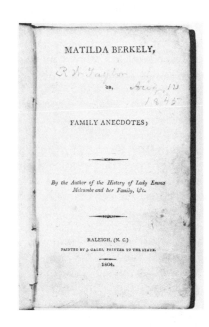

MATILDA BERKELY,

OR,

FAMILY ANECDOTES,

*By the Author of the History of Lady Emma
Melcombe and her Family, &c.*

RALEIGH, (N. C.)
PRINTED BY J. GALES, PRINTER TO THE STATE.
1804.

who pretend to know where the treasure is and are pressured into handing over to the tricksters what little cash they have. A second plot follows the misfortunes of a young gentleman named Candid, who seems to have been luckless in politics and love. But no reader need worry, for all turns out well for the virtuous Candid. Besides *Blackbeard*, Sawyer wrote a tragedy, *The Wreck of Honor* (1824); an unsympathetic *Biography of John Randolph of Roanoke* (1844); and an *Auto-Biography* (1844), in which self-revelations are embarrassingly frank.

As elsewhere, fiction trailed poetry and drama in North Carolina. In 1792 young William Hill Brown, who had written the first American novel, *The Power of Sympathy* (1789), left his Boston home and settled in Murfreesboro and Halifax. There he continued writing poetry and essays but published no more fiction. He died in Murfreesboro a year later. His humor, his patriotism, and his affection for the young women he knew are recorded in *Selected Poems and Verse Fables, 1784-1793* (1982).

In 1804 Mrs. Winifred Marshall Gales, who had published a novel in her native England, issued a second one in Raleigh, where she then lived. *Matilda Berkely, or*

Family Anecdotes, a story of the upper class in England and Russia, is noted as the first novel written by a resident North Carolinian.

A few minor efforts followed these, but it was not until 1839 that a novel with a North Carolina setting was written. In that year Senator Robert Strange of Fayetteville published *Eoneguski, or The Cherokee Chief*, which he based on material gathered when he was a judge in the courthouses of western North Carolina. Many of the characters are thin disguises of actual Indians or white settlers whom he had heard about or met. *Eoneguski* is a historical "border romance" in the James Fenimore Cooper-William Gilmore Simms tradition, with intricate love affairs and exciting incidences, and is valuable as a repository of Cherokee customs and legends. Senator Strange, though he lived most of his life in North Carolina, was a native of Virginia.

The educator Calvin Henderson Wiley, born in Guilford County, was North Carolina's first native novelist. *Alamance* (1847) describes stirring Revolutionary events in and around Alamance Presbyterian Church southeast of Greensboro in the center of the state. In *Roanoke* (1849), Wiley moved to the eastern towns of

New Bern and Wilmington for historical incidents of the Revolution. Wiley planned to round out a trilogy of novels with a western story to be called *Buncombe*, but it was never written. At a time when North Carolina was lagging in literature behind its sister states, Wiley's two books were a dedicated and conscious attempt to record for the readers of fiction some of the proud but almost forgotten episodes in his state's history.

Two less serious novels were written by an itinerant schoolmaster who worked in the homes of wealthy planters along the shore of Albemarle Sound. In *Nag's Head* (1850), George Higby Throop relates episodes during a summer vacation at the beach in antebellum times.

Horton manuscript

Bertie (1851) is a comic narrative about the jolly goings-on in the county of that name.

One of the first North Carolina textbooks was written by Charles Applewhite Hill, state senator, Methodist minister, and schoolmaster of Franklin and Warren counties, its title *An Improved American Grammar of the English Language for the Use of Schools* (1818). Hill

is credited with introducing the first Literary Fund bill in the state legislature.

The first book by a slave in North Carolina—as well as the first book by any southern black—was *The Hope of Liberty* (1829), by George Moses Horton of Chatham County, a gentle fellow who taught himself to read, then composed verses in his head until he could locate an amanuensis to write them down. He frequented the village of Chapel Hill near his master's farm, and there he sold love poems, mostly acrostics, to university students. Thus was Horton the state's first professional poet. He complained of his status:

> Must I dwell in Slavery's night
> And all pleasure take its flight
> Far beyond my feeble sight
> Forever?

In spite of such lines, Horton was not an unhappy man, for he always attracted admirers and patrons and teachers like the novelist Caroline Lee Hentz, who sponsored the first printing of his poems. After the publication of his third book, *Naked Genius* (1865), Horton moved north to Philadelphia, a free man at last.

A Wreath from the Woods of Carolina (1859), by Mrs. Mary A. Mason of

Raleigh, is the first North Carolina book written especially for young readers. Its ten stories, each illustrated by a beautiful wild flower, are highly moralistic lessons in which pious Bible-reading children are rewarded and wicked brats are punished, generally by death. Mrs. Mason also wrote a short novel, *Her Church and Her Mother: A Story of Filial Piety* (1860), with most of its setting in Raleigh's Christ Episcopal Church, where her husband was rector.

III

ANTEBELLUM WRITERS

Many writers other than those who were producing "literary firsts" were busy during the long period from the 1750s to the 1850s, especially travelers and poets.

Notable among the travelers, who meticulously recorded what they observed, was the four-times-married Anna Catharina. With her first husband, she came to the Moravian settlement at Wachovia in 1759. Adelaide L. Fries in *The Road to Salem* (1944) engagingly tells Anna Catharina's story, derived in large part from an autobiography written in German. When Anna Catharina arrived at the village of Bethabara, the furnishings of her house consisted of only a "bed, table, two or three chairs, all home-made." The village was compact, "with twelve larger and smaller houses protected by the stockade, and others near by." The pioneer travels and daily lives of such settlers are amply chronicled in the multivolume *Records of the Moravians in North Carolina* (1922-1969), edited by Fries and others. Legal documents from other sections of the state have been preserved in the ten-volume *Colonial Records of North Carolina* (1886-1890) edited by William L. Saunders, the sixteen-volume *State Records of North Carolina* (1895-1907) edited by Walter Clark, and the ongoing *Colonial Records of North Carolina, Second Series* (1963—), edited variously by Mattie Erma Edwards Parker, William S. Price, Jr., and Robert J. Cain.

A Scottish lady, Janet Schaw, was in the Wilmington area in 1775 at the time of the exciting pre-Revolutionary events.

Her *Journal of a Lady of Quality* (1921) exhibits little patience with the patriots, for she was aristocratic and loyal to the British throne. Though she praised the beauties of the countryside, she was contemptuous of the lowly, struggling settlers. Even so, her *Journal* is one of the most astute comments on the social and political upheavals of the times in North Carolina.

A more sympathetic passerby was William Bartram, a botanist like his famous father, John Bartram of Philadelphia. The younger Bartram was in North Carolina several times, often visiting his half uncle, Colonel William Bartram, at Ashwood plantation on the Cape Fear River. Though plants were William's particular study, he also jotted down notes on the animals and Indians of the backcountry. His *Travels* (1791) contains an early comment on the Venus's-flytrap, probably observed during his trip in 1777. Calling it by its scientific name *Dionaea muscipula*, he wrote that "the properties" of this "extraordinary" plant were "admirable," then continued: "Astonishing production! see the incarnate lobes expanding, how gay and sportive they appear! ready on the spring to intrap incautious deluded insects! what artifice! there behold one of the leaves just closed upon a struggling fly; another has gotten a worm; its hold is sure, its prey can never escape—carnivorous vegetable! ... they are organical, living, and self-moving bodies, for we see here, in this plant, motion and volition."

Other distinguished, though less literary, men who wrote of their travels in

North Carolina include André Michaux, President George Washington, Bishop Francis Asbury, John James Audubon, and Professor Elisha Mitchell.

Charles Lanman's *Letters from the Alleghany Mountains* (1849) is a book of incident as well as observation, and the author's accounts of his meetings with mountain people provide as good reading as his colorful, graphic accounts of Mt. Mitchell and Grandfather Mountain. Some years later, in the spring of 1856, the writer-illustrator David Hunter Strother ("Porte Crayon") began a leisurely journey through the state. In a series of articles published in *Harper's New Monthly Magazine* as "North Carolina Illustrated" and "A Winter in the South" (included in the book *The Old South Illustrated*, 1959), Strother wrote

Harper's New Monthly Magazine, XIV (March, 1857)

Drawing by "Porte Crayon"

Drawing by "Porte Crayon"

in the familiar vein of Lanman. Arriving at the shad and herring fisheries on Albemarle Sound near Edenton, he was received at a plantation "with that frank hospitality which characterizes the region, and ere long was seated at the dinner-table, where boiled rock, stewed cat-fish, white perch, and broiled shad disputed the claim on his taste and attention." After Goldsboro, Raleigh, and Salisbury, he came to the mountain village of Bakersville, whose "police force, consisting of six big dogs, is at all times uncommonly vigilant and active." Both Lanman

and Strother were men of wit and tolerance.

Of quite another sort was the narrow-minded and prejudiced Frederick Law Olmsted, whose acclaimed book *The Cotton Kingdom* (1861) was based on several journeys into the South in the 1850s. A New Englander, Olmsted condemned slavery in violent terms and thought southerners ill-mannered and their country inferior. Even so, his book was widely influential. He wrote that "North Carolina has a proverbial reputation for the ignorance and torpidity of her people"—a situation for which he blamed the "general poverty of the soil," "the almost exclusive employment of slave labour," and "the difficulty and expense of reaching markets." Education was at fault too, for the teachers were "often coarse, vulgar, and profane in their language and behaviour, who take up teaching as a temporary business, to supply the demand of a neighbourhood of people as ignorant and uncultivated as themselves."

Unfortunately, there was truth in these statements—the predicament had been noted more than a half century before Olmsted's time. Some seventy years earlier, Henry Pattillo, a Scotsman who had come to central North Carolina as a

Presbyterian minister, had begun to publish books of a practical nature in an attempt to improve the education of the citizens. In the preface to his *Sermons* (1788), Pattillo lamented the scarcity of reading material for the common people and proposed more books for educating the slaves. He had already published *The Plain Planter's Family Assistant* (1787), a practical manual for the less-than-knowledgeable farmer. Later came *A Geographical Catechism, To Assist Those Who Have Neither Maps nor Gazetteers* (1796). In the usual question-and-answer manner, the *Catechism* surveyed the world, supplying information that the almost bookless citizens might find useful. Pattillo was patriotic, for he described the United States as "the freest, happiest, most plentiful part of the globe." It was a "country in which religion is unrestrained . . . marriage honourable, and age reverenced."

At the turn of the century, in spite of Pattillo's enthusiasm, private book collections in North Carolina were either nonexistent or minuscule. Seven novels were published in New Bern during the period 1801-1804, however. At least five of these works were translated from the

François-Xavier Martin

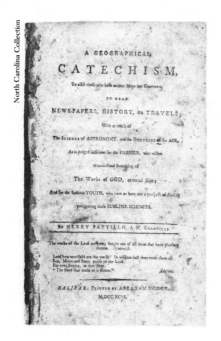

A GEOGRAPHICAL CATECHISM, To assist those who have neither Maps nor Gazetteers TO READ NEWSPAPERS, HISTORY, OR TRAVELS, With as much of The Science of ASTRONOMY, and the Doctrine of the AIR, As is judged sufficient for the FARMER, who wishes to understand something of The Works of GOD, around him; And for the studious YOUTH, who have as have not a prospect of having profligating these SUBLIME SCIENCES. By HENRY PATTILLO, A. M. Granville. HALIFAX: Printed by ABRAHAM HODGE. M,DCC,XCVI.

French, presumably by the New Bern printer François-Xavier Martin. But it is doubtful that many North Carolinians read them, for a republican frontiersman would have slight interest in such a title as *Letters of Adelaide de Sancerre to Count de Nance* (1801), an epistolary bit of fiction by Marie Jeanne (de Heurles Laboras de Mézières) Riccoboni. A more suitable novel reprinted by Martin was Maria Edgeworth's popular *Castle Rackrent* (1803), a story of oppressive Irish landlords.

One group of writers who traditionally disregard such mundane matters as the sparsity of publishers and book buyers is the poets. Poets, indefatigable and irrepressible, will dash off their verses whether or not there are readers to read them. One such was Robert Potter, "mad genius" and man of violence. When he was defeated in a Halifax County election, he returned to his native Granville County and wrote *The Head of Medusa, a Mock-Heroic Poem* (1827), in which he flayed the opposition in virulent terms. Into his poem he introduced the Devil, who "brandishes his battle-axe, / At home, alike, in Hell or H*lif*x." Potter, after surviving a number of disgraceful predicaments that he brought on himself, fled to the Southwest and became secretary of the Texas navy.

For more than a hundred years *Attempts at Rhyming, by an Old Field Teacher* (1839) baffled literary detec-

Robert Potter

The poem relates a Bertie County legend of the hanging of a Tuscarora chief for saving the life of a beautiful white girl who had been captured. In the same volume were shorter poems and a play titled *Theodosia*, which is written in blank verse and deals with pirates and lovely ladies.

Though many other poets in antebellum times achieved book publication, most were content with sending their efforts to the local newspapers or with passing their manuscripts around among friends. The famed New Bern jurist William Gaston, who in 1835 wrote the words for North Carolina's official state anthem "The Old North State," was an accomplished amateur. For private or

tives. The book had been written by an obviously well-educated man who had traveled extensively abroad and was now a schoolmaster in North Carolina. "On Chapel Hill" contained the lines

> Wood-crested hills and verdant vales among,
> See Northern-Carolina's learn'd retreat!
> Where arts and letters and the poet's song
> Adorn with majesty the Muses' seat.

It was not until a copy of the rare little book was found with the inscription "A. Hart" that the identity of Old Field Teacher became known. Research disclosed that Alban J. X. Hart was an Englishman and in 1839 director of Shocco Classical Seminary in Warren County.

Mystery still conceals the name of the author of *A Collection of Poems, by Incog.* (1845). Printed in New Bern, the book includes some tearfully romantic selections written "'twixt the sixteenth and eighteenth years of the Author's age." Of curious interest are several poetic essays in prose. "Prelude to a Song of Futurity" begins in this youthful fashion: "Onward to the future now must flow the current of my thoughts, as flows the tide of yon river glancing 'neath the morning's glow."

More talented was William Henry Rhodes of Windsor, author of the narrative poem *The Indian Gallows* (1846).

occasional purposes he fashioned such poems as "To Eliza from Her Husband" and "A May-Day Song," about which it is written that it "was composed for the scholars of an Infant School, and sung by them at one of their fêtes."

Across the state in Mecklenburg County, Philo Henderson won a reputation from the poems he frequently submitted for publication in newspapers. A favorite subject of his was "a beauteous maiden" who nevermore would return to her "bower" on the green banks of the

15

Catawba River, "Where she used to sit and dream." The Edgar Allan Poe quality is unmistakable. Like Poe, Henderson was generally melancholy and nostalgic.

The urgent feeling of a few North Carolinians that the state ought not only to create a native literature but also to see to its promotion, resulted in Mary Bayard Clarke's two-volume *Wood-Notes; or, Carolina Carols: A Collection of North Carolina Poetry* (1854). Like Wiley in writing *Roanoke* and *Alamance*, Clarke wished to prove that her region was not lagging behind its neighbors in literary energy. Among her forty-odd poets were Gaston and Henderson, as well as William Hill Brown, Winifred Marshall Gales, and Robert Strange. "Tenella" (Clarke herself) contributed seven poems and in one of them entreated the *"youth of Carolina"* to

Walk onward, then, to glory, seek literary fame,
And with the pen of History write Carolina's
    name.

But patriotic ardor was not enough. The state was still struggling with a largely uneducated citizenry. Of more value than Clarke's *Wood-Notes* was Calvin Henderson Wiley's compilation of *The North-Carolina Reader* (1851), for which Wiley supplied a history and description of the state, along with prose and verse selections by distinguished North Carolina citizens. Furthermore, he soon was traveling the state as the first superintendent of public schools and trying to see to it that his *Reader* was being used in the little short-term schools then being established.

North Carolina's advancement in matters literary would surely have been rapid at this point in the 1850s, but even then the threat of a nationwide war made the climate uncertain for those eager to devote their lives to the cause of letters.

IV

WRITERS OF THE CIVIL WAR PERIOD

Four years after her inflammatory *Uncle Tom's Cabin*, Harriet Beecher Stowe of New England wrote *Dred: A Tale of the Great Dismal Swamp* (1856), her second and final antislavery novel. The scene was Chowan County just south of the swamp, where the hero Dred, a Negro religious fanatic and outlaw, gave refuge to blacks fleeing their masters. In *Dred*, Stowe's principal purpose was to show the corroding effects of slavery on slave owners. Though there are in the book good slaves and bad, good southerners and bad, Stowe's target was the corrupting institution of slavery itself. *Dred* did not achieve the fame of its predecessor, but it was widely read; and North Carolina, trying to keep its balance in the sectional turmoil of the decade, was downgraded in northern eyes. This was particularly unfortunate, since there is no evidence that Stowe ever visited the region about which she wrote.

Of greater impact upon the state during the 1850s was the publication of *The Impending Crisis of the South* (1857), by Hinton Rowan Helper of Davie County. Second only to *Uncle Tom's Cabin* in its inflammatory effect upon the nation, the book attempted, by statistical analysis, to prove that the economic result of slavery was to force southern states into a position inferior to states in the North. Helper was no sentimentalist, no fire-eating emancipator. He had no love for the blacks. As a man from the small-farmer class of the Yadkin River valley, he simply wanted to rid the South of all slaves, to transport them to countries outside the United States. Like Stowe in *Dred*, he wrote that the system generated unproductive men and made "slaves" of the owners. He also argued that a vigorous literature could not be maintained under such a system. *The Impending Crisis* has been called "the most caustic attack upon slavery ever written by a Southerner." In rigorously condemning the society in which North Carolinians lived, Helper became the most hated man in the region. He left his home in Salisbury and never thereafter resided in North Carolina.

North Carolina has not often been disgraced by those who would censor books, but *The Impending Crisis*, written by a

Hugh C. Bailey, *Hinton Rowan Helper: Abolitionist Racist* (1965), frontispiece

Hinton Rowan Helper

17

native son, was quickly declared *litterae non grata*, and the circulation of the volume, categorized as incendiary anti-slavery literature, was prohibited in accordance with a law making illegal the dissemination of printed matter that would prompt "slaves to become discontented with their bondage." Daniel Worth, a Quaker of Guilford County, sold 120 copies of the book and, because of that offense and other pro-emancipation activities, was arrested and jailed. In Greensboro a jury found him guilty, but Worth was set free on bond and escaped to the North.

After North Carolina seceded from the Union in 1861, the state found itself cut off from the books it had been buying in the North. The situation became alarmingly acute in the schools when textbooks began to disintegrate from overuse. Local printers gradually sought to remedy the situation. Allowing their southern patriotism to flame brightly in words the children would read, authors fashioned their schoolbooks to the times. The Greensboro firm of Sterling, Campbell, and Albright published a number of elementary texts. Among the publications coming from a Raleigh shop in 1863 were Levi Branson's *First Book in Composition . . . Especially Designed for the Use of Southern Schools* and Mrs. Marinda B. Moore's *Geographical Reader for the Dixie Children.* Of the Revolutionary War, Moore wrote: "No braver men fought in the war for independence than those from North Carolina. While some few cowards refused to fight for their country, it is a notable fact, that nearly all of them, were of the ignorant class, and many of them did not know what patriotism was. We should feel as much pity for them as contempt, because they had not been properly taught." Lemuel Johnson's *An Elementary Arithmetic* (1864) posed the following mathematical problem: "If one Confederate soldier kill 90 Yankees, how many Yankees can 10 Confederate soldiers kill?"

Printers also brought out slender books of fiction. Pitt County's W. D. Herring-

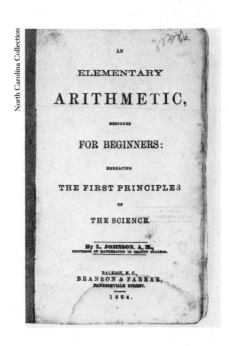

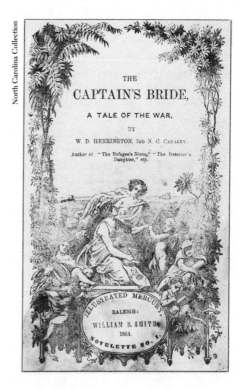

ton of the Third North Carolina Cavalry wrote several novelettes. In *The Captain's Bride* (1864), beautiful Estelle helps a Confederate captain put to rout the Union forces near Kinston by stabbing her unsavory northern suiter to death.

This twenty-two-page romantic nonsense costing $1.50 sold out its first edition of five thousand copies in thirty days, so avid were southern readers for books denied them by the blockade and northern exporters. *The Deserter's Daughter* (1865) has a foreboding word in its title, since in early 1865 its author was captured and then deserted to the Federal troops. He was provided transportation to Wisconsin. Whether he continued to turn out trite stories in Yankee Land is not known.

During the war years, poets were hard at work glorifying the southern cause and celebrating its soldier-defenders. Confederate ladies like Mary Bayard Clarke of *Wood-Notes* fame sent a steady stream of stanzas to the newspapers and periodicals, but the limitations imposed by their theme resulted in one monotonous variation after another. Only occasionally was it possible to lift a composition out of the morass, as can be observed by glancing through *Songs of Love and Liberty, Compiled by a North Carolina Lady* (1864), a 62-page anthology published in Raleigh.

It is said that the first book to be issued under copyright of the Confederate States was *Hesper and Other Poems* (1861), by Theophilus Hunter Hill of Raleigh, whose melodic stanzas project a dream world familiar to readers of Keats and Poe. In mid-century North Carolina, Hill heard "The tinkling bells of sylvan streams" and noted that in spring "The rugged hills wear emerald carcanets." In 1868, when subscriptions were being solicited for a new book by Hill, a Fayetteville newspaper, after reporting that 250 subscriptions were already at hand, made a plea for others to do their "legitimate share towards bringing into life that very rare thing, a North Carolina book, the creature of the genius of one of her own sons."

The best-known patriotic poem to survive the war years was "Ho! for Carolina!" by William Bernard Harrell, a Baptist minister and Confederate surgeon. In 1861, at the railway station in Wilson, after hearing some clamorous words of praise for the state by a soldier on his way northward to the battlefields, Harrell wrote a poem based on the shout. The refrain goes:

Ho! for Carolina! that's the land for me;
In her happy borders roam the brave and free;
And her bright-eyed daughters, none can fairer
  be;
Oh! it is a land of love and sweet liberty!

The words, set to music by Harrell's wife, were sung far and wide, and the piece came close to being chosen the official state song over William Gaston's anthem. Harrell wrote other verses reflecting the high spirits of the times, such as "Up with the Flag," "Song of Freedom," "The Confederate Banner," and "Soldier's Reverie," but they have never been collected into a book.

Another poet whose work is still remembered is Joseph William Holden, son of Governor W. W. Holden. When only seventeen he enlisted in the army, but was soon captured and put aboard a Federal prison ship. From its deck he became familiar with the treacherous North Carolina coast at Cape Hatteras. Longfellow's anthology *Poems of Places* included Holden's "Hatteras," and thus the poem achieved a modest fame that

Joseph William Holden

might otherwise have been denied it. In it Holden told of the turmoil at the cape when the north wind met the south wind there. "This is Golgotha of the sea!" he wrote. Most of Holden's better work was collected in *Hatteras and Other Poems* (1925), published a half century after his early death.

Following the end of the war in April, 1865, printers and writers continued their efforts to establish a southern market for their products, but they were generally unsuccessful. In October a Raleigh firm issued a second edition of *Mary Barker, a Thrilling Narrative of Early Life in North*

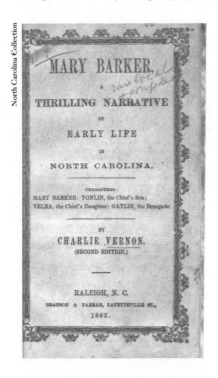

Carolina, by Charlie Vernon. Vernon was the pseudonym of Braxton Craven, head of the institution that later became Duke University. His not-so-thrilling little story has to do with some friendly Indians and a white villain. Craven later wrote a novelette titled *The Story of Naomi Wise*, whose murdered heroine has served as the subject of so many ballads that she has been called "North Carolina's principal single contribution to American folk song."

Another novel published late in 1865 was *Nameless*, by Fanny Murdaugh Downing, a resident of Charlotte. Downing avoided the stress of the times by setting her story in England and Italy. One reviewer wrote that, in the character of Lady Haughton, the book dealt "with the tragic passions of woman—her love, her pride, her duplicity and her despair— with woman's purity and guilt, with her dignity and degradation, with her glory and her shame." Though *Nameless* would hardly excite a reader today, it had no trouble reaching a second edition in those book-starved days. Fortunately, a second novel by Downing with the portentous title *Perfect through Suffering* seems never to have been published. Under the pen name "Viola," Downing was an industrious amateur verse-maker, much admired. The Charleston poet Paul Hamilton Hayne addressed two sonnets to her after receiving the gift of "a beautifully embroidered tobacco pouch."

For some years after the war, no sectional hatred or racial animosity disturbed the sensibilities of North Carolina writers, still dazed with defeat. In 1868, for instance, Dr. Benjamin Robinson of Fayetteville published *Dolores*, a lengthy, leisurely narrative based on the famous trial of Cumberland County's Ann K. Simpson, who was accused of the arsenic poisoning of her husband. It is interesting to note that Dr. Robinson had performed an autopsy on the dead man. Instead of bothering with this rambling novel, one might more profitably read the exciting court record itself, William H. Haigh's *The Trial of Mrs. Ann K. Simpson* (1851).

V

POSTWAR NOVELISTS

For several years after 1865, the writing of fiction in North Carolina was understandably a dormant preoccupation. Then up from South Carolina came distinguished William Gilmore Simms, who in the poverty-stricken South was determined to make some money as quickly as he could by selling two hurriedly written novels for serialization in New York periodicals. Notes taken on a visit to the North Carolina mountains in 1847 were pulled from his desk to refresh his memory for the background of a pair of romances. *Voltmeier or The Mountain Men: A Tale of the Old North State* (1869), set in Hickory Nut Gap and the upper French Broad River region, is replete with hunters' yarns, a gang of robbers, Gothic mansions, and other familiar Simms paraphernalia. The last novel Simms was ever to write was *The Cub of the Panther, a Mountain Legend* (1869), founded on a folk ballad. Among a gallery of characters, both North Carolina mountain rustics and haughty gentry, a snobbish braggart (the panther) is mauled by a black bear he has wounded but is rescued by his bastard son (the cub), who is then falsely accused of injuring his father.

Soon after Simms, writers in the Old North State took up their pens once again. The mainstream of their fiction at that time, and for some forty years after the beginning of Reconstruction, was dictated by Victorian standards of romantic sentimentality and lily-white propriety. It was a time when the "popular novel" was written by aggressively upright women for their equally moral

female readers. Only that which would not scandalize the tender sensibilities of young maidens was permitted on chaste parlor tables. In these novels men were either heavenly paragons or hellish scoundrels.

A somewhat typical example was *Bertha the Beauty* (1872, though serialized earlier), by Sarah Johnson Cogswell Whittlesey of Williamston, the author of

MISS S. J. C. WHITTLESEY.

two other works of fiction as well as two books of poetry: *Heart-Drops from Memory's Urn* (1852) and *Spring Buds and Summer Blossoms* (1889). In the 1872 novel, Bertha Belmont, like Whittlesey, spent her childhood in "a low brown house with a long piazza" on the Roanoke River. At the age of eighteen, upon the insistence of her father, she married a

21

handsome, jealous, worthless northerner who made her life miserable. On one terrible occasion he was even guilty of speaking some coarse language. "Our heroine had never before been so taken by surprise," wrote the novelist. "It was the first time she had ever heard him utter a profane word. Before her marriage, one of Horace Stanhope's rivals had informed her of his proficiency in the art of interlarding his language with expletives forbidden by the Decalogue, and she carried the information to her father, which was at once set down by prejudice-blinded Mr. Belmont to jealousy in a rival—a base calumny." Bertha later discovered books by Hume and Voltaire concealed among her husband's belongings and realized she had located the source of his villainy. "She consigned the iniquitous volumes to the flames, and reduced them to ashes without his knowledge." Finally she escaped the blackguard and returned to her family. Upon Horace's death, she married her virtuous childhood sweetheart, then a Confederate colonel.

The most outstanding North Carolina writer in this genre, with far more talent than Whittlesey, was Christian Reid of Salisbury. Born Frances Christine Fisher and married in mid-life to James M. Tiernan, she chose her pseudonym both to signify the ethical intention of her work and to veil her sex and true identity. To use one's real name for authorship was thought by some to be unladylike. The first of her forty-six books, mostly novels, was *Valerie Aylmer* (1870), the story of a southern coquette. One contemporary reviewer commented that in this novel the author "speaks out the moral training, elegance of manners, purity of sentiments and high moral tone of her sisters in North Carolina." *Morton House* (1871), which Reid considered one of her best efforts, concerns the involvements of a governess among plantation aristocracy. Seemingly without exertion, books thereafter surged from her pen with annual regularity. From her travels—to Mexico, Haiti, France, Italy—

she gathered material to provide a variety of setting and theme, but she did not abandon her southern heroines. Her tenth book, *The Land of the Sky* (1876), a travel novel in which young ladies and gentlemen have mild flirtations during a vacation trip to the North Carolina mountains, created in the title a nickname that has been used ever since to denote the western part of the state. This book is still the one most often associated with Christian Reid, though she wrote other North Carolina stories, such as *A Summer Idyl* (1878) and *The Wargrave Trust* (1912). The former has a scene in

"'Look at my gloves!'"

Illustration from *The Land of the Sky*

which the hero's arm encircles the heroine's waist as she slips on the brink of a mountain precipice. "It is only an instant," the author wrote, "—but an instant that he never forgets. . . . Her slight figure clinging to him, her soft hair blowing across his lips—these things thrill him suddenly with a consciousness which is like a revelation." Among her pages, Christian Reid scattered such tender moments. It is unfortunate that her popularity, tremendous at first, declined when later novels began to reflect her intense

CHRISTIAN REID
(FRANCES FISHER TIERNAN)
WROTE MORE THAN FORTY
NOVELS ODES AND POEMS
"THE LAND OF THE SKY"
HAS BEEN AN INSPIRATION
TO ALL WHO HAVE READ IT
AND MANY TRAVELERS HAVE
VISITED NORTH CAROLINA
TO ENJOY SCENIC BEAUTIES
SO GRAPHICALLY DESCRIBED
BY HER

Innis Street, Salisbury

Roman Catholicism. Even so, she remains the epitome of the "polite literature" of the era.

Operating concurrently with the school of Christian Reid and her less endowed associates were the local-color writers, whose main pursuit consisted in closely examining native customs and language for the sole purpose of discovering picturesque elements for their fiction. Practically all of the local-colorists were lady travelers from outside the state, and most of them made straight for the Blue Ridge Mountains. There they found "quaint" characters with "queer" speech habits, both of which delighted the ladies' hearts and filled their notebooks. Two Tennessee women wandered across the state line to gather material: Mary Noailles Murfree ("Charles Egbert Craddock") published *The Prophet of the Great Smoky Mountains* in 1885, and Frances Hodgson Burnett, the creator of Little Lord Fauntleroy, came along in 1899 with *In Connection with the DeWilloughby Claim*. Down from Pennsylvania came the ubiquitous Rebecca Harding Davis, and she was soon writing local-color short stories for prestigious monthlies in the North like *Scribner's*, *Appleton's*, and *Lippincott's*. And down from Maine

came Maria Louise Pool, whose depraved mountain people in *Dally* (1893) and *In Buncombe County* (1896) were no compliment to North Carolina. Up from the Deep South to join these scribbling ladies was, surprisingly, a man, Thomas Cooper De Leon, whose *Juny, or Only One Girl's Story, A Romance of the Society Crust—Upper and Under* (1890) narrates a yarn of moonshiners and assorted other characters. None of these books or similar ones, though frankly narrated from the viewpoint of the outsider, show any genuine understanding of mountain people.

Constance Fenimore Woolson, greatniece of James Fenimore Cooper, was not only a more skillful writer than her local-color sisters, but her friendship with the famous American novelist Henry James has given her a prominence never possible for the others. From visits to Asheville in the 1870s, she gathered material for a long short story, "Up in the Blue Ridge," included in *Rodman the Keeper* (1880). Her two novels, *For the Major* (1883) and *Horace Chase* (1894), also make use of the mountain scene, but the local-color aspects are only in the background. She did not try to portray the "picturesque" mountaineers but instead chose the denizens of the towns and villages. The urbane characters of *Horace Chase* lived in Asheville, where, she wrote at the beginning of one chapter, "Nothing could exceed the charm of the early summer, this year, in this high valley. The amphitheatre of mountains had taken on fresher robes of green, the air was like champagne; it would have been difficult to say which river danced more gayly along its course, the foamflecked French Broad, its clear water open to the sunshine, or the little Swannanoa, frolicking through the forest in the shade."

The local-color writers were little concerned with social or political movements. So attuned were they to the minutiae of custom and speech and scenery that, too often, the characters in their stories were mere stereotypes. Even the

23

recent Civil War was a passive historical fact with slight impact upon those about whom they wrote. Certainly this was not true for writers like Albion W. Tourgée, Charles Waddell Chesnutt, Thomas Dixon, and Walter Hines Page, who in their highly dramatic fiction drew upon the war and its aftermath to depict the turbulent social changes under way in North Carolina.

Tourgée, a courageous and intelligent northerner, settled near Greensboro late in 1865 and for the next fourteen years was hated and reviled as a leading carpetbagger and Republican. The Ku Klux Klan and conservative politicians condemned every move he made to aid the former slaves. Out of his experiences during the Reconstruction years in North Carolina, Tourgée wrote several novels. *A Fool's Errand, By One of the Fools* (1879), a best seller of its day, was the first of his Reconstruction series. The "fool" of the semiautobiographical portrait was none other than Tourgée himself, whose "errand" to rebuild the South was doomed from the start. Tourgée, while he did not hesitate to present his own points of view vigorously, was unexpectedly fair to his southern neighbors, whose biases he tried to understand as he tried to understand his own. Even

so, most southerners, traditionally proud and arrogant, could not and would not tolerate differing opinions in those desperate Reconstruction years. *Bricks without Straw* (1880), Tourgée's second important novel, showed the futile effort to educate the blacks in the face of northern indifference and southern opposition. Tourgée resented the action of a federal government that had heedlessly given political power to the blacks without first determining if they were ready for the responsibility it entailed, for "liberty could not be maintained nor prosperity achieved by ignorance and poverty, any more than in the days of Moses adobe bricks could be made without straw."

Another spokesman for the blacks was Charles W. Chesnutt, a light-complexioned Negro who spent his formative years in Fayetteville. After *The Conjure Woman* (1899), a collection of seven folk tales that remains his best-known book, Chesnutt published a group of short stories under the title *The Wife of His Youth and Other Stories of the Color Line* (1899), in which he explored the problems confronting those of mixed blood. The first of three racial novels was *The House behind the Cedars* (1900), in which Patesville (Chesnutt's name for

Frontispiece, *Bricks without Straw*

Charles W. Chesnutt

Fayetteville) was the setting for the tragic story of a beautiful girl with a fraction of Negro blood. In *The Marrow of Tradition* (1901), based on the Wilmington race riot of 1898, the author studied the hopeless situation of blacks in a white society. Chesnutt returned to Fayetteville for the scene of *The Colonel's Dream* (1905), whose hero, a Confederate veteran, is damned by the "poor whites" for his exertions to raise the economic status of the blacks. If the books of Chesnutt, like those of Tourgée, have faded with the years, the fault is not attributable to the encouragement and sponsorship Chesnutt received at the time they were written. William Dean Howells called Chesnutt's short stories "works of art," written by one who had "sounded a fresh note, boldly, not blatantly"; and Walter Hines Page, according to Chesnutt, was the one who gave "most assistance to me in publishing my first book." Chesnutt had the distinction of being the first Afro-American writer to receive serious attention as a literary artist.

Almost as if in response to the relatively temperate fiction of Tourgée and Chesnutt, Thomas Dixon wrote *The Leopard's Spots* (1902) and *The Clansman* (1905), novels of the Reconstruction era that feverishly proclaimed the doc-

trine of white supremacy and black degradation. A native of Cleveland County, Dixon attended Wake Forest College, then in quick order turned from the law to the ministry. He left the pulpit for the lecture platform and meanwhile started the writing of fiction. The first two of his many books were immediate sensations, and he became a wealthy man after turning *The Clansman* into a play. Dixon was a propagandist. His characters were admirable or despicable, his episodes the essence of sweetness or violence. In the first two books, and in the many titles that followed, Dixon presented a succession of lynchings, uprisings, house burnings, murders and the like, but whatever the events, racism was generally responsible. A preacher in *The Leopard's Spots* stated: "'In a Democracy you cannot build a nation inside of a nation of two antagonistic races; and therefore the future American must be either an Anglo-Saxon or a Mulatto.'" Dixon's readers agreed, in spite of many published refutations—for Dixon had appealed to a prejudice deeply seated in the less-than-intellectual southerner of his day. His novels shed no light; they merely inflamed.

Sunset Cemetery, Shelby

It is strange that the editor who helped Chesnutt to achieve book publication was the same man who nursed *The Leopard's Spots* through the press. Walter Hines Page, born in Cary, was a liberal more than a half century ahead of his time. As a journalist, he pointed out the three phantoms that obsessed the mind of the southerner: the ghost of the Confederate dead, the ghost of religious orthodoxy, and the ghost of white supremacy. Page wanted the South to exorcise these evil ghosts and to move forward in education, race relations, and industrial development. He loved North Carolina, but, when his program made no headway, headed north and became a successful editor and publisher. His only novel, *The Southerner* (1909), followed the career of a young man during the Reconstruction period. Nicholas Worth was not unlike Page himself. His forays into education and politics were repudiated. Men's minds were steeled against progress and improvement. Even the object of his love was spiritually warped. A leading member of the Capitol Chapter of the "Fair Daughters of the Confederacy," this sweet young woman lived in a world of "chivalry," "beauty," "heroism," "the sacred dead," and "loyalty to the Southland." At one point, she risks her life by dashing into a burning church to rescue a Confederate flag, then turns

Burton J. Hendrick, *The Life and Letters of Walter H. Page* (1922)

Walter Hines Page, 1899

on Nicholas when he expresses doubts about her rash action. Such attitudes held back the South, Worth thought. Raleigh was, he believed, "the dullest settlement of English-speaking folk in the whole world." At the end of the book, the hero, unlike Page, stayed in the South, where, as Page had advocated, a number of reforms, such as the establishment of a state-supported college for women, were instituted.

The novels of Tourgée and Chesnutt came from men whose heritage was outside the strong southern tradition, but Page spoke out as one to the manner born. It is no wonder that the friends of "Nicholas Worth" called him a "traitor" to his class.

In pleasant contrast to the serious-minded local-colorists and the agonized novelists of social and political issues were the delightful amateurs. Some of them were so amusingly artless that their books were treasured long after dozens and dozens of more solemn productions faded away.

Two novels of this kind, both written in 1883 by women of Pender County, were *Pauline, or The Girl of Piney Dell*, by Mita Leon (Mrs. Robert W. Rivenbark) and *Then and Now, or Hope's First School*, by Zillah Raymond (Miss Lou H. Frayser). Though these are charming books, the unrivaled genius of the amateur school is Mattie J. Peterson, whose *Little Pansy* (1890) is rather a glorification of the genre. Within its brief thirty-nine pages, Peterson tells a complicated story of orphans, pirates, jealous women, and pure-hearted men. When the painter Edgar Ebert proposed marriage to Little Pansy Ray, "he broke forth in passionate words, 'O, my little love, my pure white lily, I love you so. . . . I love Jesus above all, and you next. O, my darling, do not say no.'" When Little Pansy complied by saying nothing, "He leaned forwarded [*sic*], merely touched his lips to hers; then sat erect." Of course, the two were not married until they had been subjected to many harrowing misunderstandings and misadventures. In

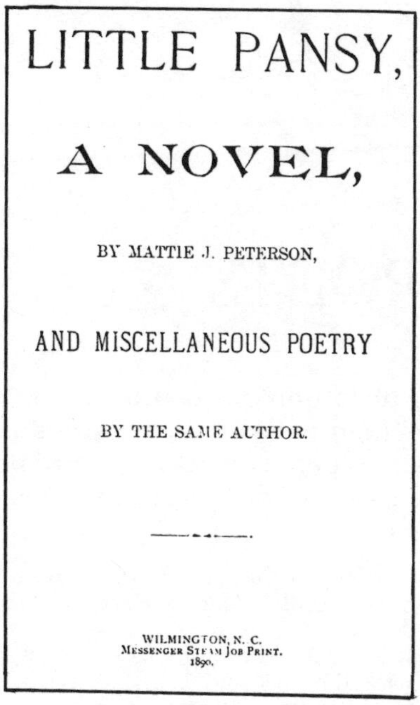

LITTLE PANSY,

A NOVEL,

BY MATTIE J. PETERSON,

AND MISCELLANEOUS POETRY

BY THE SAME AUTHOR.

——— · - · ———

WILMINGTON, N. C.
MESSENGER STEAM JOB PRINT.
1890.

sixteen pages appended to *Little Pansy* were some poems that would have delighted Mark Twain. Peterson's "I Kissed Pa Twice after His Death" contains two lines that were the joy of early nineteenth-century newspaper editors in North Carolina: "I saw him coming stepping high, / Which was of his walk the way."

VI

POSTWAR POETS

Poetry in England and America during the last part of the nineteenth century and the early part of the twentieth was frankly and unashamedly traditional. For their models, most poets everywhere, and certainly in North Carolina, looked to Burns and Shelley and Poe and Longfellow, never to Whitman and a few other savage and liberated spirits. Like Wordsworth and Tennyson, they wrote rhymed lyrics about love and nature and God. When they wanted to extend themselves, they corseted their metered words in blank verse. It would be many years before poetry broke from the restrictions of the past.

While studying at the University of Virginia, Edwin Wiley Fuller of Louisburg wrote a first version of *The Angel in the Cloud*, which, revised and lengthened, he published in 1871. For decades, this long philosophical poem about the transformation of man's cynicism into faith was considered a work of importance. In this passage, the Angel comments on riches:

Poor sordid Man! like all your gold-slave race,
You deem wealth happiness. Hence, all your
    doubts
About God's providence are based on gold.
The wicked have it, and the righteous not.
What you assert is oftenest reversed,
And in a census of the world, you'll find
The good, in every land, the wealthiest.
But Earth is not the bar where Man is judged;
But only where free-will and circumstance
May join in general progress. Gold is good!
Then good depends on use of circumstance,
And not on moral merit. Well 'tis so!
For were the righteous only blessed, all men
Would righteousness pursue, from sordid aims,—
The most devout, who love their money best;
And thus good actions' essence would be lost,
That they be done for good, within itself,
And not for benefit to be conferred.

Fuller's popular novel *Sea-Gift* (1873), containing some autobiographical chapters about undergraduate life at Chapel Hill, was known on the campus as the "Freshman's Bible." An episode in which a student is killed is probably based on the legendary disappearance of Peter Dromgoole from Chapel Hill in 1833.

The Moravian poet John Henry Boner, a native of Salem, had gifts superior to Fuller's, though he too made no attempt to break from tradition. "Poe's Cottage at Fordham," in its day Boner's most admired poem, now seems merely a clever imitation of his master. More appealing are those carefully constructed sonnets and other verses inspired by a nostalgia for happy childhood, such as Boner's reminiscence of an excursion to

Trinity Archive, IX (March, 1896)

Edwin Wiley Fuller

Old Salem, Inc.

Boner birthplace, Winston-Salem

the banks of the Yadkin River. The work begins:

There's a lone, cool nook, where the shade is deep,
  And the waves of a river softly run
To the shore where odorous muskrats creep
  From dripping roots when the day is done.

Boner's life, like Poe's, was not a happy one, for he was beset by exile from home, business failure, and sickness. In both *Whispering Pines* (1883) and *Poems* (1903) are lyrics dealing with the sadness of past enchantment:

Floating on the gentle Yadkin in an olden-time canoe,
Singing old plantation ballads—I and charming blue-eyed Sue—
  Blue-eyed, golden-tressed Sue. . . .

Years may pass, but I can never cease to dream of blue-eyed Sue
And the morning on the Yadkin in the olden-time canoe—
  Blue-eyed, golden-tressed Sue.

A few years before he died, Boner came down from Washington for a last visit to North Carolina. His happiness cannot be doubted as one reads his words when he found himself

Back in the Old North State,
  Back to the place of his birth,
Back through the pines' colonnaded gate
  To the dearest spot on earth.

Henry Jerome Stockard in *Fugitive Lines* (1897) and Benjamin Sledd in *From Cliff and Scaur* (1897) and *The Watchers of the Hearth* (1902) exemplified a somewhat different tradition, one of classic refinement. Both were men of the class-

room, Stockard at Peace College and Sledd at Wake Forest, and their love of literature and history was compounded into what they wrote. For instance, in the sonnet "My Library" Stockard imagined that the present moment had vanished and that he found himself where

the elfin horns of Oberon blow,
Or flutes Theocritus by the wimpling flow
Of immemorial amaranth-margined streams.

Sledd, though his themes were more varied, was also a devotee of classic literature. "At the Tomb of Dante" contained these lines:

Homage to thee and tribute to thy song,—
Poet who saw with awed, unquailing eyes,
Deep under deep, Inferno's dole and doom,
And glory, orb on orb, of Paradise.

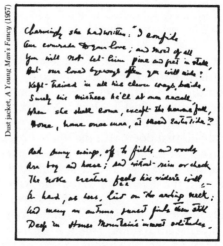

Dust jacket, *A Young Man's Fancy* (1957)

Sledd manuscript

It is unfortunate, surely, that potentially talented men like Stockard and Sledd lived in a period in which a pseudo-romantic Victorian sentimentality infected the poetry of regional America. Away from the classroom, these two poets might sometimes bravely write on a local topic, as in Stockard's sonnet "In the Lighthouse at Point Lookout, North Carolina" and Sledd's short "Vision of the Milk-White Doe." *A Young Man's Vision, an Old Man's Dreams* (1957) is a posthumous collection of Sledd's poetry.

The white doe, according to legend, was the girl Virginia Dare after her metamorphosis by a sorcerer whose courtship she had rejected. The tale so entranced Sallie Southall Cotten of Greenville that she turned it into a fifty-eight-page narrative poem, *The White Doe: The Fate of Virginia Dare, an Indian Legend* (1901), undertaken, it is said, to make money for a project sponsored by the North Carolina Federation of Women's Clubs. On Roanoke Island, wrote Cotten, the White Doe was leader of a herd of red deer, and there, in the familiar meter of Longfellow's *Hiawatha*, she eluded pursuers

> Through the tanglewood, still onward,
> Head uplifted, her feet scorning
> All the wealth of bright-hued foliage
> Which lay scattered in her pathway.
> Up the high sand-dunes she bounded,
> In the wake the whole herd followed,
> While the arrows aimed from ambush
> Fell around her ever harmless.

It was in the midst of these serious-minded bards that there sounded, just after the turn of the century, a laughing, dulcet voice. John Charles McNeill, born in the Scottish country near Wagram, wrote his first poems for the *Wake Forest Student*, later made his appearance in the *Century* magazine, and after joining the staff of the *Charlotte Observer* filled columns almost weekly with his seemingly inexhaustible lines. The manuscript of his first little book, *Songs, Merry and Sad* (1906), was the initial winner of the Patterson Memorial Cup for literary excellence. This title and his *Lyrics from Cotton Land* (1907) remained in print for more than a half century. Of the hundreds of uncollected poems in the *Observer*, eighty-seven were reprinted in *Possums and Persimmons* (1977).

McNeill's poems were a departure from the academic studies of Stockard and Sledd. He did not feel a compulsion to draw allusions from classical mythology or literary history. Though he remained a thoroughgoing romantic like his contemporaries, he was influenced by local-color and regional writers to the extent of using the black dialect and the

McNeill birthplace, near Wagram

rich but unpretentious vocabulary of the country folk among whom he had been reared. Since his down-to-earth poems and his fine-toned lyrics—and McNeill's work can be rather comfortably divided into these two types—posed no problems for the reader in spite of their ordinarily careful craftsmanship, he quickly won wide acceptance and a popularity that has not been surpassed by any other native Tar Heel poet. There was a certain adroitness in the eight lines of "'Ligion" that other dialect poets somehow missed:

> De Augus' meetin' 's over now.
>   We's all done been baptize',
> Me en Ham en Hick'ry Jim
>   En Joe's big Lize.
>
> Oh, 'ligion is a cu'i's thing
>   In its workin' amongs' men!
> We'll hatter wait a whole yur now
>   'Fo' bein' baptiz' again!

The same dexterity, but in another kind of poem, was apparent in the two stanzas of "Sundown":

> Hills, wrapped in gray, standing along the west;
>   Clouds, dimly lighted, gathering slowly;
> The star of peace at watch above the crest—
>   Oh, holy, holy, holy!
>
> We know, O Lord, so little what is best;
>   Wingless, we move so lowly;
> But in thy calm all-knowledge let us rest—
>   Oh, holy, holy, holy!

McNeill, because of such poems as these, was so beloved by North Carolinians that he was soon being called the poet laureate of the state, and the designation is engraved upon his tombstone.

But officially there was no such post as poet laureate of North Carolina until

1935, when the legislature provided for one. The position remained vacant for thirteen years. Then in 1948 Governor R. Gregg Cherry appointed to the post Arthur Talmage Abernethy, a writer of humorous rhymes from Burke County. After five years in office, Abernethy resigned, and a special committee of the North Carolina Literary and Historical Association sent Governor William B. Umstead a recommendation upon which he acted favorably. The new appointee was James Larkin Pearson, born in Wilkes County in 1879. Pearson's investiture took place on August 4, 1953, during ceremonies in the hall of the House of Representatives at the State Capitol in Raleigh.

Pearson was rather a direct literary descendant of McNeill, for he too wrote in the dialect of his region and composed lyrics uncomplicated in their meaning and direct in their presentation. His apprenticeship began quite early. "By the time I was four years old," he wrote in his autobiography, "I was uttering four-line stanzas that are as mechanically perfect as the song-poems in the old hymn-book." Pearson's boyhood ambition, from which he never swerved, was to be a poet. At the age of twelve he was taking his ambition seriously and writing constantly. In the columns of *The Fool-Killer*, which for twenty years was his personal monthly newsletter to his subscribers, Pearson generally included several poems. Evidence of his considerable productivity can be seen in six books, from *Castle Gates* (1908) to *Selected Poems* (1960), all except the last printed by him at his own press. Undoubtedly his most famous poem is "Fifty Acres,"

Fool-Killer (Moravian Falls), September, 1911

Pearson, age thirty-two

which describes his Wilkes County home. Here are four of its eight quatrains:

> I've never been to London,
>   I've never been to Rome;
> But on my Fifty Acres
>   I travel here at home.
>
> The hill that looks upon me
>   Right here where I was born
> Shall be my mighty Jungfrau,
>   My Alp, my Matterhorn. . . .
>
> My wood-lot grows an Arden,
>   My pond a Caspian Sea;
> And so my Fifty Acres
>   Is all the world to me.
>
> Here on my Fifty Acres
>   I safe at home remain,
> And have my own Bermuda,
>   My Sicily, my Spain.

On August 27, 1981, Pearson died in his native county at the age of 101.

VII

HUMORISTS

Humor is so much an ingredient of literature that it is perhaps misleading to speak of it as a separate genre. John Lawson displayed his wit on almost every page, providing a sparkle for observations and travels that otherwise might have been dull indeed. In *Blackbeard* Lemuel Sawyer turned, in several scenes, to farce. Fearing the scorn of readers who might think that all literature ought to be serious, Sawyer footnoted a passage of low comedy, "If the above scene is too vulgar for representation, it may be omitted." Both Lawson and Sawyer were well aware that humor is a necessary part of living. People love to laugh.

The writing of humor for its own sake, and not as an element of some other literary type, first became popular in North Carolina during the three decades before the Civil War. It assumed the now familiar form of the extended anecdote or humorous sketch. Often it was no more than a highly exaggerated recounting of some bizarre happening.

In 1831 Hamilton Chamberlain Jones of Salisbury, known as "Ham" Jones, printed "Cousin Sally Dilliard" in the *Saturday Evening Post* of Philadelphia. The scene is a courtroom, and a witness is asked to tell what he knows of a violent fight that took place at Captain Rice's. The garrulous old fellow, however, so persists in dragging out an irrelevant story concerning his Cousin Sally that he concludes his testimony without ever having got to the subject of the fight at all. "Cousin Sally Dilliard," known and loved by Abraham Lincoln, was one of the favorite folk sketches of the Old South. Jones wrote a number of other pieces, some of which were printed in his Salisbury newspaper, the *Carolina Watchman*.

Atkinson's Saturday Evening Post, August 6, 1831

Communicated for the Saturday Evening Post.

COUSIN SALLY DILLIARD.

Scene—*A Court of Justice, in No. Ca.*

A beardless disciple of Themis rises, and thus addresses the court:—May it please your Worships, and you, Gentlemen of the Jury, since it has been my fortune (good or bad I will not say) to exercise myself in legal disquisitions, it has never before befallen me to be obliged to denounce a breach of the peace so enormous and transcending as the one now claiming your attention. A more barbarous, direful, marked and malicious assault—a more wilful, violent, dangerous and murderous battery, and finally, a more diabolical breach of the peace has seldom happened in a civilized country, and I dare say it has seldom been your duty to pass upon one so shocking to benevolent feeling as this, which took place over at Captain Rice's, in this county, but you will hear from the witnesses. The witnesses being sworn, two or three were examined and deposed—one, that he heard the noise, but did'nt see the fight—another, that he saw the row, but don't know who struck first—and a third, that he was very drunk, and could'nt say much about the scrimmage.

Lawyer Chops.—I am sorry, gentlemen, to have occupied so much of your time with the stupidity of the witnesses examined. It arose, gentlemen, altogether from misapprehension on my part. Had I known, as I now do, that I had a witness in attendance, who was well acquainted with all the circumstances of the case, and who was able to make himself clearly and intelligibly understood by the court and jury, I should not so long have trespassed on your time and patience. Come forward, Mr. Harris, and be sworn.

So forward comes the witness, a fat, chuffy looking man, a "*leetle*" *corned*, and took his corporal oath with an air.

Ham Jones sketch

North Carolina lost one of the most celebrated of southern humorists when Wilmington-born Johnson Jones Hooper left the state for the crude Deep South in 1835 at the age of twenty. In Alabama he created his disreputably comic character Simon Suggs, whose rascally adventures delighted readers the nation over. Fayetteville's John Winslow, not so well known as Hooper, contributed a number of sketches in the mid-1840s to the *Spirit of the Times* (New York), a sporting weekly in which much of the humor by Jones and Hooper first appeared. Winslow's series on the courtship and marriage of Billy Warrick made amiable jest of the raw backwoods customs and social life of his region.

Billy Warrick's courtship and wedding

Occasionally, during antebellum times, a weekly newspaper was founded whose primary purpose was humor. The Raleigh *Rasp*, under the editorship of Wesley Whitaker, Jr., filled its columns in 1841 and 1842 with jocular concoctions and, to poke fun at the incompetent verse-mongers of the day, invented a "Poetry Machine" that was capable of turning out

Whitaker's "Poetry Machine"

some rather appalling rhymes. In 1848 Editor J. Lawrence Badger of the *Charlotte Journal*, under the pen name Jemmy Critus, instituted a "Humorous Niche" for which he wrote a number of sprightly sketches, one of them having to do with the embarrassing mishaps a country fellow has in the city. In the 1850s the *Live Giraffe* of Raleigh lived up to its startling name.

The difficult years following the Civil War were not conducive to the writing of humor. Then, providentially, in 1886, Bill Nye came to Buncombe County. Already he was a renowned American humorist ranking close to the peerless Mark Twain. At once, Nye's quips took on a North Carolina coloring. He built a dwelling not far from Biltmore House and commented that "George Vanderbilt's extensive new grounds command a fine view of my place." He wrote that "farms [in the mountains] get up and hump themselves in the middle or on one side, so that you have to wear a pair of telegraph-pole climbers when you dig your potatoes."

The humor of Shepherd M. Dugger, author of *The Balsam Groves of the Grandfather Mountain* (1892), is presumably unintentional; yet no one can help being cheered by its purple prose. Concerning the dining room of the Eseeola Inn at Linville, Dugger wrote: "Such is the variety and flavor of the food that, when you place your foot on the threshold of the masticating department, your nasal proboscis is greeted with the aroma of roasted mutton or beef, and the alimentary pupils of your orbicular instruments are fixed upon large slabs of comb honey."

After the turn of the century, the short stories of Greensboro native William Sydney Porter (O. Henry) reached a mammoth audience because of their successful blending of sentiment, surprise, and humor. In the late 1920s William T. Polk determinedly abjured sentiment and surprise but kept the humor, and, from his law office in Warrenton, wrote stories like "The Fallen Angel" and

William T. Polk

"Church Cleaning at Lickskillet," which treat the lusty antics of the village and country folk he knew so well. Polk's high jinks are in the same vein as those of Ham Jones a century earlier. Joseph Mitchell of Robeson County published in the *New Yorker* a number of humorous stories of the tobacco country. In "The Downfall of Fascism in Black Ankle County," for instance, Mitchell wrote hilariously of the stupidity of the Ku Klux Klanners. Many excellent novels, like Burke Davis's *The Summer Land* (1965), treated the joyful comedy of those who live in North Carolina's rural areas. Guy Owen's *The Ballad of the Flim-Flam Man* (1965) deals with the laughable predicaments suffered by the disreputable con artist Mordecai Jones and his innocently willing sidekick Curley Treadaway. Owen's gift for relating the scurrilous attempts of the pair to cheat those who are stupid or greedy is continued in *The Flim-Flam Man and the Apprentice Grifter* (1972) and *The Flim-Flam Man and Other Stories* (1976). The tobacco country of the Cape Fear region is Owen's locale for his stories.

In mid-twentieth-century journalism, the humorous sketch again became pop-

ular. Except for Bill Nye, it had apparently been all but buried in the debris at Fort Sumter, but after its long hiatus it was finally revived by a group of men with newspaper backgrounds. Carl Goerch established the *State* magazine in 1933, and soon his page-length feature "Just One . . . Thing after Another" appeared. Goerch's most famous sketch was "The Zipper Story," about the frenzy of a relaxed, corpulent man in a movie theater whose trouser zipper becomes caught in the dress of a lady sitting next to him. From his *State* sketches, Goerch published four books, beginning with *Down Home* (1943).

Over in Southern Pines, the ordinarily serious historical novelist James Boyd, upon assuming editorship of the weekly *Pilot*, created Mr. Hugh Dave MacWhirr, whose good-natured, outspoken opinions moved troubled minds toward comic acceptance during the distressing early years of World War II. Robert Ruark, born in Wilmington, attracted national attention as a result of his syndicated newspaper column. The column's sharpest tidbits were collected in two books, *I Didn't Know It Was Loaded* (1948) and *One for the Road* (1949). Ruark aimed his stinging wit at psychiatrists, the state of Texas, progressive schools, scheming women, and his other pet hates. In two slapstick spoofs of novels like *Gone with the Wind*, Ruark's *Grenadine Etching* (1947) and *Grenadine's Spawn* (1952) attempted to demolish the bosomy historical romance as it was then being written. In the 1950s, from his Charlotte office of the *Carolina Israelite*, Harry Golden employed a sense of comedy in defense of minority groups. Beginning with *Only in America* (1958), Golden published a book a year, each of them composed principally of essays appearing originally in his newspaper. In the early days of the civil-rights agitations, for example, he devised the Golden Vertical Negro Plan, which called for the elimination of all chairs in public schools. "It is only when the Negro 'sets' that the fur begins to fly," wrote Golden. "Provide only desks in all the public schools of our state; no seats."

The humorous sketch, relying heavily upon an autobiographical narrative line, became the medium of Willie Snow Ethridge, among whose fifteen books is *You Can't Hardly Get There from Here* (1965). One of its eleven stories is "We Get Going," relating a family's summer

Bob Parker

Illustration from "We Get Going"

morning departure from Sanford for a beach vacation. The delays encountered in getting out of town, as related by Ethridge, are as laughter-provoking to the reader as they are frustrating to the vacationers. A popular platform humorist, Ethridge tested her stories before audiences before preparing them for publication. Another kind of humor entirely is that of Greensboro's Dave Morrah, who used mock-German for his comic effects in *Cinderella Hassenpfeffer* (1948) and *Fraulein Bo-Peepen and More Tales Mein Grossfader Told* (1953). His successful series includes two humorous novels using the North Carolina scene

and a book called *Sillynyms* (1956), in which a reader will encounter such statements as "Hell hath no fury like a woman's corns."

Unique among books revealing the comic spirit of North Carolinians is *Grave Humor: A Collection of Humorous Epitaphs* (1961), collected by Alonzo C. Hall of Greensboro. Though his epitaphs come from England and throughout the United States, many are from North Carolina, like the tombstone inscription from a Snow Camp cemetery:

> Here lies a virgin with her babe
> resting in her arms.

Two distinguished politicians are among North Carolina's most treasured humorists. Regrettably, the high-flying and often bawdy anecdotes of Civil War governor and later United States senator Zebulon Baird Vance of Buncombe County have never been collected. Vance was especially well known for his amiable but cutting repartee. One example is the retort he made when, following a rather long speech in the Senate, a political opponent accosted him with "I heard your speech, Senator Vance, but it went in one ear and out the other." Vance immediately replied, "Nothing to stop it."

State Chronicle (Raleigh), August 15, 1890

Zebulon Baird Vance

North Carolinians were lucky when Morganton's Senator Sam J. Ervin, Jr., of Watergate fame was induced to collect his favorite risible stories in *Humor of a Country Lawyer* (1983). On one occasion, Ervin relates, Bob Hennessee, who "was Burke County's most cross-eyed resident with the exception of Sheriff Manly McDowell, who was equally cross-eyed," was walking along Union Street in the opposite direction from the sheriff when they bumped into each other. "Bob Hennessee," said the sheriff, "why in the hell don't you look where you're going?" "It wouldn't do a bit of good," Hennessee replied, "because you don't go where you're looking."

Richard Walser's *Tar Heel Laughter* (1974) is a 300-page anthology of North Carolina humor from 1709 onward.

VIII
HISTORIANS AND OTHERS

Though Thomas Hariot, John Lawson, and others are sometimes thought of as historians, their books are more the materials of history than they are histories themselves. The first "real" history of North Carolina was published in 1812 by Hugh Williamson, formerly of Edenton.

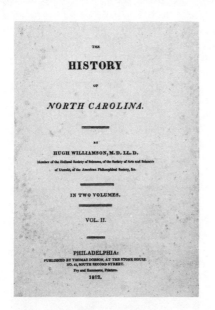

For the most part containing dull documents secured from family papers, it covered North Carolina history only up to the beginning of the colonial period. In 1829 François-Xavier Martin, the French-born printer who had settled in New Bern and brought out a number of novels there, wrote a second general history. Like Williamson's book, it was a monotonous accumulation of statements, many of them erroneous. Neither of these first two histories made a serious attempt to interpret the data they so poorly recorded. *Historical Sketches of North Carolina* (1851), though its author John Hill Wheeler of Murfreesboro disparaged Williamson and Martin, is little more than an untrustworthy succession of names and lists. The two-volume *History of North Carolina* (1857-1858), by Francis Lister Hawks of New Bern, was an improvement in that it at least dealt with social as well as political matters, but it stopped at the end of the proprietary period. Hawks was a versatile literary man who turned out ecclesiastical tracts, juvenile biographies, nature studies, and poems, though most of these writings came after he left North Carolina in 1829. John Wheeler Moore of Hertford County, two years before his popular novel *The Heirs of St. Kilda* was published, wrote a *School History of North Carolina* (1879). Because of its comprehensive sweep from the Roanoke colony through the Civil War and Reconstruction, it was for many years the standard history read by adults as well as students. Succeeding it was *Young People's History of North Carolina* (1907), by Daniel Harvey Hill, Jr., of Raleigh.

Moore and Hill tried to avoid the mistake-making habits of their predecessors, and thus their efforts were generally approved. The inadequacies of the earlier writers did not go unnoticed. In 1871 a newspaper correspondent characterized Martin "as dull as dish water" and denounced Williamson as "a blind royalist." To a prominent North Carolina judge, Wheeler's *Sketches* was simply a "Democratic Stud Book."

The fact remains that all these men, in spite of their dedication, were amateurs in that they had received no professional training for the tasks they undertook. Nor did they have available such necessary documents as those later so abundantly printed in William L. Saunders's *Colonial Records* and Walter Clark's *State Records*. Then in 1908 came Volume I of Samuel A. Ashe's *History of North Carolina* (Volume II was delayed until 1925), the first state history to make extensive use of the *Records*. Though Ashe was no trained historian, his work was exemplary, as was his editing of the valuable eight-volume *Biographical History of North Carolina* (1905-1917). It was not until 1919 that rigorously educated historians, following the good work of Ashe and using scholarly methods, produced a completely professional chronicle of the state. This was the three-volume *History of North Carolina*, for which R. D.W. Connor provided the first book on colonial and Revolutionary history, William K. Boyd the second on the federal period before 1860, and J. G. de Roulhac Hamilton the final volume. Here at last was a professionally written, reliable account of North Carolina. In 1929 came Connor's *North Carolina: Rebuilding an Ancient Commonwealth*; and in 1941 Archibald Henderson, Chapel Hill's mathematician and biographer, published *North Carolina: The Old North State and the New*, in which cultural history, given more attention than in the past, matched the usual emphases on political, military, and social affairs.

By 1940, with maximum systematic expertness, Albert R. Newsome and Hugh T. Lefler had issued a new school history, *The Growth of North Carolina*, and followed it with the convenient one-volume *North Carolina: The History of a Southern State* (1954). At that point, the indefatigable Dr. Lefler, a native of Davie County, wrote his *History of North Carolina* (1956) in two volumes. His *North Carolina: History, Geography, Government* (1959, 1966) is an updated school text. The distance from William-

son to Lefler is much more than the years of almost a century and a half. It is the distance from the dilettante and bibliophile to the scholar and historiographer. But history, by its very nature, must be constantly rewritten and reinterpreted.

Several years passed before William S. Powell of the university faculty in Chapel Hill brought out his *North Carolina: A Bicentennial History* (1977). A specialist in colonial history, Powell had endeared himself to citizens everywhere with his monumental *North Carolina Gazetteer* (1968), containing some twenty thousand entries on counties, cities, towns, deserted hamlets, inlets, sounds, mountains, lakes, rivers, creeks—each located geographically, and often with its derivation and history accounted for. Another mammoth project was his editing of a *Dictionary of North Carolina Biography*, a projected multivolume series of which only the

Gary Ward

William S. Powell

first two have appeared thus far. The 1,500 sketches, ranging from presidents to pirates and scoundrels, were written by scores and scores of contributors both in the state and elsewhere. In 1983 Thomas C. Parramore of Meredith College, an indefatigable researcher, brought out his *North Carolina: The History of an*

American State, which was quickly adopted as a text by the public schools. More than ten years went into the preparation of *North Carolina Illustrated, 1524-1984* (1983), by H. G. Jones, librarian at the University of North Carolina in Chapel Hill. It is not only a full-length historical narrative but is accompanied by nearly fifteen hundred drawings, maps, and photographs, making it unparalleled among state histories.

From the nineteenth century on, there were, of course, many historians who treated in a limited way those periods or aspects of history in which they had special competence. Among the early professionals was John Spencer Bassett of Trinity College, who wrote many studies such as *The Constitutional Beginnings of North Carolina* (1894). Notable in its day was *A Bibliography of the Historical Literature of North Carolina* (1895), by Stephen B. Weeks, a native of Pasquotank County. By the 1930s rigidly trained writers were investigating many fields previously neglected. At Chapel Hill, Samuel H. Hobbs wrote *North Carolina, Economic and Social* (1930), Howard W. Odum published *Southern Regions of the United States* (1936), and Guion Griffis Johnson completed her *Ante-Bellum North Carolina* (1937), which, based on a careful reading of thousands of books and newspapers, presents a picture of the state quite different from that engendered by the romantic recollections of old-timers. In more recent years, Lawrence Lee, Blackwell Robinson, and Alan D. Watson have been digging into dark corners of North Carolina colonial history. Christopher Crittenden, Hugh F. Rankin, and Carole W. Troxler have centered their research and writing on Revolutionary times, while the Civil War and Reconstruction have attracted Burke Davis, John G. Barrett, Glenn Tucker, Allen W. Trelease, and Richard L. Zuber. North Carolina's various Indian groups have been treated by Douglas L. Rights, F. Roy Johnson, Karen I. Blu, Vernon K. Crow, Ruth Wetmore, and Theda Perdue. On the history of blacks in North Carolina are books by John Hope Franklin, Helen G. Edmonds, Frenise A. Logan, Eric Anderson, and Jeffrey J. Crow. All of the historians here mentioned, and many others, no longer write in the stilted idiom of a Williamson or a Wheeler, whose style made no attempt at literary grace.

A unique method of writing history was employed in 1983-1984 by William D. Snider, editor emeritus of the *Greensboro News and Record*. Eighteen months before election day at the beginning of the most expensive senatorial campaign ($25 million) in American politics, he was commissioned to write about the fierce contest as it progressed. Day by day he kept up with the candidates and wrote chapter by chapter as the long, bitter confrontation ran its course. After November 6, only the last pages of his unbiased *Helms and Hunt: The North Carolina Senate Race, 1984* (1985) needed to be written, and the book was published a few months later.

Travel writing lends itself, of course, to the descriptive, but most travel books have a tendency to bolster observations of scenery and people with comments about the history of the region. Such was the case of Wilbur Gleason Zeigler and Ben S. Grosscup's *The Heart of the Alleghanies* (1883) and other books like it. The classic book about the mountains is of course Horace Kephart's *Our Southern Highlanders* (1913), which depicts, with undisguised affection, the inhabitants of the Great Smokies in the early part of the century. Relying on geography and history and hearsay, Kephart accounted for the individuality and integrity of the hill people. A similar book, valuable on many scores, is Muriel Earley Sheppard's *Cabins in the Laurel* (1935). Not only did Sheppard use local history in her study of mountain folk in the Toe River valley but, quite often, to catch the rhythm of their lives, she drifted into homespun poetry. Another book of the mountains combining history with travel and legend is Wilma Dykeman's *The French Broad* (1955), one of the

Illustration from *The French Broad*

famed Rivers of America series. This book entertainingly relates a dozen or so of those memorable stories almost always omitted from the usual histories, such as the search for Professor Elisha Mitchell's body on the mountain that bears his name, the cutting of the Swannanoa tunnel, and the coming of the Vanderbilts to western North Carolina. Dykeman has also written several novels of the mountain people and collaborated with her husband, James Stokely, on books of nonfiction. A different kind of travel book came from Marguerite Schumann, a resident of Chapel Hill, in *The Living Land: An Outdoor Guide to North Carolina* (1977) and *Tar Heel Sights: A Guide to North Carolina Heritage* (1983). Her *Grand Old Ladies: North Carolina Architecture during the Victorian Era* (1984) contains 149 photographs of Victorian buildings, captioned with excerpts from such writers as O. Henry, Jonathan Daniels, and Doris Betts.

Old Bethesda (1933), by Bion H. Butler of Southern Pines, is much more than the history of a Presbyterian church at a crossroads in the Sandhills. From the church, down the roads that dimmed to the horizon, the Scottish settlers of the Cape Fear fanned out to enact their important role in the settlement of America. Within its unique thematic frame, *Old Bethesda* is different from the usual regional studies.

It is true, and perhaps understandable, that writers have been drawn to the mountains and the coastline of North Carolina more than to the Piedmont. From the lengthy bibliography of books on the coastal region, two authors stand out. *The Hatterasman* (1958), by Ben Dixon MacNeill, is romanticized history compacted of legend and poetry, and certainly more on the side of belles lettres than history. MacNeill lived on Hatteras Island for more than a decade, and his rapturous story of the islanders is in the same tradition as Kephart's book on the mountain dwellers. Of a vastly different sort are two books by David Stick of Kitty Hawk, a fastidious researcher of the modern school depending upon reliable documents rather than upon hearsay and folklore. His account of North Carolina shipwrecks, *Graveyard of the Atlantic* (1952), is now the primary book on the subject, and *The Outer Banks of North Carolina, 1584-1958* (1958) is a definitive history of the Outer Banks from Currituck County to Beaufort Inlet. Later came *The Cape Hatteras Shore*

Illustration from *Graveyard of the Atlantic*

(1964) and *Bald Head: A History of Smith Island and Cape Fear* (1986). Though Stick was not attempting to write popular history, his books were widely read as well as widely approved.

Quite different from all of these was the approach of Bill Sharpe of Raleigh, whose four-volume *New Geography of North Carolina* (1954-1965) was aimed primarily at the wide reader audience of his *State* magazine, from which the sketches were reprinted. For each of the 100 counties, Sharpe provided, along with historical sketches, a journalist's account of the agriculture, education, industry, recreation, and population centers. Like Dykeman's *The French Broad*, Sharpe's *Geography* was crammed with miscellaneous information sidestepped by the workaday research historian.

Though all these books tried to tell the North Carolina story in their exhaustive or limited way, depending on the authors' experiences and interests and knowledge, none of them succeeded in discovering the secret of just what sort of person the composite North Carolinian was. The depth of perception necessary for such a job somehow went beyond the skills and intentions of even the most willing and energetic writers. Then Wilbur J. Cash of Shelby accepted the challenge. *The Mind of the South* (1941), perhaps the most intellectually influential book ever to come from North Carolina, encompassed all the states of the old Confederacy, but the view was clearly that of a North

Carolinian. The southerner was violent, suspicious, hasty, intolerant, and unrealistic; he was also proud, sentimental, courteous, honorable, and romantic. The southerner was, at any one moment, both democratic and aristocratic. Cash, to reinforce his analyses, had simultaneously to be psychologist, sociologist, economist, philosopher, and historian. It was a large order, and though not everyone agreed, or now agrees, with him, his tenets concerning the paradoxical southerner were ultimately acknowledged as sound. Joseph L. Morrison's *W. J. Cash: Southern Prophet* (1967) is a biography.

Cash was exceptional. But he could never have written *The Mind of the*

W. J. Cash

41

South without the tedious but necessary work of the scholars who came before him. Meanwhile, research efforts continued, not only in period histories and regional studies but also in other phases of life in North Carolina. Louis Round Wilson, for example, focused on the expansion of libraries throughout the state and the nation, an activity attested by his dozens of books and reports. In another area, Norman E. Eliason read through thousands of manuscripts in order to write *Tarheel Talk: An Historical Study of the English Language in North Carolina to 1860* (1956). He announced that *buncombe* and *scuppernong* are the only words of undoubted North Carolina origin and declared as "grossly exaggerated" those dearly beloved "claims about the antiquity of the speech in isolated sections along the coast or in the mountains, where the persistence of some older forms like *hit* for *it* or *bile* for *boil* is seized on as proof that 'pure Elizabethan' or even 'Chaucerian' English is still spoken there."

Among the more memorable bypaths of history are the biographies and autobiographies of important personages. But like the early histories, the early biographies and autobiographies were hardly standards of excellence. The *Life of the Hon. Nathaniel Macon* (1840), about a man whom many consider to be the greatest North Carolinian of his age, was written by Edward R. Cotten of Hertford and Bertie counties, but the book has had the unhappy fate to be labeled "the worst biography ever written." E. W. Caruthers's *A Sketch of the Life and Character of the Rev. David Caldwell* (1842) had better luck, though the modern reader cannot help noticing that the biographer had precious little information about the famous teacher of Guilford County and, consequently, padded his book with Revolutionary history and added more or less extraneous accounts of the Presbyterian church in eighteenth-century North Carolina. A haphazard work, but one of the mines for the research historian, was Griffith J. Mc-

Ree's two-volume *Life and Correspondence of James Iredell* (1857-1858). Though McRee knew more about his man than did Caruthers, he, like Caruthers, immersed his subject into the political and social history of the Revolutionary age in which Iredell lived.

For the next hundred years, other prominent North Carolinians sat for their biographical portraits, some successfully, some not. Again, the pattern set by the historians persisted, for it was well into the twentieth century before biographers had available the tools provided for them by large research libraries. Gerald W. Johnson, a native of Scotland County and an accomplished stylist, wrote several early novels and a trio of biographies of three Democratic presidents—Jackson, Wilson, and Franklin D. Roosevelt—then made a study of that man with the still-mysterious North Carolina background: *The First Captain, the Story of John Paul Jones* (1947). Johnson was skeptical concerning the story that the sailor John Paul added Jones to his name in honor of a North Carolina benefactor, but he did not deny the possibility of it. Among the long list of Johnson's books are a number of juveniles on American history and government.

John Paul Jones was also the subject of a biography (1927) by Phillips Russell of Chapel Hill, but Professor Russell's most admired work is *The Woman Who Rang*

Cornelia Phillips Spencer

the Bell (1949), a biography of his great-aunt Cornelia Phillips Spencer. Spencer, an author herself and a champion of education, agitated for the reopening of the University of North Carolina in postwar days, and Russell tells how, when the good news came, she mounted the steps of the deserted classroom building and rang the bell to proclaim the event.

If Jonathan Daniels of Raleigh is best known for regional books such as *A Southerner Discovers the South* (1938), he was nevertheless a renowned biographer and political commentator who roamed the national scene for inspiration. Among the few books he limited to North Carolina were *Tar Heels* (1941), a bright and happily informal portrait of the state, though now somewhat dated, and *Prince of Carpetbaggers* (1958), on the infamous career of General Milton S. Littlefield, rogue of Reconstruction days. This second book is certainly entertaining in its lively narrative about a long-forgotten rascal, but southern hero-worshipers were not amused when Daniels's honesty forced him to reveal that Littlefield would not have been nearly so successful in his money-making schemes without the collaboration of a number of eminent North Carolina conservatives still revered for their saintliness.

Notion has it that the most beloved governor North Carolina ever had was Zeb Vance, and several writers have undertaken to put him into a book. The best of the lot, by far, is *Zeb Vance: Champion of Personal Freedom* (1965), by Glenn Tucker of Fairview, whose several prior volumes concerning the Civil War served as excellent preparation for the writing of it. Even the more than five hundred pages of Tucker's biography were not enough to spell out the details of Vance's varied and action-crowded career, but Tucker managed to catch the humor and the humanity of a man whom North Carolinians adored because he could spit tobacco one moment and the next move easily and confidently among the mighty people of the nation. *Charles Brantley Aycock*

(1961), by Oliver H. Orr, Jr., and *William W. Holden: North Carolina's Political Enigma* (1985), by Horace Raper, are biographies of two governors who wielded authority during perilous periods in the state's history. Yet, the lives of many notable of the state are still unresearched and unrecorded. Perhaps they will come in time.

Some of the best books of biography are written about men and women somewhat less than celebrated. Robert Burton House's *Miss Sue and the Sheriff* (1941) is a romantic recollection of boyhood on a plantation in Halifax County, where the author's mother presided over her large household of children, relatives, and workers while his father the sheriff was away attending to law and order in the county. It is a warm reminiscence of people happy in what life had to offer. A not-so-affectionate picture of eastern North Carolina is Sam Byrd's *Small Town South* (1942), more reflection than biography. When the author returned to the town of his youth after success in the Broadway theater, he found the place economically depressed, the fine old houses turned into funeral homes, and child-brides and bootleggers everywhere.

A praiseworthy example of biography based on recollection is Pauli Murray's *Proud Shoes* (1956). As a child, the author lived with her grandparents in Durham. Many years later she wrote this beautiful and moving story about them. Cornelia Fitzgerald was an octoroon, her husband Robert an intelligent light-skinned man of color. They were useful citizens, and they and their children walked in proud shoes along the streets of Durham at the turn of the century, when pride competed with bitterness. One is again reminded, from reading a book like this, that nobility is not a commodity confined to great military and religious and political leaders, though the overwhelming number of such biographies would so seem to indicate.

The most intimate and personal "life" is undeniably written by the subject himself. Congressman Lemuel Sawyer, the dramatist from Camden County, put into his wretchedly organized *Auto-Biography* (1844) so many disreputable episodes of his selfishness and petty dishonesty that the reader is almost repelled by the outpouring. Of a different sort was the self-adulatory autobiography of Edward Warren of Tyrrell County, *A Doctor's Experiences in Three Continents* (1885). Warren's travels took him from Edenton at mid-century to France and then on to Egypt, where, according to him, he was the "most famous man" in the country, acclaimed for his surgery and honored with the title of bey.

It's a Far Cry (1937), by Robert W. Winston, viewed the social and political climate of North Carolina from a boyhood in Windsor to a legal career in Oxford and Durham, and finally, when he was past the age of sixty, a return to Chapel Hill as a freshman in 1923. As much informal history as autobiography, Winston's very readable book spoke out honestly and liberally on racial problems long before it was thought wise to do so.

Unquestionably the most ambitious and monumental autobiography ever to be written by a North Carolinian is the five-volume set by Josephus Daniels: *Tar Heel Editor* (1939); *Editor in Politics* (1941); *The Wilson Era, Years of Peace, 1910-1917* (1944); *The Wilson Era, Years of War and After, 1917-1923* (1946); and *Shirt-Sleeve Diplomat* (1947). In these books by one who was a Raleigh newspaperman and secretary of the navy under Wilson and ambassador to Mexico under Roosevelt, the sweep of state, national, and international politics is narrated by a focal participant.

Other significant autobiographies are *Businessman in the State House: Six Years as Governor of North Carolina* (1962), by Luther H. Hodges, and *My Own, My Country's Time: A Journalist's Journey* (1983), by Vermont Royster, a Raleigh native who became a noted editor of the *Wall Street Journal*.

On the opposite end of the prestige scale is the best-selling *See Here, Private Hargrove* (1942). At the beginning of World War II, Marion Hargrove arrived for induction at Fort Bragg, then reported regularly to the *Charlotte News* the "cheerful and quiet little impertinences about his new life." When collected into a book, his columns caught the fancy of American readers who were eager to know of the not-so-serious aspects of army life, and for many years Private Hargrove was the epitome of the confused but happy civilian in uniform.

Though the chapters of Hargrove's book had chronological continuity, they began as journalistic essays. The work of an earlier essayist, Isaac Erwin Avery of Morganton and Charlotte, also was written for a newspaper column before being published as *Idle Comments* (1905). Avery, the observer rather than the doer, "commented" on animals and children, on literature and manners, usually in one-paragraph passages and always with kindness and intelligence. Avery's humor and good sense were gifts inherited in a later day by Harry Golden and Thad Stem, Jr., and by Weimar Jones of Franklin, whose collection of columns in *My Affair with a Weekly* (1960) caught the essence of living happily along main street in a small mountain town.

The essayist-philosopher Horace Williams of Chapel Hill, whom Thomas

North Carolina Collection

Horace Williams

44

Wolfe immortalized as "Hegel in the Cotton Belt" in *Look Homeward, Angel,* was the subject of a biography by Robert W. Winston. Though Williams was a teacher rather than a writer, his Hegelian principles are preserved in his own *The Education of Horace Williams* (1936) and in the posthumous *Logic for Living* (1951).

Though at first it may seem surprising, the fact remains that North Carolina's best-selling writer is Billy Graham, evangelist of Montreat. His some dozen books have sold (often in translation) by the millions all over the world. A recent one, *Till Armageddon: A Perspective on Suffering* (1984), is a "spiritual survival kit" for those laboring with sorrowful experiences—personal, painful, or tragic. Most of Graham's published works were developed from his sermons.

Irene Burk Harrell of Wilson, author of books on religion and "popular psychology," has published more than forty titles. Among her more popular works are *The Opposite Sex* (1972), *Muddy Sneakers and Other Family Hassles* (1974), and *Multiplied by Love* (1976).

IX

FOLKLORISTS

Like humor, folklore is so deeply woven into a regional literature that it is not easy to separate it from other genres, to be able to say, "This is folklore, but that is a short story." Writers of imaginative literature base their work on the customs and beliefs of those whom they have known, on the manners and ways of communities where they have lived. Lore of the folk enriches the great works of Shakespeare, of Hawthorne and Melville, of Thomas Wolfe and Paul Green.

What is folklore? Arthur Palmer Hudson defines it as "that complex of knowledge which has been created by the spontaneous play of naïve imaginations upon common human experience, transmitted by word of mouth or action, and preserved without dependence upon written or printed record." Folklore comprises myths, sayings, songs, charms, anecdotes, traditions, magic, and so on. It deals with snakes, ghosts, pirates, bears, hunters, witches, and even baseball players.

North Carolina is a particularly fertile region for the creation, flowering, and preservation of folklore. First of all, the state was and is geographically congenial to folklore in that, until the coming of paved roads and wireless communications, the coastal and mountain areas of the state were relatively isolated. Especially does folklore flourish wherever intrusions from the outside world are minimal. Then, too, while there is a folklore of the towns and cities, North Carolina's stable and predominantly rural population retained its mores long after they were abandoned by those people who shifted from place to place.

While these conditions may apply somewhat to other regions, North Carolina's importance in folklore was firmly established by the publication of the seven-volume *Frank C. Brown Collection of North Carolina Folklore* (1952-1964), a vast and handsome repository unrivaled in any of the other forty-nine states. In it are recorded, in scholarly fashion, North Carolina games and rhymes, beliefs and customs, riddles, proverbs, speech, tales and legends, and popular superstitions. Four of the volumes provide the words and music for such notable folk ballads and folk songs as "Naomi Wise," "Frankie Silver," "Tom Dula," and "Nellie Cropsey."

As professor of English at Duke University, Brown early began to gather scattered bits of folklore, but it was not until after his death that his papers, magnanimously supplemented by other collectors, were published. In 1913 he had helped to organize the North Carolina Folklore Society, which still exists.

The systematic acquiring of folk materials began in 1916 when Cecil Sharp came over from England and traveled throughout Appalachia collecting ballads of British origin. He came upon much more than he had anticipated, especially in Madison County, and even discovered some distinctly North Carolina ballads that had almost disappeared.

Yet, even the first settlers were busy jotting down aboriginal beliefs, as when Thomas Hariot wrote in 1588 that the smoking of tobacco was an aid to health and as when John Lawson noted in 1709, "Some *Indians* in *America* will go out to Sea, and get upon a Whales Back, and peg or plug up his Spouts, and so kill him."

Other writers recorded similar folk beliefs. Then in 1859 came Hardin E. Taliaferro's *Fisher's River (North Carolina) Scenes and Characters, by "Skitt," "Who Was Raised Thar,"* a book consisting of tall tales from the backwoods of Surry County. Here was an entire volume of genuine folk humor. Taliaferro (pronounced Tolliver) had a lusty sense of the hilarious when dealing with his inelegant rustics, who were constantly fishing, politicking, hunting, praying, eating,

John M'Lenan (1859)

Taliaferro's horn snake

loving, fighting, and telling monstrous lies. There was an old fellow named Uncle Davy Lane, who climbed up a peach tree that was growing between the antlers of a buck deer. When the deer moved off with the ripe peaches, Uncle Davy was enraged that he had not been able to "gullup down more'n fifty." Other tall tales are just as outrageous as the adventures of Uncle Davy, who also tells two whoppers about the coachwhip snake and the horn snake.

Early on, writers of fiction recalled folk narratives and folk songs from their childhoods, then re-created them for transformation into artistic literature.

When Charles W. Chesnutt published *The Conjure Woman* in 1899, he drew on black lore of the Cape Fear country for his seven tales of slavery days. As a result of "conjuring," Sandy is turned into a tree and is then chopped down, Primus into a mule, and Dan into a wolf. The little girl in "Sis' Becky's Pickaninny" is changed into a bird in order to visit her mother on another plantation.

From the early 1920s on, Paul Green drew heavily on folklore for his first plays, as later did other writers such as John Foster West in his mountain novel *Time Was* (1965) and in the fiction of John Ehle, Guy Owen, and Manly Wade Wellman. In Green's *Words and Ways* (1968) are sections on "Folk Medicine," "Hat-Burning," and "Supper for the Dead"—all from the Cape Fear River valley. Of the songs, tales, and sketches that he printed in his *Lyrics and Legends of the Cape Fear Country* (1932), Harnett County poet-professor Hubbard Fulton Page said in the preface, "Some appear almost verbatim . . . others are improvisations built upon mere fragments of folk sayings."

Meanwhile, the recording and retelling of folklore goes on in the Sunday feature sections of the newspapers and especially in the *State* magazine. Almost every year comes some new account of the famous ballad "Tom Dula," of the Old Christmas celebration at Rodanthe, and of Jesse Holmes the Fool-Killer, a

Milton Chronicle, March 10, 1859

A Letter from the Fool Killer

Jesse Holmes in action

character originated by editor Charles Napoleon Bonaparte Evans in his antebellum weekly, the *Milton Chronicle*.

Writers of full-length books, of course, have not been inactive. Charles Harry Whedbee's *Legends of the Outer Banks and Tar Heel Tidewater* (1966) has stories about Virginia Dare and Blackbeard and Theodosia Burr, the ghost ship *Carroll M. Deering*, the devil's hoofprints at Bath, and the floating church at Swan Quarter, as well as the blasphemous fisherman Old Quork of Ocracoke and an albino porpoise known as Hatteras Jack. *The Flaming Ship of Ocracoke & Other Tales of the Outer Banks* (1971), *Outer Banks Mysteries & Seaside Stories* (1978), and *Outer Banks Tales to Remember* (1985) continue the Greenville writer's series as he tells about the "Indian Gallows," the "Dram Tree," and the "Mattamuskeet Apple."

F. Roy Johnson of Murfreesboro, an indefatigable folklorist and interviewer of informants in the field, has gathered the lore and old sagas of northeastern North Carolina in a number of books. *Legends, Myths, and Folk Tales of the Roanoke-Chowan* (1962) and *Tales from*

Bill Ballard (1969)

North Carolina devil

Old Carolina (1965) are full of ghosts, devils, and Dismal Swamp creatures. Evildoing and misbehavior by old Satan and his cronies are treated in *Witches and Demons in Folklore and History* (1969). *How and Why Stories in Carolina Folklore* (1971) and *Supernaturals among Carolina Folk and Their Neighbors* (1974) are other collections. Johnson has books on Tuscarora, Algonquian, and Cherokee Indians with their myths and legends. *The Fabled Doctor Jim Jordan* (1963) is a biography of a Hertford County black man who was noted for his successful ventures into witchcraft and spells.

At the other end of the state, the folklore of the North Carolina mountains has been amply treated by a number of writers. Traditional ballads of the region can be found in the *Brown Collection*. The books by Richard Chase of Beech Mountain, as in *Old Songs and Singing Games* (1938), are directed toward preserving those aspects of English, Scottish, and Irish folk culture handed down from generation to generation in the southern Appalachians. Many of Chase's *Jack Tales* (1943) are reminiscent of that fellow Jack who climbed the beanstalk. *Jack and the Three Sillies* (1950) is Chase's own special contribution to the Jack tales. In *Grandfather Tales* (1948) are echoes of King Lear, Robin Hood, and Cinderella.

A different approach to mountain lore is that taken by John Parris of Sylva, who has gone throughout the hills, talked to the people there, and written down what he heard. *Roaming the Mountains* (1955), *My Mountains, My People* (1957), and *These Storied Mountains* (1975) are such entertaining combinations of tale-telling and history that it is difficult always to know where folklore stops and fact takes up.

The Negro as a serious subject for folk study engaged Professor Howard W. Odum of Chapel Hill in *The Negro and His Songs* (1925) and *Negro Workaday Songs* (1926), both in collaboration with Guy B. Johnson. Then in *Rainbow Round*

My Shoulder: The Blue Trail of Black Ulysses (1928), *Wings on My Feet: Black Ulysses at the Wars* (1929), and *Cold Blue Moon: Black Ulysses Afar Off* (1931) Odum wrote a trilogy of narratives more poetry than prose. To the accompaniment of spirituals, his zestful hero saunters through life, accepting its tragedies and comedies with a happy-go-lucky philosophy said to emanate from the lore

E. T. Malone, Jr. (1985)

North Carolina ghost

Harry Knight

Odum's Black Ulysses

of his people. Odum's Ulysses is a child-like, innocent, strong man, but quite different were those who contributed to the making of J. Mason Brewer's *Worser Days and Better Times: The Folklore of the North Carolina Negro* (1965). Professor Brewer of Livingstone College, in his travels throughout the state, noted the disappearance of the old romantic image of the Negro and the emergence of a figure in the mainstream of American life, but with a folklore still somewhat apart from that of his white neighbor.

The Devil's Tramping Ground and Other North Carolina Mystery Stories (1949), by John Harden of Greensboro, ranged from the Lost Colony through Peter Dromgoole to the Missing Major. Harden's *Tar Heel Ghosts* (1954) summoned up thirty-three apparitions, some

of them odious and fearful, others mere gentle spirits who want only to be noticed. Ghost lore, indubitably one of the most popular diversions in folk studies, was further pursued, with ingenious photographs, by Nancy Roberts of Charlotte in *An Illustrated Guide to Ghosts & Mysterious Occurrences in the Old North State* (1959), *This Haunted Land* (1970), and *Appalachian Ghosts* (1978). Over in Albemarle, Fred T. Morgan concentrated on the strange doings in the thickly forested low mountains of Randolph and Montgomery counties. *Ghost Tales of the Uwharries* (1968) and *Uwharrie Magic* (1974) are filled with alarming and frightful shockers.

In Richard Walser's *North Carolina Legends* (1980) are forty-eight of the best-known, as well as a number of the less familiar, myths, folk yarns, ghost tales, and legends. This book was published by the Division of Archives and History.

Folk speech is as much an ingredient of folklore as ballads, legends, and tall tales. In *You All Spoken Here* (1984), compiled by Roy Wilder, Jr., of Spring Hope, are examples from across the South, but the emphasis is on North Carolina locutions. Wilder cites "roebuckers" (false teeth), "organ recital" (empty stomach), "snollygoster" (political shyster), and "sizzlesozzle" (a light rain). North Carolinians are gifted in hyperbole, insists Wilder, as in "Some whiskey would cause a she-baby bullfrog to spit in a whale's face."

X

DRAMATISTS

No playwrights of importance followed early figures like Thomas Godfrey and Lemuel Sawyer. Though Augustin Daly and the de Mille brothers, William and Cecil, had childhood connections with eastern North Carolina, all three achieved prominence in the world of entertainment after they left the state. At the turn of the century, Christian Reid wrote a drama of Civil War times for production by chapters of the United Daughters of the Confederacy, but her *Under the Southern Cross* (1900) was an isolated affair, as was *Esther Wake, or The Spirit of the Regulators* (1913), by Adolph Vermont of Smithfield, a historical play of Revolutionary North Carolina.

A change away from these unconnected efforts at playwriting was noted in 1918 with the arrival on the campus at Chapel Hill of Professor Frederick H. Koch with his doctrine of the folk drama. Koch preached that all one needed to do in order to write good plays was to observe the life about him, to look into the comedies and tragedies of the "folk" back home, and then to put them onto paper. Plays were not about kings and queens in faraway lands; plays were about the tenant farmers, the blacks, the hill folk, the cotton mill people, the vanishing landed aristocrats. With the Carolina Playmakers as his producing unit, Koch set up shop at the university and waited

Playmakers Theatre, Chapel Hill

for results, which were not long in coming. On the first program of folk plays in March, 1919, was Thomas Wolfe's *The Return of Buck Gavin,* in which undergraduate Tom played the role of his tall hero from the mountains. One year later came Paul Green's *The Last of the Lowries,* a tragedy about the Lumbee Indians in the swamp country. For the next decade and a half, dozens of embryonic dramatists worked under Koch, a surprising number of them achieving professional status not only in theater but also in journalism, teaching, radio, and fiction.

Koch arrived in North Carolina at a lucky time, for America was just entering the age of a New Realism in literature. Not only in Koch's classes, but all over the country as well, writers were taking fresh looks at the materials of their craft. The "folk" were to be treated with honesty and sympathy and humanity;

Frederick H. Koch

the "folk" were no longer to be looked upon as mere puppets to be manipulated. Life—the common speech, the common ways—was to be revealed as it *really* existed; it was to be laid bare by those who had lived on the farms and in the villages and consequently knew what they were writing about.

While Koch was busy with his students, a number of other North Carolina writers, caught up in the excitement, had begun work independently. Faithful to the movement was *What Price Glory?* (1924), co-authored by Laurence Stallings of Yanceyville, who had been in World War I and wanted to tell it as it

was. His tremendously successful play was set at a company headquarters in France, where two career soldiers try to outdo each other in lovemaking, swearing, and cruelty. Closer home, Lula Vollmer of Addor, after traveling with her father to lumber camps in the mountains, wrote several plays of western North Carolina. The most famous was the melodrama *Sun-Up* (1924), about a sturdy mountain woman who fights the "Guv'ment" and doesn't want her son to go off to war in France, which "wuz 'bout forty miles 'tother side o' Asheville." Other mountain plays came from Hatcher Hughes of Polkville, whose *Hell-Bent fer Heaven* (1924), winner of the Pulitzer Prize for the best American play of the year, was a comedy-drama about a fanatic preacher. Hughes's bawdily comic *Ruint* (1925) turned on events set in motion by the supposed condition of an innocent girl. A few years later, the village scene was dissected in *Coquette* (1928), a collaborative effort (with George Abbott) by Ann Preston Bridges of Raleigh. Bridges based her melodrama on an actual murder case in a small courthouse town near the South Carolina line.

Meanwhile, from the battery of Koch's young playwrights at Chapel Hill, one name leaped to prominence. *The Last of the Lowries*, no one-shot effort by any means, was followed by more one-act plays, and when *In Abraham's Bosom* (1927) won the Pulitzer Prize, everyone wanted to know more about the author, Paul Green. Born near Lillington in 1894, Green grew up on his father's farm. He attended the local academy, played baseball, and picked cotton side by side with his white and black neighbors. After graduating from Buies Creek Academy, where he said he was inspired to study literature by poet-professor Hubbard Fulton Page, Green taught school in order to save enough money to go to the University of North Carolina at Chapel Hill. His student days there were interrupted by service in World War I. Upon his return he settled down seriously to the

Paul Green

writing of plays, and though he studied philosophy and taught it for many years thereafter, he had, in accordance with a plan made in boyhood, already begun to tell the story of his people.

While the lines cannot be sharply drawn, Paul Green's career as a dramatist may roughly be separated into three periods. At first he was strongly under the influence of Koch's gospel of the folk-drama. The numerous short plays and such full-length plays as *In Abraham's Bosom* and *The Field God* (1927) belong to this period, the former a tragedy of a black educator, the latter a study of folk religion among rural whites. Both plays have characters who might have come from Green's native Harnett County, and the same can be said of the deteriorating plantation gentry in *The House of Connelly* (1931).

53

His second period, which came after a year in Europe on a Guggenheim fellowship, may be termed the experimental interval. In Germany he was enchanted by the art theater, and he began to think of writing plays that blended music, mass formations, ballet movements, and pantomime with the drama of the North Carolina people. These new techniques would, he hoped, expand the accepted concepts of time and space on the stage. As a result, he wrote three beautiful expressionistic plays: *Tread the Green Grass* (1931), *Roll, Sweet Chariot* (1931), and *Shroud My Body Down* (1935). These plays, fusing folklore and poetry, were followed by *Johnny Johnson* (1937) and *The Enchanted Maze* (1939), which moved away from fantasy toward realism. Meanwhile, essays and short stories and two novels, *The Laughing Pioneer* (1932) and *This Body the Earth* (1935), poured from his pen. Trips to Hollywood permitted experimentation with motion pictures, for which he wrote many scenarios.

A third period came with the symphonic drama, a term Green coined for an original concept of his. *The Lost Colony* (1937) was the first. It was no historical pageant presenting scenes from the past, but a play with a definite story line and warm, living characters. Here, through music and dance and sweeping movements on a large outdoor stage at Manteo, Paul Green told his audience about the American Dream, about every man's right to try to attain the best and the greatest within him. After *The Lost Colony*, which was based on Sir Walter Raleigh's settlers at Roanoke Island in 1587, Green wrote *The Highland Call* (1941) for Fayetteville on the career of the famous Scottish heroine Flora Macdonald during Revolutionary times in North Carolina. A third, *The Common Glory* (1948), with Thomas Jefferson as its leading character, was written for Williamsburg, and in the next two decades he was called on to continue his dramatic story of America in Washington, D.C., in Ohio, Texas, California, Kentucky, and Florida.

From his home in Chapel Hill, Paul Green, no longer on the payroll of the university, maintained a steady schedule of writing. He prepared other plays for Broadway, journeyed to Asia and elsewhere as "cultural ambassador," and in 1969, with *Sing All a Green Willow*, returned to the kind of play he wrote during his experimental period. Green died May 4, 1981.

The outdoor symphonic drama, as created and developed by Paul Green, lured other playwrights to try their hand at the genre. The most notable one of them was Kermit Hunter, a West Virginian who had come to North Carolina as a student. *Unto These Hills*, which opened in 1950, attracted unpredictably large audiences to the village of Cherokee to witness Hunter's dramatization of the famous mountain Indian tribe betrayed by the white man in the 1830s. At Boone, two years later, he invented for *Horn in the West* a story acted out against the western movement into Kentucky by North Carolina highlanders of the 1770s. Daniel Boone was a minor character.

Travel and Tourism Development Division, N.C. Dept. of Commerce

Scene from *Unto These Hills*

54

Both *Unto These Hills* and *Horn in the West* made use, as did all of Paul Green's outdoor plays, of sweeping movements by mimes and singers and dancers. The two plays, along with *The Lost Colony*, are revived annually in the summer months.

Other symphonic dramas, running only a season or so, were written by some of North Carolina's best literary talent. Hubert Hayes of Asheville, whose mountain comedy *Tight Britches* had been produced on Broadway in 1934, wrote *Thunderland*, with Daniel Boone this time as the central character. It was given a sumptuous production in an amphitheater on the Biltmore estate in the early 1950s. Sam Byrd's *The Duplin Story* and John Ehle's *The Road to Orange* dramatized county history, and LeGette Blythe's *Hornets' Nest* in 1968 commemorated the bicentennial year of the city of Charlotte.

In the 1970s, North Carolina, where the outdoor symphonic drama originated, became a mecca of production. So great was the activity that an Institute of Outdoor Drama was established at Chapel Hill to serve local promoters with information and advice. A number of the plays were stimulated by a desire to contribute to the celebration of the national bicentennial. Among the more durable were *From This Day Forward* (1968), by Fred Cranford for Valdese, which recites the story of the settlement of the Waldensians from northern Italy in 1893; *The Sword of Peace* (1974), by William M. Hardy, given at Snow Camp in Alamance County, which dramatizes the struggle between the peace-loving Quakers and the Regulators in Revolutionary times; *The Liberty Cart* (1976), by Randolph Umberger, Jr., for Kenansville, which recounts events in local history from before the Revolution through the Civil War; *Strike at the Wind* (1976), a second outdoor drama by Randolph Umberger, this time at Pembroke, which features the Lumbee Indian folk hero Henry Berry Lowry and his outlawed

"Lowry Gang" from 1864 to 1874; *First for Freedom* (1976), written for Halifax by Maxwell B. Williams, which deals with the Fourth Provincial Congress held there in April, 1776, a body that authorized its delegates to concur with other colonies in declaring independence from Great Britain (North Carolina was the first colony to make such a resolution); and *Blackbeard: Knight of the Black Flag* (1977), by Stuart Aronson, at Bath in Beaufort County, which tells of North Carolina's favorite pirate in 1718. Aronson also wrote *Blackbeard's Revenge* (1985), which utilizes a large amphitheater near Swansboro in Onslow

News and Observer (Raleigh), 1985

County to dramatize the beginnings of the legends surrounding the pirate, whose real name was Edward Teach (or Thatch).

Among the many plays by Howard Richardson of Black Mountain, the one most often revived is his poetic fantasy-drama *Dark of the Moon*, which had a successful New York run in 1945 and has been constantly restaged by both amateur and professional groups. A Koch

alumnus, Richardson based his play on the Scottish ballad "Barbara Allen," beloved by generations of mountain singers and long since transformed by them into a North Carolina folk legend. The play turns on the love of John the witchboy for bonny Barbara Allen of Buck Creek.

Romulus Linney, scion of a prominent family from the mountainous counties of Alexander, Wilkes, and Watauga, spent much of his youth in Boone. He first wrote two novels, each of them a tour de force quite different from the other, then turned to playwriting. After several full-length dramas set variously in Germany, Hawaii, and Washington, D.C., he ventured into his familiar and beloved North Carolina hills for *Holy Ghosts* (1974). This comedy-drama, performed throughout the United States, has as its heroine an unhappy wife who joins a pentecostal cult that practices the handling of rattlesnakes. When her husband comes to rescue her, he too is converted to the dangerous excitation. *Appalachia Sounding* (1975), Linney's contribution to the bicentennial celebration, follows a mountain family through two hundred years of rugged but enduring vitality. *Old Man Joseph and His Family* (1977) is a biblical folk play that dramatizes the childhood of Jesus. After *Just Folks* (1978), another

mountain comedy, came *Tennessee* (1979), a short sketch concerning an overcredulous woman of the hills who late in life discovers that she was misled by her young husband who, promising to take her to Tennessee, instead moved her merely to the other side of an adjoining mountain. Linney continues to write plays and novels on a variety of subjects. "That he is a major talent among contemporary dramatists," wrote a critic, "is a fact the future will acknowledge."

Laura Linney

Romulus Linney

In the autumn of 1974 guitar-playing Jim Wann, a recent graduate of the University of North Carolina at Chapel Hill, collaborated there with his friend Bland Simpson on a "saloon musical" performed at an off-campus location. *Diamond Studs*, a burlesque on the life of Jesse James, filled the air with country music by the Red Clay Ramblers and the Southern States Fidelity Choir. It hit the mood of the times and was so successful that the company moved on to New York for 230 performances, thereafter playing at Ford's Theater in Washington and taking a tour of Alaska. The following year Wann wrote the text as well as some of the lyrics and music for *Hot Grog*, set on the coast of North Carolina in the 1710s, where Blackbeard meets up with such other notorious pirates as Anne Bonney, Calico Jack Rackham, Mary (Mark) Read, and Israel Hands. North

Scene from *Hot Grog*

Carolina's notorious Governor Charles Eden is also present. The musical ran for several months in New York. The success of *Diamond Studs* was repeated by *Pump Boys and Dinettes* (1981), with gas-station jockeys and diner waitresses singing country music to each other across "Highway 57." Its fame crossed the Atlantic, as evinced in the borrowing of its title for an "American" restaurant in Spain. These Jim Wann musicals were followed by other presentations, and on the part of Bland Simpson by a country music novel entitled *Heart of the Country* (1983). In December, 1985, Wann and Simpson got together again, writing and producing their unconventional *King Mackeral &*

Advertisement for Spanish restaurant

The Blues Are Running, for which they abjured plot to tell stories and sing songs to their own accompaniment at the fictitious Corkcake Inlet Inn on an offshore North Carolina island. Their subjects varied from a climb up Jockeys Ridge to shag dancing; pier fishing; a hurricane; and the headless, lantern-carrying ghost of Maco Light.

Though not a science-fiction gaze into the distant future, Nicholas Kazan's *April 2, 1979: The Day the Blanchardville, North Carolina, Political Action and Poker Club Got the Bomb* did indeed anticipate its ultimate fate by eleven months when it opened off-Broadway on March 2, 1978. The plot of this comedy, with a cast of six men and two women, is rather adequately suggested in the wording of its long title.

One of the most significant playwrights to come out of North Carolina in recent years is Pender County's Samm-Art Williams, who grew up near Burgaw. After graduating from Morgan State University in Baltimore, he went to Philadelphia, then on to New York to try his luck

Samm-Art Williams

in the theater. By 1974 he was a member of the Negro Ensemble Company as actor, director, and dramatist. One of his first five plays, *Welcome to Black River* (1975) dealt with North Carolina share-croppers in 1958. But it was *Home* (1979) that catapulted him into top-rank recognition. Cephus, the protagonist, is a strong believer in God and in the land he tills beside the "White Stocking River" at "Cross Roads," North Carolina. When anything goes wrong, Cephus tells himself that God must be on vacation in Miami. A man of integrity—his grandfather and his Uncle Lewis had taught him the precepts "Thou shall not kill" and "Love thy neighbor"—Cephus refuses to go soldiering in Vietnam and is sent to prison in Raleigh. On his release he heads north to work in the city, but his seven years there prove to be disappointing and degrading. "I love the land," he reminds himself, and takes a bus on Christmas eve for North Carolina and his persevering sweetheart, Pattie Mae. His eyes to heaven, he intones, "You finally came back from Miami. Welcome Home." The play had long runs on and off Broadway and was widely toured across the country. The *New York Times* opined that "*Home* was a play from the heart, about the heartline of America." Samm-Art Williams has written other dramas, was author of a television series, has acted in several Hollywood motion pictures, and plans more plays about the black experience in North Carolina.

Country Songs (1986) by Judy Simpson Cook of Charlotte centers on Mildred Cato Privette, the "best hairdresser in Hemby Springs, N.C.," who wants one of her songs sung by the Catawba River Musicmakers at the local VFW dance. The comedy is enriched by its sympathetic portrayal of rural characters in North Carolina's western piedmont. An instant hit when produced on regional stages, the play caught the mood of the mid-1980s.

The state squeezed briefly into the Broadway scene when the eminent American playwright Tennessee Williams chose "Highland Hospital on a windy hilltop near Asheville, North Carolina," as the setting of *Clothes for a Summer Hotel: A Ghost Play* (1980). The actual Highland Hospital was a mental institution where Jazz Age novelist F. Scott Fitzgerald's disturbed wife Zelda spent many of her last twelve years and where she died when the building was destroyed by fire in 1948. Williams's characters, "ghosts" of the famous couple and such of their friends as the Hemingways, recall, long after their deaths, those frivolous days of prosperity, notoriety, and dissipation during and after the 1920s.

Meanwhile, original plays from local writers, produced by campus groups, little theaters, and community dramatic societies, popped up from east to west. Theater by North Carolinians, in and outside the state, was a thriving adventure in the latter part of the twentieth century.

XI

THOMAS WOLFE

Thomas Wolfe, rather generally acclaimed as the greatest writer North Carolina has produced, was born in Asheville on October 3, 1900. His place in the history of American fiction now seems assured, for none of his predecessors and contemporaries—Hawthorne, Melville, Twain, James, Fitzgerald, Hemingway, Faulkner—brought to the novel his combination of vivid character portrayal, his feeling for American immensity, and his lavish poetic rhetoric. If his four enormous novels, as is sometimes said, fall short of perfection, it is a result of their attempt "to put all the experience of the human heart" (in the words of Faulkner's high estimate of Wolfe) "on the head of a pin, as it were."

Wolfe's Pennsylvania father, a tombstone cutter who was fond of quoting Shakespeare and the Bible, went to Asheville from Raleigh with his second wife, who was ill with tuberculosis. But the pure mountain air did not save her, and less than a year after her death, he married Julia Westall, a schoolteacher and native of the hill country. The third Mrs. Wolfe, from the beginning, was a woman of keen intelligence and good business sense.

Thomas Wolfe, youngest of the children, had two sisters and four brothers. He started to public school before he was six and always made good grades. A year or so later, he began selling magazines on the streets of Asheville and shortly afterward took on an early-morning newspaper route. When he was twelve, his teachers opened a private school in Asheville and asked the boy's parents to allow

Wolfe, age fifteen

him to attend. It was there he did his high school work, and there, under the eager direction of his teachers, he fell in love with literature and language. His English compositions indicated that young Wolfe was no ordinary student.

His family decided that his good school record warranted more education, and they chose for him the university at Chapel Hill. His freshman year there was not a happy one, for he was so thin and tall and strange that the other students made fun of him. In order to make the time pass, he studied long and hard. But in his sophomore year, with upperclassmen leaving the campus to join the army after America entered World War I, his prospects began to change. Wolfe's talents were recognized, and he was asked to take on campus responsibilities. In his senior year he was editor of the college newspaper. By the time he graduated in 1920, he was the "biggest man on the Hill." Besides his major in English, other important undergraduate influences were his courses in philosophy and, under "Proff" Koch of the Carolina Playmakers, his writing of folk plays.

Secretly he decided to become a dramatist and convinced his parents to let him go to Harvard, where he planned to study under a famous professor of playwriting. He stayed at Harvard for the next three years, then went to New York to seek producers for the dramas he had written. Because these dramas were so very long, and because they were so unlike the successful Broadway plays of the day, he had no luck. In order to "buy time" until he could make his name in the theater, he accepted a job teaching English at New York University.

Like his father and mother, Wolfe had a passion for travel. In 1926, during his second trip to Europe, he began to write down some of his childhood memories of Asheville. He forgot about playwriting and filled page after page after page with rich prose narrative. Three years later, following many changes and copious revision, his work was published as *Look Homeward, Angel: A Story of the Buried Life* (1929).

Look Homeward, Angel, among the great novels of maturation written in English, is based on the first twenty years of Wolfe's life. Like his creator, Eugene Gant is a boy in a little mountain city called Altamont (Asheville), where his father is a stonecutter and his mother a boardinghouse keeper. A sensitive youth, little appreciated by his parents and friends, Eugene has a newspaper route and is a good student at school. His big family scorns his seriousness, and he withdraws into a "buried life" of his own imagination and desires. There he finds protection from the coarseness and bru-

Wolfe's angel, Hendersonville

tality around him. The only one who really understands him is his brother Ben, a moody and sensitive fellow like Eugene. When Eugene falls in love, when Eugene goes to college at Pulpit Hill (Chapel Hill), it is Ben who sympathizes with his adolescent problems. Some of the most intense chapters in American literature are those about Ben's illness and death. It is then that Eugene is sacrificially freed to a new life, and the novel ends with his planning to move into a larger world.

The success of *Look Homeward, Angel* enabled Wolfe to give up his job at New York University. First he traveled in Europe, then moved to Brooklyn to write a second novel. This he found a much more difficult task than the writing of the first, and he turned from one idea to another without conviction. Finally he decided to continue Eugene's adventures— a sensible and fortunate choice—and, when *Of Time and the River* (1935) was published, he found himself with a best seller on his hands.

The action in *Of Time and the River* begins the day after the closing chapter of *Look Homeward, Angel*. At the Altamont railway station, Eugene awaits the train that will take him off to Harvard, where he will study for a master's degree. Further episodic adventures are set in Europe, New York, and elsewhere in America. No plot, at least in the traditional sense, holds the varied sections of the book together. Rather, as implied in his subtitle *A Legend of Man's Hunger in His Youth*, Wolfe links the episodes of the narrative by other means. Here is Eugene, hungry for life and the meaning of life, coursing across lands and oceans in what seems to be an unending search for certainty. In a little book called *The Story of a Novel* (1936), Wolfe told about the way *Of Time and the River* was created. He made clear that the "central legend" of the novel was that "the deepest search in life . . . was man's search to find a father, not merely the father of his flesh . . . but the image of a strength and wisdom external to his need and superior to his hunger, to which the belief and power of his own life could be united." If *Look Homeward, Angel* is a story of maturation, *Of Time and the River* is a modern odyssey, somewhat in the tradition of Twain's *Huckleberry Finn*.

Wolfe was a restless man and, though committed to his art, generally on the

Belinda Jelliffe

Wolfe, about 1935

move. He was often in Europe and occasionally came back to North Carolina for visits. Even so, he found that New York was the place where he could most satisfactorily do his writing. For the next three years he worked on a long manuscript and turned it over to his publisher before leaving for the West Coast. There he became ill with an old infection and was hospitalized in Seattle, then was brought across the continent for an operation at Johns Hopkins. He died in Baltimore on September 15, 1938, and was buried in the family plot at Asheville's Riverside Cemetery.

From the huge manuscript, his publishers blocked out two novels. The first was *The Web and the Rock* (1939), a book in its initial sections similar to *Look Homeward, Angel*. Monk Webber, a hero not unlike Thomas Wolfe and Eugene Gant, grows up in a southern mountain town now called Libya Hill. After college, he goes to New York to be a writer, makes a trip to Europe, and falls in love with a woman considerably older than he. In America, he resents his dependence upon her and goes back to Europe, thereby reestablishing an emotional stability. *You Can't Go Home Again* (1940) follows the life of Monk upon his return. He finally gives up the woman, then is caught up in the Great Depression years of the 1930s. Amid harrowing circumstances, Monk (meaning Wolfe, of course) learns to love his fellowman, even when it means the rejection of home, privilege, and fame. Concluding *You Can't Go Home Again* is a lengthy optimistic statement, the essence of which is that "America and the people in it are deathless, undiscovered, and immortal, and must live."

That the four novels are based on the life of their author even the casual reader will be aware. But Wolfe was right to protest the charge of autobiography, for the books are far more than what the author did and saw. Along with a highly charged poetic style is a set of symbols giving meaning and richness to the adventures of Eugene Gant and Monk

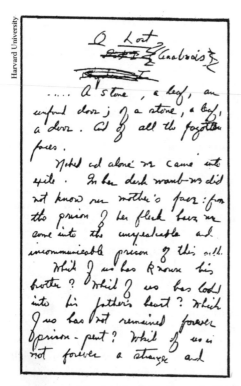

First manuscript page, *Look Homeward, Angel*

Thomas Wolfe died before his artistic researches were completed. But even at the time of his death, he was already recognized as the greatest talent North Carolina had given to American literature, though there were still many people in Asheville who had not forgiven him for the uncomplimentary, but truthful, things he had written in *Look Homeward, Angel* about his native town, where at first the novel was viewed as resentful gossip.

Wolfe Memorial, Asheville

Webber. The angel in the first book represents man's spiritual quality, and the beautiful recurring phrase—"a stone, a leaf, a door"—symbolizes the unchanging as well as the changing essences of life, then the entranceway into fulfillment. The river, the web, the rock are key words in the later books. Wolfe's symbology was the artist's way of expressing his love and devotion to America, whose literature has rarely proffered a writer so committed to an exploration and understanding of its vast geography and varied peoples.

In addition to the tetralogy, books of his short stories, plays, essays, notebooks, and letters have been issued. Book-length biographies of Wolfe are by Elizabeth Nowell (1960), Andrew Turnbull (1967), and David Herbert Donald (1987). Among the many critical studies, the most indispensable is Richard S. Kennedy's *The Window of Memory* (1962). Headquarters of the Thomas Wolfe Society and editorial office of the semiannual *Thomas Wolfe Review* are at the University of Akron in Ohio.

XII
WRITERS FOR YOUNG READERS

The books that came after Mary A. Mason's *A Wreath from the Woods of Carolina* (1859) were, for the most part, boring little moral stories with only slight relevancy to the lives of the young readers for whom they were intended. In those days, it is no wonder children turned to Scott and Dickens. In *Grandfather's Tales of North Carolina History* (1901), Richard Benbury Creecy of Elizabeth City wrote, as he said, "for the private instruction of my children and grandchildren," but his sentences were so graceless and his "tales" were told so uninterestingly (and often inaccurately from a historical point of view!) that it is doubtful that any child could get much pleasure from reading the book. Not until after the literary revival of the 1920s

GRANDFATHER'S TALES

OF

NORTH CAROLINA HISTORY

BY
RICHARD BENBURY CREECY

Look abroad throughout the land and see North Carolina's sons contending
manfully for the palm of honor and distinction.   —*Gaston.*

RALEIGH
EDWARDS & BROUGHTON, PRINTERS
1901

did juvenile literature make up for lost time. Then in 1930 Elizabeth Janet Gray of Chapel Hill published *Meggy Mac-Intosh*, its historical background peopled by the Scottish Highlanders and Flora Macdonald. The book was a harbinger of good things to come, for it was followed by the same author's *Jane Hope* (1933), a novel about a tomboy growing up in a university town just before the Civil War.

From then on, the writing of juvenile books was pursued with the same seriousness and craftsmanship given adult books. Veterans in other fields—such as Carl Sandburg, Gerald W. Johnson, Bernice Kelly Harris, James Street, Jonathan Daniels, Randall Jarrell, Burke Davis, Ben Haas, William S. Powell, Max Steele, and Thomas C. Parramore—all renowned in various genres like poetry, adult fiction, history, or biography, have discovered and maintained that putting together a book for young people is not so easy as it might seem to nonwriters but requires an ultimate know-how and perception.

Early on the scene was Ellis Credle of Hyde County, whose *Down, Down the Mountain* (1934) and *Tall Tales of the High Hills* (1957) deal with folks living along the Blue Ridge. *Across the Cotton Patch* (1935), *Little Jeems Henry* (1936), and *Here Comes the Showboat* (1949) shifted to eastern North Carolina. Most of the other dozen or so books by Credle, including her folklore ghost story *Big Fraid, Little Fraid* (1964), were for youngsters of grammar-grade age. *Big Doin's on Razorback Ridge* (1956; new

Illustration from
Big Doin's on Razorback Ridge

Photograph from *Tobe*

edition 1978) focuses on the day the president of the United States comes to the North Carolina mountains to celebrate the completion of a new dam, the occasion to feature a prize competition among such local entertainers as the two kids who dance old-fashioned jigs and flips and clogs.

Mabel Leigh Hunt, an Indiana Quaker, during a visit to the environs of her ancestors in Guilford County, was inspired to write *Benjie's Hat* (1938), the story of an eight-year-old boy who, when his worn-out chapeau is eaten by a horse, gets a new "real hat," and *Matilda's Buttons* (1948), whose nine-year-old heroine causes trouble when she dispenses with a set of buttons that picture the family forebears.

An example of the uncompromising realism that sometimes underlies juveniles is *Tobe* (1939), by Stella Gentry Sharpe of Hillsborough. Instead of imaginative drawings, the book is illustrated with more than seventy photographs, their purpose being to emphasize the realism of Sharpe's sympathetic story about a little black boy and his family on a North Carolina farm.

A number of storytellers delved into history for subject matter and background.

In *The Middle Button* (1941), Kathryn Worth, born at Wrightsville Beach, wrote of the 1880s and a Cape Fear River schoolgirl who wanted to study medicine. *They Loved to Laugh* (1942) moves back to the 1830s and a jolly Quaker family in Guilford County, while the climax of *Sea Change* (1948) comes at the time of a destructive hurricane at Wrightsville Beach in 1893.

The Society of Friends seems to produce juvenile writers more than any other sect. Stephen W. Meader, a Rhode Island Quaker, came to the state briefly but managed to add to his long list of titles four new ones featuring coastal North Carolina locales. In *The Sea Snake* (1943) a Kitty Hawk boy is captured by the Germans and put aboard a submarine; his escape from the U-boat early in World War II is thoroughly exciting and entertaining. The city boy in *Wild Pony Island* (1959) forgets his loneliness when he makes friends with the Ocracoke herd, and *Phantom of the Blockade* (1962) has to do with life on a Confederate blockade-runner out of Wilmington. *Topsail Island Treasure* (1966) is the last of Meader's tetralogy of North Carolina stories for boys.

In spite of the good work that had been going on, it was during the decades after World War II that juvenile writing in North Carolina sprang to life with extraordinary vitality. Two husband-wife teams moved into western North Carolina and set the pace. Corydon Bell and Thelma Harrington Bell purchased a house deep in the forest near Highlands. The character named Randy in Mrs. Bell's *Mountain Boy* (1947) and *Yaller-Eye* (1951) was an actual youngster whom she taught to read, and other characters in the books were based on real-life friends. *The Two Worlds of Davy Blount* (1962) poses the old question of which is better, the beach or the mountains, and concludes with a surprising decision made by Davy. Mr. Bell's *John Rattling-Gourd of Big Cove: A Collection of Cherokee Indian Legends* (1955) was inspired by his frequent visits to the reservation in

Illustration from *John Rattling-Gourd*

the Great Smoky Mountains not far from his home. Mrs. Bell turned from fiction to meteorology in *Snow* (1954) and *Thunderstorm* (1960). With her husband, she collaborated on an even more difficult subject in *The Riddle of Time* (1963). The wizardry of scientific experiments is explained in four books by Asheville's Bob Brown: *Science Circus* (1960), *Science Circus No. 2* (1963), *Science*

Treasures (1968), and *200 Illustrated Science Experiments for Boys and Girls* (1974).

Hardly had another experienced husband-wife team, Ruth and Latrobe Carroll, moved to Asheville than they began a series of word-and-picture books using North Carolina scenes and characters. The hero of the first one, its title *Peanut* (1951), was a puppy. Many of the

Latrobe Carroll

later books featured a mountain boy named Beanie Tatum and his dog Tough Enough, though there were cats and bears and ponies too. *Digby, the Only Dog* (1955) is set on Ocracoke, an island with a large cat population. *The Managing Hen and the Floppy Hound* (1972) was the Carrolls' tenth book, all of them written for preschool tots and those in elementary school. On this team, the husband wrote the first draft of the stories, and his wife was the artist-collaborator.

The writing careers of Mebane Holoman Burgwyn of Jackson and Peggy Hoffman of Raleigh are similar. Both began writing when their children were small, then moved their books smoothly upward on the teenage ladder as the children became young adults. At first Burgwyn combined realism with adventure and romance. *River Treasure* (1947) and *Lucky Mischief* (1949), both of whose central character is a black boy, have exciting chapters about buried treasures and escaped convicts. For teenagers Burgwyn wrote some stories dealing candidly with young people's problems. In *True Love for Jenny* (1956), for instance, she tells almost painfully of a sophomore girl's admiration for "Charlie Ross, the biggest wheel in the senior class," and of the girl's anguished disagreements with her mother about a dress for the Harvest Ball. In *The Crackajack Pony* (1969) Burgwyn reversed her course and wrote again for the younger reader. Peggy Hoffman's *Miss B's First Cookbook* (1950) and *Sew Easy!* (1956) were written with her young daughter in mind, while *The Wild Rocket* (1960) and *Shift to High!* (1965) are adventures for teenage boys. When her children entered college, Hoffman turned to adult fiction.

On May 21, 1983, Manly Wade Wellman, resident of Chapel Hill, said: "Today is my eightieth birthday, and I've written eighty books. That's pretty good, don't you think?" Of these eighty, thirty-five were written for boys who have a liking for swampland adventures, mountain mysteries, and military heroics. Wellman was one of the most prolific and certainly the most versatile writer ever to work in North Carolina. In addition to science fiction and detective stories, history and biography, folklore and true murders, and radio dramas and adult novels, his long list of juvenile books is decidedly impressive. Some half of them are set in North Carolina and are tidily arranged in several groups. First came a round of boys' adventure stories taking place along the waterways of the Lumber River in the southeastern part of the state: *The Raiders of Beaver Lake* (1950), *The Haunts of Drowning Creek* (1951), and *Wild Dogs of Drowning Creek* (1952). At this point Wellman's interest was directed to the richness of Appalachian history and lore, and over the years he wrote seven novels using mountain material. The first of the seven, which cover time from the eighteenth century to the pres-

ent, was *The Last Mammoth* (1953), in which a surviving member of the now-extinct family of beasts is found still alive in the depths of the forest. After *Lights over Skeleton Ridge* (1957) and *The Master of Scare Hollow* (1964), Wellman wrote a trilogy on pioneer life in the mountains: *Mystery of Bear Paw Gap* (1965), *The Spectre of Bear Paw Gap* (1966), and *Battle of Bear Paw Gap* (1966). *Mountain Feud* (1969) is set in the Great Smokies in 1906. In the third group are historical novels, principally Wellman's tetralogy of the American Revolution. Their titles suggest the historical content: *Rifles at Ramsour's Mill* (1961), *Battle for King's Mountain* (1962), *Clash*

Frontispiece, *Battle for King's Mountain*

on the Catawba (1962), and *The South Fork Rangers* (1963). *Settlement on Shocco: Adventures in Colonial Carolina* (1963) won the literary award sponsored by the Carolina Charter Tercentenary Commission for prose fiction dealing with North Carolina history prior to the American Revolution. *Carolina Pirate* (1968) is Wellman's sixth novel based on events in the state's history. Among his other juveniles are several Civil War stories of the Virginia battlefields, as well as two sports stories, *Third String Center* (1960) and *Fast Break Five* (1971).

Another writer of sports stories for boys is Burgess Leonard of High Point. Beginning with *Victory Pass* (1950) and continuing through *Stretch Bolton, Mister Shortstop* (1963), his ten novels deal with football, basketball, and baseball. Many of his settings are easily recognized as the campuses at Wake Forest University, the University of North Carolina at Chapel Hill, and North Carolina State University.

Julia Montgomery Street of Winston-Salem was a grandmother before the publication of her *Fiddler's Fancy* (1955), a lively mountain story that utilizes the folklore, speech, and customs of Mitchell County in the late nineteenth century. Street's four novels were written only after lengthy research into specific periods of North Carolina history. *Moccasin Tracks* (1958) centers on the "Great White Chief" of the Cherokee, *Drover's Gold* (1961) on the driving of farm animals down the Buncombe Turnpike before the railroads were built, and *Dulcie's Whale* (1963) on the enemy submarines at Cape Lookout during World War I. *Judaculla's Handprint and Other Mysterious Tales from North Carolina* (1975) was published at a time when readers in the state were becoming increasingly curious about North Carolina folklore. Street was coauthor in 1966 of *North Carolina Parade*, which included not only familiar legends but also such accounts as "Dr. Mitchell's Mountain," "Tobacco and Buck Duke," and "Young Thomas Wolfe."

The stimulation to write for young people came to Ina B. Forbus after she and her husband bought an old gristmill in Orange County and converted it into a home. Girls and animals and birds, with sometimes a touch of fantasy and enchantment, enliven her four novels from *The Magic Pin* (1956) to *Tawny's Trick* (1965).

The North Carolina coast is not only home but also the fictional setting for five books designed by Nell Wise Wech-

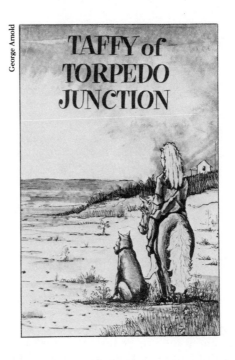

George Arnold

ter of Stumpy Point to please the middle-school reader. *Taffy of Torpedo Junction* (1957) is a World War II tale of Cape Hatteras. *Betsy Dowdy's Ride* (1960) is based on a North Carolina legend about the girl who rode all night through the marshland to warn the patriot Revolutionary soldiers of an impending British attack. In *Swamp Girl* (1971), a blend of local color and mystery, a twelve-year-old Dare County girl solves the enigma of the Lost Colony. The two youngsters in *Teach's Light* (1974), searching for Blackbeard's treasure, suddenly find themselves transported back into the pirate's life in the early 1700s. *Winddrift* (1983) depicts the young master of a Tyrrell County plantation protecting his family and slaves during the Civil War. Thus far, Wechter has not brought forth a book with its heroine as Virginia Dare, whose appearance in juveniles has fascinated dozens of writers such as Jean Bothwell in *Lady of Roanoke* (1965).

The nature books by Glen Rounds are rather in a class by themselves. Before he arrived in Pinebluff, he had already started a series about Whitey, a bantam-sized cowboy. With *Swamp Life* (1957),

Glen Rounds

Illustration from *Lone Muskrat*

Rounds began to relate aspects of wildlife along the boggy little streams of the Sandhills, then in *Wildlife at Your Doorstep* (1958) gave close attention to such creatures as wasps, spiders, toads, snakes, birds, and ants. After *Beaver Business* (1960) came *Wild Orphans* (1961), which centers on the struggle of a solitary young beaver to survive in the wilderness. *Rain in the Woods* (1964) is based on observations at Rounds's own pond and records the activities of turtles, otters, caterpillars, and others when the rainy days come. Opossums, flickers, foxes, and milkweed bugs are among the forest inhabitants he tells about in *The Snake Tree* (1966). Among his many other books are *The Day the Circus Came to Lonetree* (1973) and *Mr. Yowder, the Peripatetic Sign Painter: Three Tall Tales* (1980). A consummate artist as well as a writer, Rounds illustrates his own books and those by others.

Rain Makes Applesauce (1964) and *Upside Down Day* (1968), by Julian Scheer of Charlotte, are charming fantasies based on children's nonsense talk. "The stars are made of lemon juice," writes Scheer, and "Monkeys mumble in a jellybean jungle . . . and rain makes applesauce"—musical phrases that bypass the adult world to find happy meaning within a child's imagination.

From his hidden retreat among the mountains of Macon County, Alexander Key transferred his mature interest in science fiction into books for young readers. *Sprockets: A Little Robot* (1963), *Rivets and Sprockets* (1964), and *Bolts: A Robot Dog* (1966) were written for very young folk. *The Forgotten Door* (1966), considered by the author his best book, tells of a boy from another planet who falls into western North Carolina, where he is able to read the minds of Earth people. *The Golden Enemy* (1969) is a story of the future after an atomic war. *Escape to Witch Mountain* (1968), made into a Walt Disney motion picture and Key's best-known book, is a science fantasy of two children who roam through North Carolina towns in search of their barely recollected home. Its sequel was *Return from Witch Mountain* (1978). Key, who began his career as a painter, illustrated these and other juveniles.

Alexander Key

Illustration from *Rivets and Sprockets*

After Vera and Bill Cleaver settled in Watauga County, they began a series of stories about North Carolina mountain children who have serious problems. *Where the Lilies Bloom* (1969) tells of four youngsters who are unswerving in their decision to stay together after the death of their parents. In *The Mimosa Tree* (1970), five children and their poverty-stricken stepmother and blind father leave their "Goose Elk, North Carolina," mountainside home for Chicago, but since conditions for them are even worse there, they return to the high hills. *Trial Valley* (1977) is a sequel to *Where the Lilies Bloom*. In their concentration on physical and emotional disabilities, these "grim" problem novels are quite different from the usual juveniles.

Among the books for ages eight through ten by Charlotte's Betsy Byars are *The Midnight Fox* (1970), its theme the beauty one absorbs in loving a wild animal; *The Summer of the Swans* (1970), about a girl's tender but passionate protection of her brain-damaged younger brother; *Go and Hush the Baby* (1971), in which an overworked mother is fascinated by the many ways her son manages to quiet the family's crying infant; *The Lace Snail* (1975), about a well-disposed mollusk's providing for the individual needs of those who require her services various kinds of lace such as a "heavy strong lace for the hippopotamus's size and light fine lace for the hippopotamus's nature"; and

Something about the Author, IV, 41

Betsy Byars

The Computer Nut (1984), a science-fiction yarn about a girl and her brother's experimenting with their father's computer and surprisingly getting in touch with an extraterrestrial fellow named BB-9 who is planning to visit Earth because only on Earth do the inhabitants laugh. Byars's two dozen books, all keyed to social and moral problems, include *The Horror Film Freak* (1981) and *The Two-Thousand-Pound Goldfish* (1982). In her *The Not-Just-Anybody's Family* (1986), the older boy has sneaked into jail to be with his grandfather, incarcerated there for banging away at several destructive teenagers. The younger brother is in the hospital with broken legs from flying off the barn roof on homemade wings. The dog Maud has disappeared. Sister Maggie is seeking to locate their out-of-town mother and get everybody home again, and she does.

Theodore Taylor, a Statesville native who works in the Hollywood film industry, wrote, among many other books, what he calls his "Hatteras trilogy." The three adventurous survival stories are *Teetoncey* (1974), in which a brave boy lives through a destructive shipwreck; *Teetoncey and Ben O'Neal* (1975); and *The Odyssey of Ben O'Neal* (1977), an exciting tale of the seafaring experiences of a girl, a boy, and a dog.

In recent times, the most consistent and successful worker in the field of juveniles has been Suzanne Newton, a native of Bunnlevel and mother of four. She spent her childhood in the sleepy coastal towns of Beaufort County—Bayview, Bath, and Washington. "I'm happy," she said. "I'm making my living doing what I want to do." The titles of her books are not only unusual but downright delectable as well. *Purro and the Prattleberries* (1971) is about a tomcat and his disturbing habit of running away, and *C/O Arnold's Corners* (1974) tells of the struggle of an unconventional girl and some conservative townfolks to make peace with each other. In *What Are You Up To, William Thomas?* (1977) the practical jokes played by a high school boy turn out to be not so funny after all. *Reubella and the Old Focus Home* (1978) is a sympathetic story of how the elderly have much more knowledge about the art of living than young people may think. In *M. V. Sexton Speaking* (1981) a lonely, studious girl learns from her summer job in a bakery how to blend more easily into the life of her classmates and family. *I Will Call It Georgie's Blues* (1983) concerns two sons of a minister in eastern North Carolina, the older a secretive jazz artist who composes "Georgie's Blues" to relieve his mind about the

Ted Lewin

trauma of his younger brother's fast retreat into a make-believe world. *An End to Perfect* (1984) has at its center a twelve-year-old girl who resists growing up in a world of people who become "ugly and hard to live with even if they'd never been that way before"; eventually, of course, she has to face being a teenager.

One of the most popular of juvenile writers in North Carolina is Sue Ellen Bridgers, born in Winterville. The girl of a migrant family in *Home before Dark*

(1976) returns to her father's childhood home and fights against her new stationary life. In *All Together Now* (1979) an eleven-year-old girl in eastern North Carolina happily discovers a friendship with a thirty-three-year-old woman. The terror of a North Carolina boy who wonders if he is afflicted with the same mental illness as his father is the theme of *Notes for Another Life* (1981). An adult novel by Bridgers is *Sara Will* (1985), set in a small fictional North Carolina town called Tyler Mills. To the home of a disconsolate spinster and her widowed high-spirited sister comes a young relative with her illegitimate child, bringing about a requisite examination of three generations in the family.

One of the dozen juveniles by Caroline B. Cooney, who lived in Rocky Mount for a number of years, is *Safe as the Grave* (1979), in which twin sisters, picnicking in their family's cemetery in

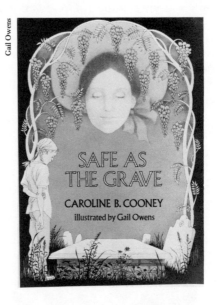

Gail Owens

eastern North Carolina and puzzled by a flat stone bearing only the name "Cornelia," set about ascertaining her identity, thereby unearthing a long-lost treasure.

The first book by Statesville's Belinda Hurmence was *Tough Tiffany* (1980), in

Belinda Hurmence

I got some butter on my hands
And they were good and slick,
And then I drank my milk the way
I've seen a kitten lick.

My milk was in a cup, and I
Leaned down and drank it so—
The way I've seen a kitten do,
Like-it, lap-it, low.

Illustrated with the gentle line drawings of Cricket Taylor, Russell's soothing, sprightly, and inventive rhymes appeal especially to the preschool and kinder- garten set.

Cricket Taylor

Illustration from *Iris Hill*

which a girl from a poor rural North Carolina family takes a first step toward adulthood. The pampered black girl in Hurmence's *A Girl Called Boy* (1982) is transported back into slavery days and fights to escape her bondage. At the end of the Civil War, the young house servant in *Tancy* (1984) leaves an Iredell County plantation to go in search of her mother. Hurmence edited *My Folks Don't Want Me to Talk about Slavery* (1985), a col- lection of interviews with former slaves transcribed by various writers in the 1930s.

Among North Carolina books there are few like *Iris Hill: Poems for Little Children* (1975), by Mary Margaret Rus- sell of Chapel Hill. Of the twenty-five selections, here is "Butter and Milk":

An overview of North Carolina juve- niles indicates that, though books for the very young reader in kindergarten and elementary school are in short supply, those for older readers are bountiful, with an almost equal division between titles written especially with boys in mind and those written especially for girls—not that many boys' books don't appeal to girls, and vice versa.

XIII
HISTORICAL NOVELISTS

Following Robert Strange's *Eoneguski* and Calvin Henderson Wiley's *Alamance* and *Roanoke*, many novels with a background of North Carolina history came from the press, but few if any of them bore marks of distinction. A hasty survey shows that certain figures and periods from North Carolina's past were especially favored. Raleigh's colonists on Roanoke Island, along with Manteo and Virginia Dare, were particularly attractive to writers, as were Blackbeard and Daniel Boone, fascinating fellows with conveniently obscure biographies. The War of the Regulation, the events leading up to the Battle of Kings Mountain, and the western movement across the mountains—all served historical novelists for place and time and sweeping action. That the resulting books were inconsequential was not attributable to the undramatic materials at the writers' disposal but rather to the low standards of American historical fiction during the long decades after Cooper and Simms.

It was James Boyd's *Drums* (1925), one of the classic works of North Carolina literature, that established new rules for the genre and lifted the historical novel out of its mediocrity. Boyd was a scholar no less than a writer. Before penning even the first sentence of his great story of eastern North Carolina just prior to and during the Revolution, he read deeply and thoroughly into all the documents and histories of the period. He visited New Bern and Washington and Edenton and Hertford and Elizabeth City. His friend, the novelist Struthers Burt, explained how the two of them

Pilot (Southern Pines)

James Boyd

"drifted down the lonely roads in a car or walked through the cemeteries deep in ivy and moss, or visited the old plantations." Only when Boyd was saturated with the actualities of the past was he willing to attempt a first chapter. *Drums*, in Burt's opinion "by far the best and most re-creating and human American historical novel ever written," was no swashbuckling romance of heroic derring-do careless about facts and details, but rather a work compounded of meticulous historical realism.

Its hero, Johnny Fraser, is sent away from his home in the pinewoods to attend school in Edenton, where he becomes a young gentleman. When the war begins, he, like most run-of-the-mill North Carolinians, is still loyal to England. In London his fidelity begins to waver, and finally he goes off with John Paul Jones and is present during the sea battle between the *Bonhomme Richard* and the *Serapis*. Back in North Carolina he becomes an ardent patriot and, forgetting the ladies of Edenton and London, is reunited with his Sally, his first sweetheart. Boyd's handling of the shift in Johnny's political allegiance is deft and subtle. In this book, commented Ernest E. Leisy in *The American Historical Novel*, "the everyday hopes and tribulations of the common people are fully realized—*Drums* is social history in the best sense."

Boyd, a native of Pennsylvania, attended Princeton and Cambridge in England. His health was impaired after service in France during World War I. In the 1920s, on a piney ridge overlooking the town of Southern Pines, he built his home, Weymouth (now an arts center),

Weymouth

on an estate once owned by his grandfather. At Southern Pines he took up fox hunting and writing. *Drums* was his first novel. *Marching On* (1927), his second, again employed historical realism. James Fraser, a descendant of Johnny, joins the Cape Fear Rifles during the Civil War and, after participating in several battles, is taken prisoner. Though from the small-farmer class, he eventually wins the beautiful daughter of an aristocrat whose mansion is destroyed by the Yankees. *Long Hunt* (1930), Boyd's third novel, begins in North Carolina about 1800 but soon takes its trapper hero westward into

the raw Tennessee country. Before Boyd's death in 1944, he wrote several other novels, a manuscript of poems, and more than a dozen short stories.

An author's careful research, including even an investigation of unpublished manuscripts, continued to undergird the best historical novels. In *Alexandriana* (1940) LeGette Blythe of Huntersville sketched the panorama of Revolutionary years in North Carolina, with his focus on

LeGette Blythe

the brave actions of heroic whigs in Mecklenburg County. Scores of illustrious characters from history fill in the background of Blythe's pages, while the foreground is occupied by David Barksdale, once a "bound boy" on a Mecklenburg plantation but now seasoned into a whig fighter and leader, and Jethro O'Flannagan, a rough-and-tumble frontiersman. The theme of *Alexandriana*, published the year before Pearl Harbor, is that democracy has always been preserved by the joint struggle of the aristocrat and the common man. Blythe's *Call Down the Storm* (1958) recalls the destruction of a proud family by miscegenation in nineteenth-century North Carolina, then leaps to the 1950s in order to suggest how history might repeat itself. Blythe, a versatile writer of drama, biography, and history, is perhaps best known for his eminently successful Biblical novels, the sixth of which was *Brothers of Vengeance* (1969), a story of the conflict between a Greek slave and Barabbas.

Not to every historical novelist were the American revolutionaries always the heroes. Often the "enemy" was glorified. *Tory Oath* (1941), though similar to *Alexandriana* in method, showed the other side of the war in North Carolina. Written by Tim Pridgen of Bladen County, who was steeped in the history of his region, *Tory Oath* deals with Flora Macdonald and the Scottish Highlanders who fought the whigs during the early days of the struggle. The Scots' obstinate loyalty to the crown ended in their defeat by men who seemed to them a disarray of upstart rabble backwoodsmen. The Scotsmen's heroism and dignity in military ruin make for noble chapters in the history and literature of the Cape Fear country.

Raleigh's Eden (1940) was the first of twelve novels in Inglis Fletcher's popular Carolina Series. Like Boyd and Blythe and Pridgen, Fletcher was committed to the doctrine that research must precede composition. She was not satisfied to frame a plot until she knew exactly how people had lived, with what their houses were furnished, and exactly how they dressed and what they ate. For instance, in the early pages of *Men of Albemarle* (1942), her second novel, Roger Mainwaring stops at the Red Lion tavern in Queen Anne's Town (Edenton):

He walked into the tavern ordinary, ducking his head as he went through the low door. The room was packed with men in butternut brown, buckskin jerkins and heavy boots. . . . He ordered a tankard of ale from a slovenly potboy. . . . Across the room at a long trestle table were seated eight or ten men. They were dressed carelessly, yet they had the look of soldiers. Every man carried a poniard at his belt, and a stack of muskets leaned against a wooden bench close at hand. Roger's eyes lingered longest on a tall young man seated at the end of the table. He was of a different class from the rest, by his bearing and his clear, strong features. He was garbed as a Quaker, in drab smallclothes, but he wore a soldier's leather jerkin and high loose boots on which heavy spurs were visible. He was talking to a strangely attired man, a foreigner, dark and swarthy, with long, greasy black hair escaping from a red Turkish tarboosh.

Fletcher's passion for factual detail, as illustrated in these sentences, gave a nimbus of stark realism to what were otherwise extravagantly romantic novels in which highborn ladies and gentlemen of the North Carolina tidewater underwent one exciting adventure after another. Yet Fletcher's pervasive theme was ever present: man's freedom as symbolized by the ownership and love of the land he masters, protects, fights

Inglis Fletcher

for, and passes on to his children. The history retold in each of the novels, she trusted and believed, gave meaning to the modern problems of America and North Carolina during the years in which the books were being written and published.

The Carolina Series, as Fletcher planned it, tells of the founding of a democratic state from the first attempt at colonization through the ratification of the Constitution in 1789. The twelve novels in their historical order are *Roanoke Hundred* (1948), 1585-1586, Sir Walter Raleigh's colonists at Roanoke Island; *Bennett's Welcome* (1950), 1651-1652, the first permanent settlers coming down from Virginia; *Rogue's Harbor* (1964), 1677-1689, the first revolt against overbearing officials; *Men of Albemarle* (1942), 1710-1712, the evolution of law

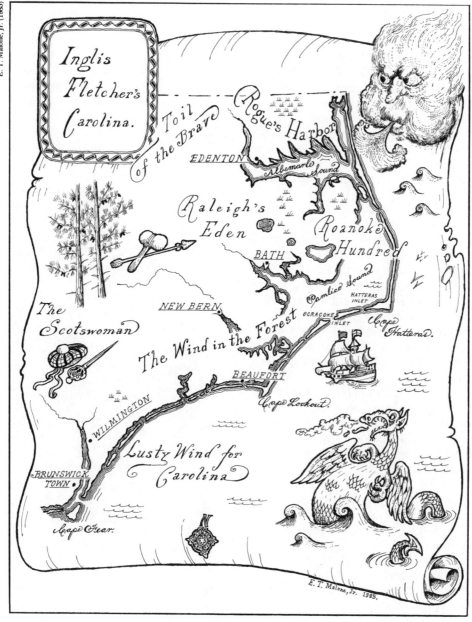

Inglis Fletcher's Carolina.

Toil of the Brave

Rogue's Harbor

EDENTON

Albemarle Sound

Raleigh's Eden

Roanoke Hundred

BATH

Pamlico Sound

HATTERAS INLET

The Scotswoman

NEW BERN

The Wind in the Forest

OCRACOKE INLET

Cape Hatteras.

BEAUFORT

Cape Lookout.

WILMINGTON

Lusty Wind for Carolina

BRUNSWICK TOWN

Cape Fear.

E. T. Malone, Jr. 1985.

and order in the colony; *Lusty Wind for Carolina* (1944), 1718-1725, a dramatization of trade illustrated by the struggle of the Huguenots on the Cape Fear as they fight off predatory buccaneers; *Cormorant's Brood* (1959), 1725-1731, the establishment of responsible government in the Albemarle; *Raleigh's Eden* (1940), 1765-1782, the causes of the Revolution; *The Wind in the Forest* (1957), 1770-

1771, the fight for freedom as symbolized by Governor William Tryon and the Regulators at the Battle of Alamance; *The Scotswoman* (1955), 1774-1776, loyalists versus insurgents, Flora Macdonald and the Scots as opposed to the whig patriots; *Toil of the Brave* (1946), 1778-1780, the critical contests of the Revolution in North Carolina; *Wicked Lady* (1962), 1781-1782, the final years of the

75

war as affecting the people of the Albemarle; and *Queen's Gift* (1952), 1783-1789, the aftermath of the war and the struggle for constitutional liberties. The dozen books of the Carolina Series are linked not only geographically and thematically. Certain of Fletcher's favorite characters frequently reappear in novel after novel. Adam Rutledge, for example, was created in *Raleigh's Eden*, but he is seen again and again for more than twenty years until his final appearance in *Wicked Lady*.

That the impressive Carolina Series exists at all is a matter of accident. Its author, born in Illinois and a resident of California, had gone to a San Francisco library to do some genealogical research on her Tyrrell County ancestors. It occurred to her that she might write a novel based on the data she found. In 1940, six years and four long-hand drafts later, *Raleigh's Eden* was published. From then on, Fletcher and her husband were frequently in North Carolina, and in 1944 they purchased Bandon plantation on the Chowan River fourteen miles north of Edenton. It was there that she wrote most of her other novels. Inglis Fletcher died May 30, 1969, at the age of ninety.

The appeal of the historical narrative is attested by four other writers who brought to the genre their own distinctive gifts. Dr. Frank G. Slaughter of Oxford, whose more than forty books make him one of North Carolina's most prolific authors, has written two novels of the nineteenth-century Cape Fear country. Both *In a Dark Garden* (1946) and its sequel *The Stubborn Heart* (1950) have that popular, irresistible blend of history, medicine, and romance. In the first, Confederate surgeon Julian Chisholm, married to a Yankee spy, is constantly engaged in hair-raising adventures, while in the second he is faced with the problems brought on by Reconstruction, the Ku Klux Klan, and the ever-present, ever-disturbing beautiful women. These two books, depending little on factual history, might properly be defined more as "period fiction" than historical novels in the restricted sense of the term.

From the frequent visits of Connecticut-born Don Tracy to North Carolina in the 1950s came four novels woven less out of history than sensationalism. In *Roanoke Renegade* (1954), Manteo is a traitor to his people rather than a friend of the English colonists, while Wanchese, instead of a villain, is admired for his tribal loyalty. No writer has ever portrayed Blackbeard as a virtuous fellow, but in *Carolina Corsair* (1955) North Carolina's favorite pirate is depicted as the vilest,

Jules Gottlieb

most degenerate creature one can imagine. *Cherokee* (1957) is a story of racial hatred among the mountain Indians of the 1820s and 1830s rather than the usual narrative of confidence betrayed. In *On the Midnight Tide* (1957), the goings-on in war-booming Wilmington of 1863 are as sinful as the outrageous capers of the white trash Grayson brothers, newly rich pilots for the blockade-runners.

Burke Davis, a native of Durham, has an impressive bibliography of more than

Burke Davis

twoscore books, including juveniles, biography, and, most of all, history. His very first title, however, was *Whisper My Name* (1949), a novel for mature readers that deals with a prominent businessman in Charlotte; so thinly disguised was it that Mecklenburg tongues buzzed excitedly over the fictional disclosures. Davis's two historical novels of the Revolution, *The Ragged Ones* (1951) and *Yorktown* (1952), carry historical realism far beyond the point that even James Boyd was willing to go. In these two narratives, the action of the second of which follows hard upon that of the first, the campaign of Lord Cornwallis is pursued from Cowpens to the Virginia peninsula. For the first book, with General Nathanael Greene as Cornwallis's adversary, Davis gathered a huge file on various topics: uniforms, geography, firearms, personalities. He even compiled a weather calendar for the first months of 1781 so that he could know when it was cold or mild and when it rained. He outlined a minute chronology of battle marches and an extensive catalog of names and places. Principal source for much of this material was Cornwallis's order book, whose authenticity is unchallenged. Honesty forced Davis to picture the Americans not as the heroes of legend,

but as dirty, illiterate, reluctant soldiers who had to be threatened by sharpshooters to keep them from fleeing the battle lines. When they could, many of the North Carolina troops deserted in shameful fashion and dallied with "camp followers." In these novels and in his other books, Burke Davis belongs to the school of unvarnished realism.

Before John Ehle began his series of historical novels set in western North Carolina, he completed a task, perhaps unconsciously, left unfinished more than a century ago by Calvin Henderson Wiley, who had planned to write a trilogy portraying life in the three geographic sections of the state. Like Wiley, Ehle began with the piedmont, and in *Move Over, Mountain* (1957) told of a black man in Leafwood (Carrboro) who succeeds in overcoming numerous obstacles in keeping firm his family bonds. In this book no clang of racism is sounded, for the ever-present concerns of the father could be those of a black man as well as those of his white neighbor. The scene of the second, *Kingstree Island* (1958), is easily identified as Ocracoke, where an outsider battles with the "boss" of the island to be accepted. For the third, *Lion on the Hearth* (1961), Ehle chose his native Asheville in the mountains for his story of a sensitive young

John Ehle

man (shades of Eugene Gant in *Look Homeward, Angel*) isolated in an unfeeling environment.

The first of Ehle's historical mountain novels is *The Land Breakers* (1964), a lusty narrative of settlers beyond the Blue Ridge in 1779-1784. For such a time and place, fact is less important than the procedures of living—how to kill for food, how to cut down a tree, how to build a house, how to make clothes. These how-to activities are described in minute, thorough detail. *The Road* (1967) has a fictitious plot to serve as foreground for those Herculean men who in the late 1870s laid a railway track up the Blue Ridge from Old Fort to Ridgecrest,

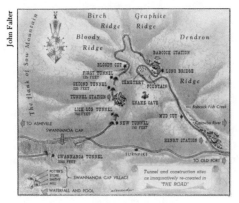

Illustration from *The Road*

digging tunnels as they ascended, including the final 1,800-foot Swannanoa Tunnel at a cost of 120 lives. *Time of Drums* (1970) has two brothers, both Confederate colonels from western North Carolina, in love with the same lass, their lives inexorably leading them toward the Battle of Gettysburg. Ehle turned back to the early nineteenth century for *The Journey of August King* (1971), which a critic defined as an "unsentimental story that comes across like a classic folk tale . . . full of poetry and beauty." The work centers on a widowered mountain farmer as he aids a fifteen-year-old runaway slave girl to escape northward. Two neighboring mountain families during the Great Depression

in *The Winter People* (1982) reconcile their animosity toward one another through the intermediary of a traveling clockmaker. Like the previous novel, *Last One Home* (1984) has fewer earmarks of the conventional historical novel than the other four, since it begins at the turn of the century and progresses into almost contemporary times. Here, an ambitious young man from the backwoods, after settling his family in Asheville, becomes a prosperous businessman at cross purposes with his wife, who longs for the slower, pastoral life in her native hills.

Tom Wicker, born in Hamlet and now associate editor of the *New York Times*, walked a long, slow literary road before writing his mammoth (642 pages) historical novel of the Civil War. It was a road paved with four murder mysteries, three of them under the pseudonym "Paul Connolly"; studies of John F. Kennedy and Lyndon B. Johnson; a political commentary; the firsthand account of the Attica prison riots; a book on journalism; and three works of fiction. First of the three was *The Kingpin* (1953), a hardfisted story of political deception based on the vicious, race-stimulated second primary campaign between Frank P.

Tom Wicker

78

Graham and Willis Smith for the Democratic candidacy to the United States Senate in 1950. *The Judgment* (1961) is a subtly symbolic novel about the terror that comes to a small town (Rockingham?) with the arrival there of a satanic stranger during a November snowstorm. In *Facing the Lions* (1973), a Washington journalist reviews his past on a flight southward to the funeral of a favored politician. It was some time later that Wicker spent four years researching and writing *Unto This Hour* (1984), which presents a panoramic view of the Second Battle of Manassas in August, 1862, with forty characters, both historical and fictional, moving to center stage at one time or another. Lee, Jackson, Longstreet, Stuart, Lincoln, McClellan, and Pope, as well as preachers, slaves, newspaper correspondents, Confederate and Yankee soldiers by the dozens, a southern beauty left alone on her plantation, two men who find love amid the turmoil of war—all pass in review during those two gladiatorial summer days at Manassas. Tenderness and dignity, comedy and faith, gore and death commingle in Wicker's tragic specter of war, a useless squandering, he would tell us, of sacred mankind.

The all-too-few books mentioned here are representative of hundreds of other historical novels about North Carolina or by North Carolinians. The genre is a pliant one, bending to the will and intention of any writer who assays it. That every one of the hundred counties in North Carolina has a history, written or unwritten, suitable for fictional treatment should be a consoling thought to those who may have believed that local materials for use in imaginative literature were fast being used up.

XIV

NOVELISTS AT MID-CENTURY

The four middle decades of the twentieth century were, even discounting historical fiction, extraordinarily fruitful in the publication of novels by North Carolinians. Almost every year some new writer of merit issued an impressive first volume and promptly joined the group of veteran performers. The names are so many, the books so numerous, that only the most successful can be cited here.

Even as early as 1920, after the arrival in Southern Pines of Struthers Burt and Katharine Newlin Burt, it was obvious that a new breeze of competent professionalism was blowing. They and their friend James Boyd were no village amateurs but skilled craftsmen working for the lucrative New York market. While Burt was producing serious books, his wife wrote light novels of adventure and mystery, such as *The Red Lady* (1920) and *Beggars All* (1933), in which no reader is surprised to meet jewel thieves and smugglers at wisteria-draped southern mansions. It was during this time, too, that Laurence Stallings was beginning those famous books drawn from his experience in World War I. His semi-autobiographical *Plumes* (1924) tells of a wounded veteran's agonized adjustment to civilian life in a town closely resembling Wake Forest. Stanley Olmsted of Murphy wrote *At Top of Tobin* (1926), a sensitive, now inexplicably forgotten novel of a mountain town in the 1880s. Olmsted's chronicle is important not only as a work of literary merit but also as vivid social history. Like the Asheville experience of Wolfe's *Look Homeward, Angel* three years later, Olmsted's roman a clef was condemned in Murphy.

In 1929 textile union troubles in Gastonia, followed by the stock market crash, ushered in the Great Depression. The first of a number of proletarian novels based on the struggle between the Gastonia workers and the millowners was *Strike!* (1930), by Mary Heaton Vorse of Massachusetts, which told of a northern newspaperman's eventual sympathy for and understanding of a strike leader. Grace Lumpkin came up from Georgia, and in *To Make My Bread* (1932) she wrote strictly from the Marxist point of view about the violent death of an actual person, Ella Mae Wiggins. Yet, it remained for the equally sympathetic Olive Tilford Dargan to translate those convulsive times into vital literature. In *Call Home the Heart* (1932) and its sequel *A Stone Came Rolling* (1935), she wrote, under the pseudonym of Fielding Burke, of her beloved mountain people, lured down to the mills by promises of prosperity and a better life and then betrayed and impoverished by the capitalistic system.

The urban scene in North Carolina, this time among the upper crust, was pictured in the novels of Marian Sims of Charlotte. The heroine of *Call It Freedom* (1937), for instance, is a divorcée caught up in a country-club atmosphere of bridge, golf, and attractive men, and *Memo. to Timothy Sheldon* (1938) is made up entirely of a series of notes written by a romantic woman to her prosaic rich husband after she has met a man who "understands" her. Sims's most significant novel is *The City on the Hill* (1940), in which a right-thinking man loses his fight against corruption in "Medbury" to the forces of religious orthodoxy and political apathy. *Storm before Daybreak* (1946) deals with a Marine veteran's return to his home city after World War II.

Just how close the "Medbury" people and events in *The City on the Hill* were to certain actual citizens in Charlotte and to well-known civic scandals in that city is speculative, but certain it was that church leaders and police officials were offended by the book, and everyone knew that the author's husband was a local judge well informed on the subject of public evils. The drawing of recognizable characters in familiar situations is, as Thomas Wolfe and Stanley Olmsted discovered after their romans à clef were published, a hazardous course for a novelist to take. But the temptation is always there.

Margaret Culkin Banning, a Minnesotan, was a prolific writer of light romances. After she began spending winters in Tryon in 1933, she set some of her novels in the North Carolina foothills. In the resort village of De Soto (Tryon), the reader meets up with local tradesmen, well-behaved servants, and of course the "country-club aristocracy." For example, *I Took My Love to the Country* (1966) moves in on numerous complications among the De Soto horsey set at the Riding and Hunt Club. *Such Interesting People* (1979), Banning's last novel, has to do with a frustrated New York writer who has retreated from the city to De Soto in order to examine the reasons for his failures.

James M. Shields's novel *Just Plain Larnin'* (1934) criticizes a public school system that is an outmoded nonprogressive pawn of industry and privilege in a tobacco city, but what Shields wrote was too much like what was going on in Winston-Salem to suit the school board, which fired him from his job. Gastonia over a seventy-five-year span came to life in Evan Brandon's masterful *Green Pond* (1955), which treats several generations of a prominent doctor's family, their friends, their townspeople, and their associates in the Presbyterian church. Readers identifying the models of Bran-

don's many characters were somewhat put off by his sweep and poetic style. A more publicized and turbulent aftermath than any of these, however, came in response to the publication of *The Education of Jonathan Beam* (1962), by Russell Brantley of Zebulon, director of communications on the Wake Forest campus at Winston-Salem. In the novel, Jonathan Beam, a fundamentalist boy from the backwoods, goes to a Baptist college and discovers that dancing and drinking, as well as modernism in religious views, are not so bad after all. The resulting furor, during which the book was denounced at the Baptist State Convention, helped to sell out several editions quickly, and for almost a year *The*

Baptist Groups Attack WF Plan; Claim Brantley's Book 'Offensive'

Baptist groups have strongly attacked a proposal to put non-Baptists on the Wake Forest College board of trustees and have criticized Russell Brantley for an "offensive" book written by him in statements published Thursday in The Biblical Recorder official publication of The Baptist State Convention.

The attack on the trustee proposal came from the Baptist ministers and laymen. The proposal was described as the first step toward complete loss of control of the institution by the Baptist State Convention.

"Some are being led to believe," the statement said, "that if we elect 16 non-Baptists and out-of-state trustees the prospect is bright" for obtaining $80 million.

Brantley Criticized.

A Baptist committee has strongly criticized Russell Brantley, director of communications at Wake Forest College.

The executive committee of the General Board of the Baptist State Convention said "certain living Baptist leaders were held up for ridicule" by the book, "The Education of Jonathan Beam."

Education of Jonathan Beam was the most discussed literary work in all North Carolina. Brantley heroically held on to his job.

Such explosive books as these did not, even so, mean that novelists no longer wrote, with their traditional dedication, of the seemingly placid small towns. Gerald W. Johnson's first novel, *By Reason of Strength* (1930), was based on pioneering days in the life of the author's great grandmother along Drowning Creek. Then Johnson turned, in *Number Thirty-Six* (1933), to the small-town newspaper editor and the conflicts that ensue with industrial development. Readers recognized the town as Thomasville, which also served as the setting of Eugene Armfield's *Where the Weak Grow Strong* (1936), a plotless novel with slice-of-life episodes about various types of inhabitants—factory hands, blacks, business folk, millowners, and farmers. Fred Ross and James Ross, brothers, were born in Stanly County. James Ross's *They Don't Dance Much* (1940), showing the seamy side of piedmont North Carolina, is naturalistic fiction set for the most part in a roadhouse, where the town's worthless humanity come to eat, drink beer, play the slot machines, and plot to do each other in. They dance a little, but not much. Fred Ross's *Jackson Mahaffey* (1951), almost as if by contrast, is a frolicsome yarn about a whiskey-drinking, cockfighting fellow on a round of pranks that includes getting himself elected to the state Senate. The book is an irresistible combination of storytelling, humor, folklore, and myth.

One of the most distinguished writers of mid-century North Carolina was Bernice Kelly Harris, whose book of plays, Christmas gift books, autobiography, and seven novels epitomized the rural areas and the small towns of the eastern part of the state. Born in Wake County, a graduate of Meredith College, and a teacher of high school English, Harris married in 1926 and thereafter called Seaboard home. At first, upon attending classes taught by Frederick H. Koch, she was a writer of folk plays; but editor Jonathan Daniels noted the touching human-interest news items she sent to his paper and suggested that she write a novel. *Purslane* (1939), a quite remarkable first novel, is a nostalgic evocation of rural life at the turn of the century among the independent, landowning small farmers of her native county. With only the most necessary plot line, it is primarily a succession of tobacco curings, spring-cleanings, hog-killings, Sunday school excursions, and box suppers accenting the otherwise quiet days of churchgoing, right-living country folk. With *Portulaca* (1941), Harris moved into town, the Nannie Lou of *Purslane* now Nancy Huntington, the wife of a man strongly attached to his well-to-do family. It helps to know that portulaca is the cultivated variety of the vigorous but common herb called purslane. So, instead of cotton pickings and coon hunts, the succession

Bernice Kelly Harris

in *Portulaca* is one of bridge parties, minor infidelities, and business deals. Though occasionally Harris's satire can be harsh, it most often is gentle and understanding. After all, these are the people she loves.

Portulaca was Harris's only trip into town. The other five novels have rural settings. For *Sweet Beulah Land* (1943), she chose a familiar southern literary theme: the contrast between seedy, landweary aristocrats and sturdy, enterprising sharecroppers. *Sage Quarter* (1945) is a Cinderella-like love story of the girl who patiently waits in her bucolic surroundings for the arrival of the comely young man who will once more set up a medical practice in the deserted doctor's office. *Janey Jeems* (1946) has a gimmick: though race is never mentioned, the novel is about a hardworking black family aspiring to improve itself and its community and to bring up its children to be industrious and God-fearing. Harris's only novel dipping into history for background is *Hearthstones* (1948), which concerns the consequences throughout the years of a Civil War deserter's being "read out" of the Baptist church for his disloyalty. In *Wild Cherry Tree Road* (1951), the novelist returns to the setting of *Purslane*, this time focusing on the crude and homeless but vigorous Kalline, a character she had introduced in two of her previous works.

The inventiveness of these seven novels is amazing, and each one has its own distinctive quality. They easily move back and forth in time and place, without repetition. They deal with human behavior, with human weakness, with human strength. They treat broad, recognizable segments of society, yet do not overlook the strange and unusual. As much as any series of books can, they encompass a people and a region with warmth and perception.

Use of the remembered or re-created past, observable in so many of the works by Harris, is a dominant quality in the fiction of a number of other North Carolinians during the period. Peirson Ricks, a native of Mayodan, set *The Hunter's Horn* (1947) in the eastern Carolina plantation country of 1895, and his story turns on a seventeen-year-old boy's guilt about his relationship with a sharecropper's daughter. Like many of his literary predecessors, the boy leans to patrician pleasures like fox hunting, but, deep inside, a love of his ancestral lands exacts his devotion and labor. In *Bright Leaf* (1948), Chapel Hill's Foster Fitz-Simons brings back the early days of empire building in the tobacco industry. His characters, loosely based on members of the Duke family, are ruthless in business and personal affairs but eventually manage through their wealth to initiate progressive programs and institutions for their people. *Bright Leaf* deals with the big world, but not so *Love Is a Wound* (1952), by Worth Tuttle Hedden, born in Raleigh in a Methodist parsonage. Two earlier novels preceded her now-neglected masterwork, which from three points of view narrates with intense artistry the tangled relationships of a minister and two sisters, the younger of whom he marries while permitting the older to live with them.

For his novels, Ovid Williams Pierce of Weldon chose the horse-and-buggy past. In muted rhetoric, *The Plantation* (1953) tells what happens after the death of a landowner so conscious of his responsibilities to others that he turns aside any

D. Schwarts

THE PLANTATION

a novel

Ovid Williams Pierce

assertions of personal wishes and ambitions. *On a Lonesome Porch* (1960) reveals the sad aftermath of the Civil War as reflected in the strength and sacrifice of two women intent on rebuilding a plantation. In *The Devil's Half* (1968) Pierce's central character is a soft but strong-willed woman determined not to let postbellum dissolution corrupt the values of a happier time. From a present-day point of view, *The Wedding Guest* (1974) looks into the past. *Old Man's Gold and Other Stories* (1976) reprints six short narratives written before the publication of Pierce's first novel.

Race consciousness quickly reasserted itself in the 1950s, resulting in a kind of fiction that was indeed a far cry from the opinionated ethnic novels of the past. In those first years after the Supreme Court decision of 1954, Lucy Daniels of Raleigh, in *Caleb, My Son* (1965), wrote of the clash between a conservative black father and a son unwilling to accept the old patterns. A backward look at two generations of blacks, at their long suffering and patience, at the effect upon whites who come among them, was taken by Hoke Norris from Holly Springs in *All* the Kingdoms of Earth (1956), a casually developed novel with obvious Biblical parallels. Lettie Rogers of Greensboro faces head-on the differences separating whites and blacks in *Birthright* (1957), in which racial tensions divide the people in a small town. Charlotte native Ben Haas tells in *Look Away, Look Away* (1964) of two friends—one white, one black— growing up together in harmony with each other until racial strife divides them, one becoming the segregationist candidate for governor, the other a national leader in the civil rights movement. A sympathetic white man in Haas's *The Troubled Summer* (1966) joins the blacks' civil rights campaign, whose leader spies on the Ku Klux Klan, confronts its members, and succeeds in abrogating their obnoxious schemes.

Lucy Daniels and Hoke Norris, Lettie Rogers and Ben Haas made, through the medium of their fiction, such earnest and thoughtful comments on the tense racial question that readers welcomed *The Jub Jub Bird* (1966), by William M. Hardy of Chapel Hill. In this satire set in a university town torn by civil rights agitation, Hardy pounds with good humor the bigots and the intellectuals, the blacks and the whites, the liberals and the conservatives, the do-gooders and the do-nothings. In the mid-1960s the time was ripe for just such a novel as this.

Race relations behind them, these writers had other fictional areas to explore. Lettie Rogers's *Landscape of the Heart* (1953) and Lucy Daniels's *High on a Hill* (1961) are stories of life in mental institutions. Norris's *It's Not Far but I Don't Know the Way* (1969) relates an unusual love affair.

A decidedly professional writer who depended upon his typewriter for subsistence, Ben Haas was the author of more than a hundred books under the pseudonyms John Benteen, Thorne Douglas, Richard Meade, Ben Elliott, Ben Stone, John Michael Elliott, Quinn Reade, and perhaps others. These were for his "lesser works," he said, reserving his Ben Haas by-line for "those books

important to me." Among them are *The Foragers* (1962), a Civil War novel about a Confederate captain's raid during the final days of the war on a luxurious plantation presided over by a stubborn old lady and her beautiful daughter; *The Last Valley* (1966), which sets forth the conservationist's point of view in a narrative that speaks out against the destruction of irreplaceable North Carolina mountain forests by predatory business and industrial interests; *The Chandler Heritage* (1971), presumably based on the colossal Cannon Mills textile empire; and *The House of Christina* (1977), a dramatic novel of Austria during the Anschluss and World War II.

Among William M. Hardy's other half dozen novels are three adventures involving submarines and *Year of the Rose* (1960), in which a North Carolina professor falls in love with a graduate student, thus risking his professional status.

Three writers from outside the state who, after residence in North Carolina, achieved national reputations were Betty Smith, James Street, and Richard McKenna. All found Chapel Hill a good place to do their work. Smith's *A Tree Grows in Brooklyn* (1943) and other books by her, none of which uses a North Carolina setting or characters, brought her abundant royalties and much fame. She once said that whereas Thomas Wolfe had gone to Brooklyn to write about North Carolina, she had come to North Carolina to write about Brooklyn. James Street was author of a dozen best sellers, among which *Tap Roots* (1943), *The Gauntlet* (1945), and *The Velvet Doublet* (1953) were best known. He often remarked, with a sly grin, that his books were not works of art but, he had very good reason to believe, solid professional productions. Concerning the second statement, he was of course right, but no one can read the Columbus story he tells in *The Velvet Doublet*, for instance, without realizing what a master craftsman he was in every narrative requirement. Richard McKenna died before he completed his second book, but *The Sand*

Pebbles (1962), his long novel of the United States Navy in China during the 1920s, so caught public attention that his became a noted name. It was reprinted in 1984 in the Naval Institute Press's "Classics of Naval Literature" series.

In these middle years of the century, four outstanding American novelists with limited ties to North Carolina found in the state exactly the right settings for at least one title among their corpus of works. Carson McCullers, who lived for a while in Fayetteville, wrote *Reflections in a Golden Eye* (1941), a novella of psychoneurotic horrors at a peacetime army post (Fort Bragg) at which a number of pathological characters with diseased minds—two officers, two women, a soldier, a Filipino—are pushed to the ultimate limits of tragedy, leaving a noble horse the only untainted living creature in the denouement.

Based on a wrenching incident experienced by William Styron when he was recalled to the Marine Corps at Camp Lejeune in 1950, *The Long March* (1952) is a blunt narrative about a sadistic thirteen-hour forced trek through the swamps and forests with devastating effects on both officers and men.

In Jack Kerouac's *The Dharma Bums* (1958), the semiautobiographical protagonist, a serious Zen Buddhist seeking dharma (eternal truth) through meditation, spends several months near Rocky Mount with his mother and brother-in-law's family, periodically escaping into the nearby fields and a pine grove to commune with infinity.

The Second Coming (1980), the fifth novel by Walker Percy, a Chapel Hill graduate thoroughly acquainted with the state, has as its leading character a millionaire, mentally troubled about his past, who returns to his summer home (in Asheville?) and regains his lost peace of mind upon meeting up with a secretive young woman then living in a deserted greenhouse after slipping away from an asylum.

Plot, style, and atmosphere are dominant factors in *Little Squire Jim* (1949), a

Fayetteville Observer-Times, June 16, 1985

Bookmark
BY ROY PARKER JR.

The McCullers Link

Reeves and Carson McCullers

THE LONELY HUNTER. A Biography of Carson McCullers. By *Virginia Spencer Carr. Carroll & Graf Publishers. New York. 598 pages. $12.95. Paperback.*

•

Forty-six years ago this month, neighbors in the courthouse town of Fayetteville often saw that strange McCullers girl banging away at her portable typewriter from her summer perch — the second-floor veranda of the old Cool Spring Tavern, then a private residence.

More than a year later, a few of them who learned about it would be surprised that she was writing a novel.

And they would be shocked that the story — titled **Reflections in a Golden Eye** — was a biting tale of homosexuality, rage, and cruelty on an Army post which strongly resembled Fort Bragg, the small artillery post a few miles down the two-lane blacktop road from the town.

And, of course, she gave Fayetteville a place on the American literary map which serves well to decorate the heritage of the new All-America City.

The McCullers came to Fayetteville from Charlotte. Reeves McCullers worked for a "credit bureau" operation, but the young couple were both bent on a literary career. The end of their relationship is not part of this portion of their story. Once they moved from Fayetteville in mid-June, 1940, they never returned.

They "hated the place," according to the biographer.

Reeves explained to a friend that Fayetteville was a place where:

"It is the same today as it has been for years ago and probably would be years from now. All a man could do was work all day, go home, read, go to bed, get up, and work all day again. The only slight change was getting a little bit drunk on Saturday night. But just a little bit — just a little bit."

Nonetheless, it was where Carson not only whipped out **Reflections in a Golden Eye** in two summer months, but also put final touches on **The Heart is A Lonely Hunter.**

This is the description of the Cool Spring scene:

"From their homes and yards the neighbors listened to Beethoven's Third (and other classical pieces), amazed that the strange girl of whom they were so critical could play the beautiful music they heard daily coming from the landlady's piano in the downstairs parlor. Then, incongruously, they saw a tall, straggle-dressed figure emerge with a portable typewriter and sit at a small table on the railing of the wide upstairs veranda, which ran across the front of the house.

The picture illustrating this Bookmark is published for the first time in the new edition. It was taken during the Fayetteville months, probably in the winter of 1939-40. (And Carson is not wearing her "winter outfit")!

gothic tale by Mt. Airy native Robert K. Marshall as he romanticizes the daring and superhuman exploits of a handsome young folk hero in the Surry County hills; its sequel, *Julia Gwynn* (1952), continues

85

the lives of the youth's extraordinary family with further extraordinary events. Both novels depend upon superstition and mystery and unnatural occurrences for their effect.

The name of Robert Ruark of Wilmington was a household word, principally because of his syndicated newspaper column. Though his two long novels of Africa, *Something of Value* (1955) and *Uhuru* (1962), were his most popular books, his best one, undoubtedly, was *The Old Man and the Boy* (1957), the heartwarming reminiscences of a youngster in Southport learning from his grandfather to hunt and to fish and to respect the natural world that makes such sports possible. It was followed by *The Old Man's Boy Grows Older* (1961). *Poor No More* (1959) is a rags-to-riches novel about a North Carolina young man, and *The Honey Badger* (1965) is the story of a North Carolina writer torn between work and women.

Many writers at mid-century found it satisfying to work on college campuses, where they could combine teaching and writing. The arrangement permitted a relaxed writing schedule and provided a rather constant forum for criticism. The best teacher-writers could also profit from the stimulation that always comes from active young minds. Among this group of teacher-writers, some of whom have been previously mentioned, were Stanley Olmsted, James M. Shields, Bernice Kelly Harris, Foster Fitz-Simons, Ovid Williams Pierce, Lettie Rogers, William M. Hardy, John Ehle, Robert K. Marshall, and Romulus Linney.

At the university in Chapel Hill, the long career of Jessie Rehder was devoted more to teaching than to writing, but her novel *Remembrance Way* (1956) gave her students a skillful model in the technique of how recollected experience—in this case, that of a girl at a summer camp—might be handled for narrative purposes.

At North Carolina State University, English professor Guy Owen achieved a popularity with his humorous Flim-Flam

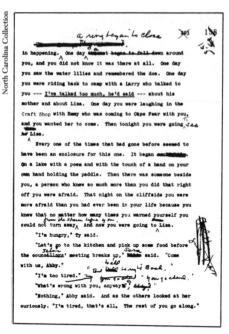

Manuscript page, *Remembrance Way*

Man stories, which delighted his worshiping students, the many neophyte writers he was always encouraging, those who attended his public lectures, and Owen himself, who took his popularity in stride and loved every minute of it. His native southeastern North Carolina was almost his private literary domain. *Season of Fear* (1960), his first novel, however, was not comic. Though it dealt with a lower-class, retarded tobacco farmer obsessed by sex and religion, it was so deftly constructed along classic lines that it was, like Rehder's *Remembrance Way*, a prototype of thematic form.

The rascally but lovable flimflam artist Mordecai Jones in *The Ballad of the Flim-Flam Man* (1965) enlists willing young folk singer Curley Treadaway, AWOL from Fort Bragg, to be his sidekick while traipsing the countryside and hamlets in the Cape Fear River basin. Though constantly on the run from the simple-minded sheriff, Jones and Treadaway manage to cheat the local residents at lightning-rod sales, card games, liquor dealings, revival services, and other seemingly straightforward proceedings. As the flimflam man makes clear, an honest person can never be tricked in the "skin trade," the two imposters succeeding only when their victims are gullible or greedy and deserve to be flimflammed. The rogues' extravagant swindles are continued in *The Flim-Flam Man and the Apprentice Grifter* (1972) and *The Flim-Flam Man and Other Stories* (1980). Owen's *Journey for Joedel* (1970) tells of the painful awakening, during one long day at a small-town tobacco auction, of a right-thinking thirteen-year-old Croatan Indian boy to the shabby, dishonest adult world of his father. Owen's love of poetry (see chapter 17) is manifest in *Cape Fear Country and Other Poems* (1958) and *The White Stallion and Other Poems* (1969).

A curious twist played first fiddle to William E. Cobb's novel *An Inch of Snow* (1964). Two years before its publication, the Morganton author, called at that time "the glamour boy of the North Carolina GOP," withdrew from a political race following the exposure of his "double family," a wife in Morganton and a common-law wife and two sons in Virginia. In the novel the Republican protagonist of Jeffersonville (Morganton), certain to win a seat in the state legislature, throws the election to the Democratic father of the girl he has made pregnant. The sensational background of Cobb's book is the primary reason for its being remembered.

XV

WRITERS OF WHODUNITS AND SCI-FI

Though at the turn of the century North Carolinians, like everybody else in the English-speaking world, were avidly reading the adventures of Sherlock Holmes, they were not producing detective stories or murder mysteries of their own. True, Eugene Hall (Mrs. Emma Baker of Louisburg) had written *The Master of L'Étrange* (1886), about mysterious organ music and murder upsetting a lovers' romance at a Gothic castle near Swannanoa, and Thomasville's Nancy King Brown told in *A Broken Bondage* (1911) of a lady-killing rascal who does in several innocent maidens; but both books were strictly amateur. Except from an acknowledged genius like Edgar Allan Poe the genre was considered subliterary. This situation soon changed, however.

First in the professional field was James Hay, Jr., of Asheville, who used his mountain city as the setting for three novels. In *The Winning Clue* (1919) authorities must solve the crime involving a strangled woman, in *The Bellamy Case* (1925) the manager of a candidate for the state legislature is murdered, and in *The Hidden Woman* (1929) a neighbor uses her wits to find the killer of a tubercular victim. Meanwhile, down in the Sandhills country, Ernest M. Poate in *The Troubles at Pineland* (1922) portrayed three doctors (in Southern Pines), one of them murdered, a second accused, and a third who runs down the assassin.

The most gifted of the early murder storytellers was Dorothy Ogburn of High-lands, who in *Death on the Mountain* (1931) wrote of the strangling of a wealthy man on the lawn of his summer home at Thunder Falls (Highlands) during a windy night in July, 1925. A beautifully authentic locale provides summer visitors, town residents, innkeepers, and an idiot boy. Ogburn is best remembered, however, for *Shake-speare: The Man behind the Name* (1962), which denies the country bumpkin from Stratford his authorship of the greatest literary works of all times and instead argues that the true playwright and poet was heroic, talented Edward de Vere (1550-1604), seventeenth earl of Oxford.

Early on, western North Carolina seemed especially inviting to architects of murder mysteries. Kathleen Morehouse of North Wilkesboro in *Rain on the Just* (1936) turned back to the days following the Civil War when several murders, a suicide, and other unpleasant goings-on take place amid the Brushy Mountains. In *Kill 1, Kill 2* (1940), Walter Anderson has a business executive murdered at a cloud-topped lodge while the Brown Mountain Lights keep flashing a warning. Dean Hawkins's *Skull Mountain* (1941) includes three alarming murders that upset both the suspicious natives and the frightened tourists. Asheville resident Thomas Polsky tells in *The Cudgel* (1950) of a young woman beaten to death in a swimming pool on an ancestral estate atop a mountain west of Asheville. Talmage Powell, born in Hendersonville, wrote copious whodunits, the first of which was *The Smasher* (1959), whose murderer is apprehended by the victim's husband. Over in Tryon, Richard Lockridge, author of the numerous Jerry North series, wrote *Death in a Sunny Place* (1971), in which the body of a guest is pulled out of the lake at a tourist inn called the Hilltop Club.

Finally at mid-century it was Tom Wicker who lured a coterie of those western North Carolina murderers and detectives down to the piedmont. His first three excursions into the mystery field were paperbacks written under the pseudonym Paul Connolly. *Get Out of Town* (1951) has a World War II veteran and a newspaperwoman in Hampton (Wicker's native Hamlet) solve a string of murders committed by drug racketeers; *Tears Are for Angels* (1952) combines fighting, sex, and homicide in a tobacco-growing county; and *So Fair, So Evil* (1955) aligns a Korean War veteran against his wife's murderer at her former plantation house jammed with her violent, decadent family and friends. Wicker used his own by-line for *The Devil Must* (1957) as he solves the witchcraft killing of a farmer near Marion (Lumberton?) and frees the young black man accused of the crime. Upstate a hundred miles Robert Turner, native of Eagle Rock in Wake County, tells in *The Tobacco Auction Murders* (1954) of a New York policeman's return to Wilsboro (Wendell) in order to find the murderer of his wife, who was done in while visiting her father on a tobacco farm. Turner followed up this mystery with *The Night Is for Screaming* (1960) and, under the pen name Mercer B. Cook, *In Hot Blood* (1966).

Murderers moved onto the university campuses when Ian Gordon wrote in *After Innocence* (1955) of sex and homicide in a professor's family at Southern University (the University of North Carolina). Another Chapel Hill murder mystery, *Du Sang sous les Magnolias* (Madrid, 1982, no English translation), came from the pen of Jacques Hardré, native of France and professor of French at the

university. In this novel a young Frenchman follows his fiancée from Montpellier to Chapel Hill, where he becomes a lecturer at the university. Against his will, he finds himself involved in four murders committed by a dope ring; though the police seek his assistance, he is reluctant to reveal his private discovery of the gang leader's identity. In Chapel Hill, readers were delighted with the murder plot, but even more so with the game of identifying the models on whom many of the characters were based. One local reviewer wrote that he "recognized composites of a dozen folks I know about town!"

In *Lady Killer* (1957) Chapel Hill faculty member William M. Hardy tells of a mathematics professor who disguises the murder of his wife by strangling a number of other people. For *A Little Sin* (1958, retitled *The Case of the Missing Co-ed*, 1960), Hardy moved over to Dryden (Duke) University to depict a mathematics professor's horror in discovering the body of the student who had a crush on him, then watching her murderer vanish into the shadowy shrubbery. *A Time for Killing* (1962) is another Hardy murder mystery.

Amanda MacKay (Mrs. James David Barber) of the Duke faculty was on familiar ground when she wrote *Death Is Academic* (1976), in which Hannah Land, professor and detective, solves the mystery of a scholar's dropping to the floor during a dinner attended by members of the political science department. No one can understand why anyone would want to murder mild Bradley Brown, until she deduces that a fruit cocktail laced with cyanide, which killed him, was really meant for someone else. Hannah's apperceptions are once again kept busy when in *Death on the Eno* (1981) she looks into an "accidental" drowning in the Eno River north of Durham and brings to justice the gunmen who had been hijacking tobacco trucks loaded at Durham warehouses.

Death and violence moved to the coastland in Ben Haas's *Daisy Canfield* (1973), based on an actual unsolved murder of a young stage seamstress in Manteo.

Hugh Zachary of Yaupon Beach, after producing *Second Chance* (1976), a novel of spine-chilling experiences during a North Carolina hurricane, turned to whodunits, first in *To Guard the Right* (1980),

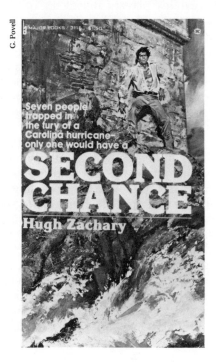

G. Powell

like Haas's *Daisy Canfield* based on a real-life situation. A retired admiral in Clarendon (Brunswick) County, reputed to have valuable coins, is set upon by ruffians. Though they torture him, tie his hands behind his back with leather thongs, and push him face-down in a bathtub, he survives, only to be murdered while recuperating in a hospital. In *Bloodrush* (1981), the Clarendon County sheriff hires a black deputy to help him with a mess of troubles: a black prostitute and others are murdered, thirteen teenagers disappear, and farm animals are disemboweled. The deputy finds that witchcraft is involved. The sheriff and his deputy reappear in *Murder in White* (1981) when the staunch admirer of a drug-habituated doctor in the Clarendon County hospital resolves that, in order to protect the reputation of his medical friend, he must murder the only other persons who know of the doctor's addiction. Zachary transports his readers from the North Carolina coast to Paris for his sensational tale *The Venus Venture* (1986), which hinges on the theft of the world-famous Greek marble statue of Venus de Milo from the Louvre.

Another novel set in the east is *A Country Killing* (1981), by Max F. Harris of Monroe, who has a county sheriff and two city cops moving about the swamplands and competing against each other in finding out whether or not a son has murdered his father, meanwhile unmasking a batch of blackmailers and professional criminals.

An unlikely writer of whodunits is Miles Wolff, owner of the Durham Bulls baseball team. The setting of *Season of the Owl* (1980) is Centerville (Greensboro), where a fourteen-year-old boy searches for the killer of his father, whose body is found in a baseball park. Readers praised Wolff's evocation of Greensboro in the 1950s more than his plotting of the crime and its solution. Murder travels up and down country roads in Nearing River (Nash) County in *Rear-View Mirror* (1980), by Caroline B. Cooney of High Point. This is no who-did-it, for the

A novel by
Miles Wolff, Jr.

Ted Bernstein

murderers in this "terror" novel are known from their first killing. A savage convict and his vicious cousin steal a station wagon, smother with a big black plastic sack a baby girl left in the back seat and throw her body into a river, then kidnap a young dentist's receptionist and force her to drive them down remote byways as they go on a haphazard, gory spree of slaughter.

Caroline B. Cooney

John Goodwin Cooney

Uncivil Seasons (1983), by Michael Malone, Tar Heel born, is narrated by a detective whose socially prominent aunt has been savagely murdered in a fictional industrial city in the piedmont. "Two things don't happen very often in Hillston, N.C.," says the detective. "We don't get much snow, and we hardly ever murder one another." But murder has been done, and during the investigation by the police detective, himself a scion of wealth, and his less affluent partner, the city's secrets are uncovered, the substratum of characters on all levels revealed. The rednecks, the rich and powerful, and those in between speak, if variously, with accent and flowing measures true to the North Carolina vernacular. A comic interchange between the pair of policemen brightens the otherwise grim goings-on.

In *Bloody Kin* (1985), Margaret Maron of Willow Springs set her third mystery in colorful Colleton (Johnston) County, to which an attractice widow returns from a New York career in modeling and fabric design to plunge into a network of cousins, courtship, and homicide while investigating the murder of her husband and his Vietnam War comrade. The Tar Heel Scene—barbecue, basketball, and Raleigh's shopping malls—is as engrossing to read about as the sleuthing tactics of the winsome widow.

In the midst of the whodunits mentioned here and scores of others, the strangest book of all is *The Flesh of the Orchid* (1948), by James Hadley Chase, pseudonym for the enormously popular British writer of "thrillers," René Raymond. This is a horror tale about a beautiful, wealthy, deranged woman who falls into the hands of two bloody killers. Nothing unusual about that, of course, but since Raymond freely admitted that he had never in his life been even close to North Carolina, his geography to anyone familiar with the contours of the state is flawed and unreal. For true-hearted Tar Heel readers, this murder mystery is more a comedy than a hair-raising "thriller."

The flourishing of detective novels in North Carolina was soon matched by a companionate genre—fantasy and science fiction—that attracted the general reader along with a loyal cult, members of which, according to a knowledgeable bookseller, purchased copies for their home libraries. Such readers were unlike the "murder" enthusiasts, who swapped their paperbacks or disposed of them to friends on a no-return basis.

The earliest two sci-fi titles with a North Carolina locale came, like the odd *Orchid* opus, from one who never set foot in the state. Jules Verne, the famous Frenchman, rarely moved out of his restricted environs into the worldwide geography of his creations. Rather, at Amiens he collected maps, travel books, encyclopedias, and other helpful references for his workshop, then almost every day walked to the public library to read and take notes. In *Face au Drapeau* (1892, English title *Facing the Flag*) a crazed French inventor is kidnapped from a New Bern asylum by a pirate and taken to Bermuda to construct a death-dealing apparatus one hundred times more devastating than anything then known. Verne's protagonist in *Maître du Monde* (1904, English title *The Master of the World*) is Robur the Conqueror, who at his base atop a mountain near Morganton keeps in readiness his "Terror," a machine that combines the attributes of automobile, boat, submarine, and airplane. An explosion at the Conqueror's eyrie convinces the local denizens that the mountain is a volcano. Verne undoubtedly had read about a succession of earthquakes that rattled the countryside of Rutherford and Burke counties in 1874, the more than fifty shocks seemingly coming from Rumbling Bald Mountain.

After Verne, sci-fi was dormant in the state till Manly Wade Wellman took up the gauntlet. Wellman's very first book publication, written fifteen years before he moved to North Carolina, was *The Invading Asteroid* (1932), a fantasy of the thirtieth century continued in other titles such as *The Devil's Planet* (1951), a Martian murder mystery that teams up two detectives, one a human being, the other an android. Meanwhile Wellman had moved on to other kinds of books that interested him as a writer, but from time to time he returned to his early love, as evinced by his more than a score of fantasy and science-fiction titles.

North Carolina Collection

Manly Wade Wellman

George Roux, Paris

Illustration from *Maître du Monde*

In 1951 Wellman struck a vein of gold. In the *Magazine of Fantasy and Science Fiction* appeared "O Ugly Bird!" which features a virtuous, selfless, and conscientious fellow who, while fearlessly combating witches and warlocks and various evil creatures in the North Carolina mountains (Wellman had a summer retreat in Madison County), goes in search of genuine old ballads, then sings them accompanied by his playing on a silver-stringed guitar. In his encounters with the supernatural, the hero, Silver John, is ever defending those who are innocent, timid, and afraid. John is a strong, a good man, a very good young man. Nine other Silver John fantasies (as differentiated from science fiction) were included in *Who Fears the Devil?* (1963), an unquestioned classic among the thousands of books that make up North Carolina's literature.

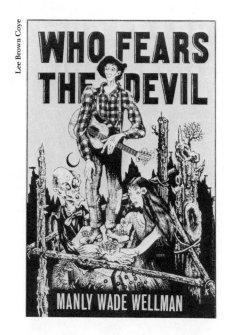

Lee Brown Coye

The critical success of *Who Fears the Devil?* prompted Wellman to write book-length adventures of Silver John. An Indian medicine man joins John in *The Old Gods Waken* (1979) to attack two blood-sacrificing twentieth-century druids who are attempting to arouse prehistoric spirits asleep on top of a nearby mountain. In *After Dark* (1980) "Shonokins" in the North Carolina mountains, survivors of the humanoid race that dominated the continent before their

defeat by the Indians who crossed over Bering Strait, want John to be their leader in a plot of destruction, but instead the incorruptible John turns against them. The government hires John in *The Lost and the Lurking* (1981) to look into the suspicious doings of folks in an apparently quiet, desolated mountain village, where things are not at all what they appear to be. In *The Hanging Stones* (1982), a millionaire who is constructing a replica of Stonehenge on a mountaintop refuses to believe that the obstacles he encounters are caused by resident devil worshipers, but he is finally convinced when John and a seventh son of a seventh son use their magic against a tribe of paleolithic cavemen. Why does Cry Mountain cry? asks Wellman in *The Voice of the Mountain* (1984), and ballad-singing Silver John, with only his purity of heart and his courageous self-reliance to protect him, unriddles the weird things that make the mountain cry. In all of these stories and novels Wellman was careful to use authentic mountain dialect, and his place names (e.g., Lake Lure) are as often real as fictitious.

Silver John did not occupy all of Wellman's time. *The Dark Destroyers* (1959) reports the struggle of fast-disappearing human beings aligned against snaillike Cold People who have become potentates of Earth and whom no weapon can exterminate. Among other titles are *Island in the Sky* (1960), *The Solar Invasion* (1968), and *The Beyonders* (1977), in which loathsome vermin from the galactic void invade the North Carolina mountains. One critic opined that *Twice in Time* (1957), whose protagonist falls back into the fifteenth century and realizes he has become Leonardo da Vinci, is Wellman's top achievement in science fiction.

Dead and Gone: Classic Crimes of North Carolina (1954) records grisly true accounts of poisonings, hangings, murders, and other atrocious iniquities perpetrated by citizens of the state. Some terror-fraught supernatural goings-on among American Indians as well as Civil

War soldiers are reprinted in *Worse Things Waiting* (1973). *Lonely Vigils* (1981) is a second collection of Wellman's short fiction. His last two novels are *The School of Darkness* (1985), in which devil worshipers at Buford State University (undoubtedly Chapel Hill) interrupt the weekend sessions of a folklore survey symposium until their lair is discovered by a scholarly foe of the powers of darkness and their ages-long efficacy at the campus site destroyed, and *Cahena* (1986), for which Wellman leaves the Carolina scene for north Africa in the seventh century. Wellman died on April 5, 1986.

In time, Wellman's solitary position in North Carolina fantasy and science fiction was challenged by younger practitioners in friendly competition, always with admiration and deep respect for the Old Master.

Early on, Philip José Farmer explained in *Dare* (1965) how Roanoke Island's Lost Colony disappeared when its settlers were transported to another planet by its grotesque inhabitants, there to establish an Elizabethan community in conjunction with other sixteenth-century human captives.

Four years later, Ben Haas, then living in Raleigh, wrote three fantasies under two pen names—the first and third as Richard Meade, the second as Quinn Reade. In *The Sword of the Morning Star* (1969) a wizard makes use of a "morning star" (medieval mace) to replace the dismembered arm of the hero, who thereupon slays the enemies of those who are innocent and unprotected. Haas's other "sword and sorcery" fantasies of medieval times are *Quest of the Dark Lady* (1969) and *Exile's Quest* (1970).

Karl Edward Wagner, with the degree of Doctor of Medicine and a residency in psychiatry to his credit, lived near Wellman in Chapel Hill and in 1975 began full-time free-lancing in sci-fi. By then he had already created his superhero, Kane, a swashbuckling "Mystic Swordsman." In a dark empire centuries ago, described in *Darkness Weaves with Many Shades* (1970), Kane offers his powerful military services to an evil, revengeful sorceress who keeps monsters at her command in the deep. *Bloodstone* (1975) has Kane

disinterring from a swamp a token of the time when scourges from a remote constellation ruled Earth—a diabolic prize, a bloodstone that will allow Kane dominion over the world. Kane's wicked exploits continue in several more books, including *In a Lonely Place* (1982), a collection of Kane stories. Wagner, called "the master of contemporary horror," collaborated with his friend David Drake, also of Chapel Hill, on *Killer* (1985), a saga of ferocious contests in the Roman Coliseum. For these savage sports, a hunter of beasts—tigers, lions, elephants—captures a hellish, intelligent animal loosed from an extraterrestrial body so far away that its light has not yet reached Earth. In Drake's military science-fiction novel *Hammer's Slammers* (1979), a relentless mercenary has a band of soldiers available to fight on any planet at any time. Similar novels led to *Cross the Stars* (1984), in which one of Colonel Hammer's veterans is determined to make his way back home to the planet Tethys. A sequel to these novels is *At Any Place* (1985). The setting of Drake's *Bridgehead* (1986) is an engineering building at a North Carolina university (Duke). A professor's team has built a machine by which humanoids arrive on Science Drive from the planet Skius, its civilization resembling Earth's in A.D. 12000. Unknown to those at the university, the Skiuli are planning to use Earth as a "bridgehead" from which to attack their belligerent, spiderlike archenemies on the mesozoic planet Vrage.

Among the group of sci-fi writers in the Asheville area, the most experienced is Ian Wallace, pen name for John Wallace Pritchard. *Croyd* (1967) and *Dr. Orpheus* (1968) are novels in which complex applications of philosophy and psychology underlie the actions of a madman resolved to drug the human race into slavery. More recent Wallace books are *The Lucifer Rocket* (1980) and *The Rape of the Sun* (1982). Also in the Asheville group is Ralph Roberts, whose speciality is complex situations analyzed by intricate and unusual employment of

computers. And there is mathematician Martin Gardner, whose dozens of titles include *The Incredible Dr. Matrix* (1977), which stars a fictional numerologist who exposes bogus rituals, and *The Magic Numbers of Dr. Matrix* (1985), which exposes a scoundrel's attempts to get rich by using "mathematics-based scams, frauds and extortion schemes." Gardner's *Science Fiction Puzzle Tales* (1981) is a book of delightful exercises for the cognoscenti.

Winston-Salem psychologist Felix C. Gotschalk said he wrote sci-fi simply because it pleased him—"an egocentric luxuriation," he insisted. For *Growing Up in Tier 3000* (1975) and *The Last Americans* (1980) he concentrated on "horribly precocious children" living in "an electronic future that is almost incomprehensible in current terms."

In the 1970s two Greensboro businessmen—M. A. Foster and Orson Scott Card, the first a native, the second a transplanted Mormon from Utah—took up the writing of science fiction. Foster's *The Warriors of Dawn* (1975) introduced the "Ler," supermortal humanoids related to earthlings. In its sequel, *The Gameplayers of Zan* (1977), considered his best work, the "Ler" are dispatched by an overpopulated Earth in the twenty-sixth century to a barricaded encampment, and from there, though constantly watched, they escape and clash with the earthlings. Thousands of years after the "Ler" of the *Gameplayers*, four young men in *The Day of the Klesh* (1979) take a spaceship to the planet Monsalvat "to wander and explore, to see new things," just as do all curious young men in all ages. At Monsalvat, inhabited by many different species, including the "Klesh," descendants of the Warriors of Dawn, the young men confront secrets of time and space. With abundant footnotes to explain curious linguistic terms of the future and to explicate questions of physics and mathematics, Foster may be labeled "the erudite man's Jules Verne."

Among Orson Scott Card's half dozen or so books are his initial *A Planet Called*

Illustration from *The Day of the Klesh*

Treason (1979); his fantasy *Songmaster* (1980), in which a nine-year-old boy betrays his unprecedented genius to exact an absolute authority over everybody and everything far and wide; and *Ender's Game* (1984), a forecast of the time when, to prevent aliens from extinguishing Earth's creatures, military geniuses are bred to fight off the invaders.

On the coast, Hugh Zachary, best known for *The Beachcomber's Handbook of Seafood Cookery* (1970), began writing a series of science-fiction novels under the pseudonym Zack Hughes. *The Book of Rack the Healer* (1973) set the course and tone for more than a dozen books, many dealing with a future when interstellar civilizations are governed by an organization called the United Planets. Zachary believes the best of them is *Killbird* (1980), whose Eban the Accursed, in a bleak age following nuclear destruction, comes upon a still-active atomic station with calamitous results. *Gold Star* (1983) presents a man and wife who operate a salvage tug in deep space. Zachary's earlier *A Feast of Fat Things* (1968), a non-sci-fi novel with its setting

in Southport, tells of middle-age love against a background of curious townspeople and strict but endearing local customs.

Though Wellman's Silver John fantasies were firmly anchored in the geography of western North Carolina, science-fiction writers at first were too busy with planets and asteroids, with millennia in the past and millennia in the future, to settle down at home. Thus, an added pleasure came to North Carolina readers with Zachary's *Gwen, in Green* (1974), described as a "plant novel," whose heroine lives on a foliage-lush island off the North Carolina coast. So identified has she become with the greenery that she begins to act eerily, seducing youths met by chance and killing bulldozer operators on nearby properties. Even a psychiatrist who analyzes the cause of her diabolic behavior cannot stay her metamorphosis.

The setting of Zachary's *Tide* (1974) is Southport and the Atlantic Ocean stretching fifty miles beyond the fishing village. At a marine laboratory, the government is conducting a radiation experiment that accidentally produces mutant plankton. Formerly benign fish, after consuming the plankton, are changed into belligerent predators upon other fish. On land, those who chance to eat the contagious marine life become aggressive and homicidal. The president of the United States considers detonating a nuclear explosion in order to purge the world's oceans of the "dinoflagellate" curse. In this novel the Clarendon (Brunswick) County local color is genially painted on Hughes's tension-charged canvas.

Another North Carolina setting is used by Durham's Allen Wold in *The Crivit Experiment* (1985), which, though loosely written and its narrative background insufficiently glossed, has the attraction of running its course in the Research Triangle Park. Once again invaders from a faraway orb, in this instance in the form of lizardlike "Visitors" outfitted to resemble human men and women, are intent upon the destruction of Earth's inhabitants. The "Visitors" have an office in the Park, another directly on the campus at Chapel Hill, and a prison compound only a "sky fighter" away at Fort Bragg. Their pernicious undertaking is the breeding of fiendish "crivits," a bloodthirsty, sand-burrowing abomination with lengthy tentacles capable of pulling animals, and men and women, deep into the smothering sand. Also being bred is the noxious "verlag," an insatiable vegetable-consuming putrescence spawned to feed the "crivits." When the "crivits" and "verlags" finally, as planned by the "Visitors," extinguish Earth's inhabitants, the triumphant lizard-invaders will possess the globe.

John J. Kessel of the Department of English at North Carolina State University won the 1982 Nebula Award of the Science Fiction Writers of America for his novella *Another Orphan*, a literature-inspired story of a Chicago businessman with a love for Herman Melville. One morning the businessman awakes aboard the *Pequod*, possessing, having read *Moby Dick*, a foreknowledge of the eventual sinking of the ship by the great white whale. Kessel collaborated on the writing of *Freedom Beach* (1985), which projects a case of "dream therapy." The protagonist finds himself at a tropical resort where marble statues hand out advice and trash cans amble about to serve food to the guests, where visions come intermittently to puncture his

John J. Kessel

amnesia with sparks from his past, and where all-powerful "dreamers" control him. The novel is a highly sophisticated work that some readers may wish had been provided with footnotes to identify the many classical and literary allusions.

Most writers of murder mysteries and science fiction are rapid craftsmen, sometimes turning out several books a year. They have brisk, incisive, inventive minds, often leaping far beyond the seemingly slow pace of the keys on their typewriters. In the 1980s their successful, moving-ahead productivity is one of the features of North Carolina fiction.

XVI

SHORT-STORY WRITERS

Writers of short stories were early on the literary scene. In 1799, for instance, a certain "J. S." of Raleigh published in the local weekly a tale called "The Modern Lover." Newspapers of the antebellum years were receptive to filling their columns with prose narratives by village storytellers. Occasionally one of the better writers might place his offerings in a northern periodical. In 1849 *Sartain's Union Magazine of Literature and Art* in Philadelphia printed "The Haunted Chamber; or, How They Chose a May Queen in the School of Parson Cole" and "The Poor Student's Dream; or, The Golden Rule," two stories by Calvin Henderson Wiley. Five of the seven selections in Christian Reid's *Nina's Atonement and Other Stories* (1873) have southern settings. For the local-colorists of the late nineteenth century, North Carolina provided attractive characters for use in short fiction: fisher folk of the coastal region, eccentric blacks from mid-state, and the "quaint" mountain people. Most of these stories have long since been forgotten.

Still remembered, and previously noted, are seven black folk tales in Charles Waddell Chesnutt's *The Conjure Woman* (1899) and nine selections in *The Wife of His Youth and Other Stories of the Color Line* (1901), five of them set in and around Chesnutt's Fayetteville. Of far less literary importance are three other books of short stories issued in the first decade of the century: *The Eyrie and Other Southern Stories* (1905), by Bettie Freshwater Pool of Elizabeth City, an amateur effort to preserve the legends of the Albemarle Sound and Outer Banks areas; *The Triumphs of Ephraim* (1907), by James Ephraim McGirt, black poet of Greensboro, who portrays the black man

James E. McGirt

in his struggle for improvement; and *Tar Heel Tales* (1910), by Charlotte's H. E. C. Bryant, who, under the pen name "Red Buck," produced dialect sketches of "good old days."

It was during this period of the early twentieth century that North Carolina, almost as if to offset the work of its minor writers, gave to the United States the most popular short-story writer in the literary history of the nation. William Sydney Porter was born September 11, 1862, on Polecat Creek in Guilford County. He grew up in nearby Greensboro, attending his aunt's private school and working

Birthplace of O. Henry

in an uncle's drugstore. At the age of nineteen he went to Texas, first began to call himself O. Henry, and spent some time in an Ohio prison as a result of circumstantial evidence against him in connection with a bank shortage. Between 1901 and 1910, most of which time he was living in New York, his productivity was tremendous. For two years in 1904 and 1905 he wrote a story a week for the *New York Sunday World*, and the name O. Henry became a household word. In 1907 he was married a second time, to his childhood sweetheart Sara Lindsay Coleman of Weaverville, where he lived for a while before his death on June 5, 1910. Thomas Wolfe was later buried not far from O. Henry's grave in Asheville's Riverside Cemetery.

In the hundreds of short stories, collected in more than a dozen books, O. Henry's talent for inventing plots is amply illustrated, though the stories are sometimes criticized for their sentimentality and surprise endings, both of which later became unfashionable. Yet no one can doubt his affection for human beings, as evinced in such famous titles as "The Gift of the Magi," "The Ransom of Red Chief," and "A Municipal Report." Among the stories in which O. Henry employed his North Carolina background are "Let Me Feel Your Pulse," "A Blackjack Bargainer," and "The Fool-Killer."

Greensboro was the birthplace in 1886 of another famous short-story writer, Wilbur Daniel Steele. During his youth

Steele's family lived in Berlin and Denver. As a young man, Steele turned from a career in art to one in literature and was five times cited for excellence by the O. Henry Memorial Award committee. Five books of short stories appeared between 1918 and 1929, followed by *The Best Short Stories of Wilbur Daniel Steele* (1946) and *Full Cargo* (1951). For two years in the early 1930s he again lived in North Carolina, renting a house in Chapel Hill. From this period came a number of stories with a North Carolina theme and background: "Light," the much admired "How Beautiful with Shoes," "A Way with Women," and "Man and Boy" (which was previously titled "The Man without a God" and "Town Drunk"). Steele's more than 250 stories have varied settings in the United States, Europe, North Africa, and the West Indies—wherever

Wilbur Daniel Steele

Steele lived and traveled—but all are distinguished by a deliberate technique and a scrupulous exposition of character, with action more in the mind than in events. His curiosity about the psychopathological aspects of human beings is basic to "How Beautiful with Shoes," a North Carolina mountain story that attempts to define the distinction between sanity and insanity.

James Boyd, Thomas Wolfe, Paul
Green, and Olive Tilford Dargan wrote
enough stories to fill one or more volumes
apiece, but they were unlike O. Henry
and Steele in that they made their literary
reputations in other fields. Two years
after James Boyd moved to Southern
Pines, his first short story appeared in the
Century magazine for March, 1921. "Old
Pines" tells of a spur-line railroad and its
engineer in the pine forests of the Sandhills. Other stories similar to it appeared
during the next two decades, filling in the
time between the writing of Boyd's
better-known historical novels. As Boyd
grew older, he often used the short story
to experiment with narrative technique,
as in "Bloodhound" and "Civic Crisis."
Old Pines and Other Stories (1952) is a
posthumous collection.

In order to capitalize on the tremendous popularity of his second novel, *Of
Time and the River*, Asheville's Thomas
Wolfe hurriedly supervised the publication, eight months later, of *From Death
to Morning* (1935). Some of the fourteen
titles in it are mere essays, but then Wolfe
was uncommonly insensitive to traditional literary definitions. In addition to
"Circus at Dawn" and "The Men of Old
Catawba," *From Death to Morning* contains "The Web of Earth," an extensive
monologue by Eliza Gant about superstition and mountain violence. Many critics
consider "The Web of Earth" to be one
of Wolfe's most successful pieces of writing. After his death, other short narratives by Wolfe were collected in *The
Hills Beyond* (1941), and among them
were "The Lost Boy" and "Chickamauga,"
two memorable but quite unorthodox
stories. Most of the material in both
books fits somewhere into the Gant-Web-
ber chronicle of his four great novels.

Olive Tilford Dargan was one of those
versatile writers who composed easily in
several genres. Though she is better
known for her poems and novels, she
published several volumes of short stories about the Great Smoky Mountain
people among whom she lived. To the
eight stories in *Highland Annals* (1935) a

Asheville Citizen-Times

Olive Tilford Dargan

ninth was added in a revision of the earlier book, which then was titled *From
My Highest Hill* (1941). Such stories as
"Sam" and "Evvie: Somewhat Married"
reveal Dargan's understanding of her
mountain neighbors and her love for
them. *Innocent Bigamy and Other Stories* (1962) contains more mountain
sketches in which Dargan, as usual, sides
with the underdog.

Paul Green, the dramatist, published
five volumes of short stories: *Wide Fields*
(1928), *Salvation on a String and Other
Tales of the South* (1946), *Dog on the Sun*
(1949), *Home to My Valley* (1970), and
Land of Nod and Other Stories (1976).
For the most part, the subject matter of
the stories is similar to that in his one-act
and full-length plays. Green writes about
the farm tenants and the landowners of
the Cape Fear valley country; the young
people and the old; the good people and
the bad; the blacks, both hapless and
resourceful; and the unfortunate half-
breeds. He writes about love and happiness, about drabness and tragedy. In his
hands, the people of the valley become
the people of the world.

In a collection titled *McSorley's Won-
derful Saloon* (1943) Joseph Mitchell of
Fairmont included several humorous
stories based on events from a boyhood
in the North Carolina low country. The
outlandish shenanigans of Mitchell's

eccentric characters brighten the pages of "The Downfall of Fascism in Black Ankle County," "Uncle Dockery and the Independent Bull," and "I Blame It All on Mother."

Unlike the three preceding writers, with their emphasis on the lives of rural folk, Frances Gray Patton wrote of urban dwellers in the towns and small cities of North Carolina. Raleigh and Durham appear in thin disguises. Her characters, educated and socially presentable and often even sophisticated, move in a world of events that, if not earthshaking, disclose the minutiae of weaknesses and strengths in their lives. The stories in *The Finer Things of Life* (1951) and *A Piece of Luck* (1955) were re-collected in *Twenty-Eight Stories* (1969). Patton's style is precise and disingenuous, her point of view ironic. Despite a successful and only novel, *Good Morning, Miss Dove* (1954), expanded from her short story "The Terrible Miss Dove," Patton's literary acclaim has come almost entirely from her short stories.

The usual practice for the fiction writer is to publish short stories in periodicals and books before moving on to the larger form. The first book from University of North Carolina professor Max Steele, however, was his novel *Debby* (1950), whose central character is a feeble-minded woman taken into the affluent southern household of a mother and five children. In spite of occasional dark moments when the woman recalls a shameful past, her customary disposition is one of childlike innocence—a humor that makes her a delightful companion to the five youngsters. In *Where She Brushed Her Hair and Other Stories* (1968), the thirteen selections written over a period of twenty years "range from rich humor to supernatural fantasy to poignant sentiment—often, indeed, a remarkable blend of all three," remarked a critic. Among them are many that take place in North Carolina, but in truth the settings are quite varied. In "The Cat and the Coffee Drinkers" a patrician kindergarten teacher trains her wards to take

their dram black without such vulgar ingredients as cream and sugar; and all goes well until the preceptress's cat, "Mr. Thomas," returns home from a feline battle so mortally wounded that the lesson that particular day is how to kill a cat without hurting it. Steele is especially skilled in depicting childhood experiences. Fantasy prevails in "Hear the Wind Blow" when a fifteen-year-old wife of a forty-year-old farmer gives birth not to a baby but to a light blue egg. In the title story, Steele evokes a dream to reveal the essense of a southern lady (the narrator's mother) who is most herself when brushing her hair "not a hundred times, but a thousand" and while so doing "persuades her soul back into her body, recoups her strength, apportions her energy to the one most in need of it at the moment."

Leon Rooke, a native of Roanoke Rapids, has written three novels and six collections of short stories. Many of these narratives are macabre as well as lyrical, surrealistic as well as superrealistic. In his novel *Fat Woman* (1981) a corpulent wife in a rundown southern town wonders why her husband is nailing up the bedroom windows; in *The Magician in*

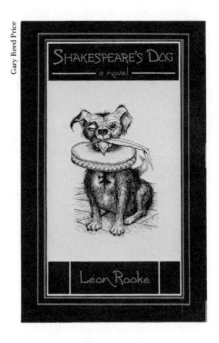

Gary Reed Price

Love (1981) none of the protagonist's tricks keeps his wife from running off with a less enigmatic youth; and in *Shakespeare's Dog* (1983) a talking canine belonging to the twenty-one-year-old henpecked husband of Anne Hathaway absorbs his master's gift of words and may perhaps be the author of *Macbeth* and *Othello*. Rooke's short stories, beginning with *Last One Home Sleeps in the Yellow Bed* (1968) and carrying through *The Love Parlour* (1977), *The Broad Back of the Angel* (1977), *Cry Evil* (1980), *Death Suite* (1981), and *Sing Me No Love Songs, I'll Say You No Prayers* (1984), are as comically neurotic and grotesque, as expertly detailed, as his novels. Rooke's imagination is unrestricted. But it is his verbal dexterity that is his most distinguishing characteristic. Though Rooke moved to Canada many years ago, the liquid purl of his phrases and sentences remains distinctly southern.

The Great Saturday Night Swindle (1984), by Stephen E. Smith of Sandhills Community College in Southern Pines, is a first collection of six stories that emphasize the often eccentric natures of believable characters: a prosaic instructor without inner convictions, a handsome though crippled shoe salesman, a widower who moves from his comfortable house to a mobile home. Smith is concerned with everyday personalities who are not what they seem to be on the surface.

Ruth Moose, of Albemarle, formerly more at home in poetry than in short stories, has included in *The Wreath Ribbon Quilt and Other Stories* (1986) a selection of her best work. "The Eyes of Argus," the unusual "A Biography in Seven Lives," and similar brief narratives focus on the misunderstandings and entanglements within the family and with neighbors. Like many of her contemporaries, Moose sets her stories in the North Carolina countryside so familiar to her.

XVII

CONTEMPORARY POETS

Mary C. Williams, poetry anthologist and professor of English at North Carolina State University, said in a 1980 *North Carolina Historical Review* article that North Carolina poetry now has at least four "voices," rather than just the one traditional voice or viewpoint usually attributed to southern poetry. Some of the people who have tried to define southern poetry have said that it often has a "sense of place" and relies very much on memories of rural life. This is the traditional poetry, the voice that recalls the locations, values, objects, and emotions of the past. Three other voices are those of the universal poet, the woman poet, and the black poet. Obviously, these sometimes overlap.

What is poetry? Often, even poets themselves disagree on its definition. The poet whose work is tightly bound to any one of the "voices" named above may discount the value of the others. Perhaps one may define poetry by saying what it is not. Poetry does not have to rhyme. It does not have to be pretty. It does not have to teach a lesson, although wisdom or special insight is certainly imparted in various ways through some poems.

What is left is experience. A poem is a concisely built attempt to communicate the author's experience or vision to the reader. The poet shares experience by creating mental pictures that will conjure up a sympathetic response in the reader. With or without rhyme, poetry differs from prose in that it is more condensed. Images, similes, metaphors, ironic devices, symbols, and so on, which may all occur at various places in any good novel, are crowded into the "loaded words" of a poem. Its concentrated nature is part of what makes it different from prose. North Carolina poets speak from the experience of living in this very particular place.

Among the hundreds of North Carolina poets active since 1930, there are only a few who could be called artists. Many have been good craftsmen, but unfortunately most have been ineffectual amateurs whose poems have suffered from being derivative or imitative despite their sincere love for a form often ignored and financially unprofitable. As advances in technology have made printing less difficult, however, the number of poetry volumes published by North Carolinians has steadily increased, as has the quality of the writing. Mentioned here are not only the artists and a number of the good craftsmen but also several of the more interesting and enthusiastic amateurs.

In recent years Tar Heel writers have received honors such as the Bollingen Prize in Poetry, large National Endowment for the Arts fellowships, and even National Book Awards. Earlier in the century the situation was quite different. Between 1917, when Olive Tilford Dargan of Swain County was awarded the Patterson Cup for her sonnet sequence

The Cycle's Rim, and 1953, when Frank Borden Hanes of Winston-Salem won the Roanoke-Chowan Award for his poetic narrative *Abel Anders* (1951), no awards were given to any North Carolina book of poetry. For the most part the volumes produced were slim and inconsequential. Exceptions included the following lyrical works: *Released* (1930), by Anne Blackwell Payne of Charlotte; *Spring Fever* (1935), by Lucy Cherry Crisp of Falkland; and various works by Dom Placid Kleppel at Belmont Abbey. Annarah L. Stewart, a one-time resident of Wilmington and teacher at St. Mary's College in Raleigh, wrote poems that were printed in *Atlantic Monthly*, *Cycle*, and *Commonweal* during the early 1930s.

One evening in 1932, during the worst months of the Great Depression, a small group of poets gathered in Charlotte and established the North Carolina Poetry Society. This still-flourishing organization, like the later Poetry Council of North Carolina in Asheville, has been generally traditional in its approach, but nevertheless it has managed to nourish a variety of writers who otherwise might have foundered in solitude. Stewart Atkins of Gastonia sounded a fresh voice with free-verse poems on industrial topics, such as "Love in a Cotton Mill," included in his *The Halting Gods* (1952). Among the few men active in the society was Charlotte's Andrew Hewitt. His *Traveler to April* (1949) and *Pickapot* (1956), with stanzas more delicate and restrained than Atkins's, projected a child-like world part magic and part luminous innocence. Another member was Dr. William Thornton Whitsett of Whitsett, author of *Saber and Song* (1917). Zoe Kincaid Brockman of Gastonia, prominent member of the society during its first score of years, became a popular poet when her *Heart on My Sleeve* (1951) went through five printings. Over the years, some of the more active producers in the society included Charlotte Young of Asheville, whose sixth volume of verse was published after her one hundredth birthday; Paul Bartlett of Guil-

ford College; Merle Price of Forest City; Sallie Nixon of Stanley; Dorothy Edwards Summerrow of Gastonia; Howard Gordon Hanson of Ruffin and Buies Creek; Mary Louise Medley of Wadesboro; Sidney Ann Wilson of Raleigh; H. Glen Lanier of High Point; John Moses Pipkin of Greensboro; and Emily Sargent Councilman of Burlington. *A Time for Poetry* (1966) anthologized thirty-seven of the society's members.

Meanwhile, Carl Sandburg and Randall Jarrell, two poets with reputations already firmly established, came to live in North Carolina. In 1945 Sandburg, sixty-seven years old, bought Connemara Farm near Flat Rock, where he lived until his death in 1967. Though his best creative years had passed, he continued to write poems occasionally and to work on his book of memoirs, *Always the Young Strangers* (1953). The mountains

Travel and Tourism Development Division, N.C. Dept. of Commerce

Connemara Farm

among which he lived may have inspired him, but they did not become subject matter for his verse. Accounts of his residence in North Carolina can be found in Harry Golden's lively *Carl Sandburg* (1961) and numerous newspaper and magazine interviews and feature articles.

Randall Jarrell, having already published two books of poems that received national acclaim, was only thirty-three in 1947 when he came to the University of North Carolina at Greensboro (then the Woman's College) to teach English. Critics praised his descriptions of the horrors and distractions of World War II. Settling into his adopted home, he began a very productive period in which he wrote a novel, three children's books—including *The Bat-Poet* (1964)—and several volumes of poetry. Jarrell's literary essays appeared in leading national journals, and many of them were gathered in 1953 into a seminal book called *Poetry and the Age.* Jarrell was also an avid translator of the works of foreign poets. His poetry volume *The Woman at the Washington Zoo* (1960) won the National Book Award, and from 1956 to 1958 he was consultant in poetry at the Library of Congress.

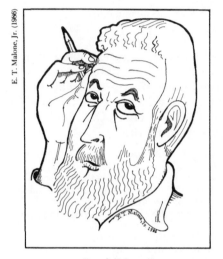

Randall Jarrell

Twenty-one years after his death in 1965, when at age fifty-one he was struck by a car, Jarrell's literary stature is still debated. The number of critical studies of his poetry continues to increase, but some experts think he was a better essayist than poet. In his poems on war, childhood, and modern America, this immensely talented man of letters was sympathetic though often ironic. He fell, some believe, just short of first rate because he was still, at his death, a poet of surfaces and hence only a "major minor poet." Others classify Jarrell as a figure of undisputed national importance. *The Complete Poems* was published in 1969.

In contrast to Jarrell's universality, native-born poet Thad Stem, Jr., of Oxford was the supreme regionalist who was described affectionately by Guy Owen as the last of America's small-town poets. Stem's richly wrought evocations of the countryside, quiet streets, and flesh-and-blood population of his Granville County home would easily have made him poet laureate of North Carolina had the post been vacant during his lifetime. His volumes of essays, such as *Entries from Oxford* (1971), and his colorful feature editorials for the Raleigh *News and Observer* reinforced this regional emphasis, which had begun in 1949 with his *Picture Poems.* Stem regretted the dull sameness and bad taste that television, shopping centers, and urbanization brought to American life and language.

The poem "Next Year, With Luck," from *Journey Proud* (1970), captures the spirit of the impoverished small farmer's lifelong battle with the land:

His eyes are yellow glass marbles, burned
    hollow,
And his bones a squeaking shambles of rusty
    wagon.
His broken fingers are the twisted harvest
That never seemed to measure out, and his face
The grass burning up and beyond all aid of rain.

The land is a leech charting each day's bloody
    stint,
Watering and feeding its bottomless gullies from
    his heart,
The land is a serpent always holding forth an
    apple
In such a way the sun conceals the rioting
    worms.

But still:
With a stub pencil he scrawls portentous figures.
Always the figures . . . Now, next year with good
    luck
He'll make a killing, sure as hell. And then
He'll square the merchants and the banks, and
    buy Martha
That bunch of curtains whose spangled promises
Have fought the chills of long winters past.

Stem was typically more lyrical, as when he wrote of Oxford on a summer night "gone to velvet dreams / Like a child spent from play," where "There's hardly a whir among the linden trees / Where the moon goes walking on tiptoe." The content and consistency of his

Thad Stem, Jr.

Sam Ragan

art is revealed in the titles of some of his other volumes of poems: *The Jackknife Horse* (1954), *Penny Whistles and Wild Plums* (1962), and *Spur Line* (1966). He died in 1980.

A leading force in North Carolina poetry for several decades has been Sam Ragan, editor since 1969 of the *Pilot* in Southern Pines and formerly on the editorial staff of the Raleigh *News and Observer*. After printing his poems anonymously for many years in his Sunday literary column, he published three books—*The Tree in the Far Pasture* (1964), *To the Water's Edge* (1972), and *Journey into Morning* (1981), which was nominated for a Pulitzer Prize. Appointed by Governor Robert W. Scott, Ragan served in 1972-1973 as the first secretary of the state's new Department of Art, Culture and History, now the Department of Cultural Resources.

In 1982 Governor James B. Hunt, Jr., appointed Ragan to the post of poet laureate to succeed the recently deceased centenarian James Larkin Pearson. As a teacher of creative writing, adviser to poets, and organizer of literary events, Ragan transformed what had been a largely moribund ceremonial office into a lively, creative, and useful position. His own poems are composed in a lean, re-

strained manner, often telling of human stoicism in the face of blind tragedy, or in observation of the ancient seasonal changes that sweep over the land. The poem "I Watched October" is from *Journey into Morning*:

> I watched October
> Flare today.
> The flames spread along the highway,
> Across the ridges, along the creek banks
> Where sycamores marched naked.
> October raced before me, red and yellow,
>   orange,
> And the purple of sweetgum.
> I traveled through the sun
> Into the night's silences,
> Marking the moment of no consequence,
> Stapling it down for keeps.
> I feel it burning, the last hurrah—
> Who tends the ovens of October?

In contrast, a poet who has more often taken an artful notice of life's comedies is Helen Bevington at Duke University, author of well-received books such as *Nineteen Million Elephants* (1950) and *A Change of Sky* (1956). Mae Woods Bell of Rocky Mount has written humorous verse on a more folksy plane. Other newspaper book-page editors who, like Ragan, have taken to writing poetry, are Goldsboro's Margaret Baddour, author of *A Murmuration of Purrs* (1982), and Harriet Doar (*The Restless Water*, 1983) and Dannye Carol Romine, both of Charlotte.

A whimsical move was made by two East Carolina University English instructors—Luke Whisnant and Alex Albright—when they suggested to the organizers of the Ayden Collard Festival that a Collard Poetry Contest be held in conjunction with the festival. Fred Chappell was chosen as guest celebrity poet. To everyone's surprise, more than two hundred entries were received. The entries were published as a book entitled *Leaves of Greens: The Collard Poems* (1984).

Whiteville native A. R. Ammons has been the most prolific and most successful twentieth-century North Carolina

A. R. Ammons

poet, although he has lived most of his adult life out of state in New Jersey as a businessman and since 1964 at Cornell University, where he is now Godwin Smith Professor of Poetry. Ammons, who has published seventeen volumes of poems, started out as principal of Hatteras Elementary School on the Outer Banks following his graduation from Wake Forest College. Some of his titles and awards include *Corson's Inlet* (1965); *Collected Poems: 1951-1971* (1972), winner of the 1973 National Book Award for Poetry; *Sphere: The Form of a Motion* (1974), winner of the 1973-1974 Bollin-

gen Prize in Poetry; *A Coast of Trees* (1981), winner of the National Book Critics Circle Award for Poetry, 1981; and *Worldly Hopes* (1982). Ammons resembles his junior fellow Tar Heel poet Robert Morgan at Cornell in that knowledge of science is evident in his poems. Although the influence of his upbringing in Columbus County shows from time to time in his poems, Ammons is clearly a poet of national rather than regional stature. Some critics consider him one of the most distinguished American poets writing today.

The following lines are from Ammons's poem "Immortality" in *Worldly Hopes*:

> The double lanceolate
> needlelike
> hemlock leaf
>
> will, falling, catch on
> a twitch of old
> worm-silk
>
> and, like a fall worm,
> dingledangle breezy
> all day in the noose.

Guilford College professor of classics Ann Deagon began writing late but made up for lost time by being a prolific producer and winning literally scores of awards. Among her books are *Carbon 14* (1974), *Poetics South* (1974), *There Is No*

Ann Deagon

Balm in Birmingham (1978), a volume of short stories entitled *Habitats* (1982), and a novel called *The Diver's Tomb* (1985). A founder and codirector since 1980 of Poetry Center Southeast, a nonprofit organization at Guilford that aids and promotes North Carolina writing—and one that prefigured the more ambitious North Carolina Writers' Network (1985)—Deagon won a 1981-1982 National Endowment for the Arts Literary Fellowship. Her poems have appeared in several recent anthologies of American poetry, and in 1978 Sam Ragan called her "one of the foremost poets of our time."

Charles Edward Eaton, born in Winston-Salem but a longtime resident of Chapel Hill, had published nine volumes of poetry by 1985. He attended the University of North Carolina at Chapel Hill,

Alex Darrow

Charles Edward Eaton

Princeton, and Harvard, where he studied with Robert Frost. For four years he was American vice-consul in Rio de Janeiro, a position that provided material not only for his poetry but also for some of his three collections of short stories, which include *Write Me from Rio* (1959) and *The Girl from Ipanema* (1972). *The Man in the Green Chair* (1977), *The Thing*

King (1983), and *The Work of the Wrench* (1985) are among his most recent collections of poetry. Eaton's lyrical gift has been called fresh, civilized, and beautifully articulate.

Clarkton native Guy Owen was a poet who almost gave up his own poetry to promote the work of others. Better known as a novelist, Owen taught at several colleges throughout the state, ending his career at North Carolina State University in Raleigh. He was the cofounder and longtime editor of *Southern Poetry Review*. A voracious reader of poetry, Owen and fellow faculty member Mary C. Williams edited several anthologies of state and regional verse. Tar Heel readers may be particularly interested in *North Carolina Poetry: The Seventies* (1975) and *Contemporary North Carolina Poetry* (1977). Owen always played down his own poetry, but his *The White Stallion* (1969) was an impressive selection of his best work. From that book comes the following poem, "Abandoned Plow":

> Whoever left this plow
> to warp in wind and rain
> (in a field of broom sedge now)
> unhitched in dark despair—
> and knowing he'd never return
> to finish the furrow again,
> left it: worn handles, beam and sweep,
> for only the quail to keep.

Guy Owen

Owen's work was widely praised, and partly because of his willingness to assist younger writers, he was one of the most popular figures in state literary circles when he died in 1981 at the age of fifty-six. His prose work is discussed in chapter 14.

By 1985 Canton native Fred Chappell had emerged as the most widely acclaimed and versatile writer living in the state. Already well known as a novelist and essayist, Chappell published his first book of poems, *The World Between the Eyes*, in 1971. His subject matter often is

Fred Chappell

the usual material for traditional southern poetry; but he is not limited by his mountain background, nor does he limit its universal potential: he is a virtuoso of poetic forms, from terza rima to Shakespearean monologue (*Castle Tzingal*, 1985). A boy's imaginative brooding while angry with a parent, his resentment toward a stern and sterile religiosity, or his dissatisfaction with the circumstances of his hometown have been embodied by Chappell in western North Carolina. But Chappell's evocations are also without time or place. His language is at once wise and graphic; he often thinks of new and striking ways to paint familiar pictures, as in these lines from "The Farm":

The hay, the men, are roaring on the hill, July
Muzzy and itchy in the field, broad sunlight
Holds in its throat the tractor's drone, dark bees
Like thumbs in the white cut bolls of clover.

Summer in the fields, unsparing fountain
Of heat and raw savor. Men redden and boil
With sweat, torsos flash, talk, and the laughing
Jet up cool, single cool sound in saffron air,
Air like a yellow cloak. The land is open,
At the mercy of the sky, the trembling sun and
    sky.
One cloud drives east. Cattle plunder the
    brackish pools,
Drop awkward shadows while black flies
    fumble on their skins;
Ruminate; and observe the hour with incurious
    eyes.

The mouths of the men are open, dark medals
    dangling.
They gulp fierce breath. If a breeze lift the field,
    skins cloy
With dust. Grin and gouge; neck muscles first
    tire;
Exhaustion laps the bodies, the mouths are
    desperately open.
The woman brings water, clear jar echoing
Rings of light fluttering on her apron.

Chappell's major poetic work is a tetralogy, published first as four separate books—*River* (1975), *Bloodfire* (1978), *Wind Mountain* (1979), and *Earthsleep* (1980)—and then combined into a single book called *Midquest* (1981). Each of the composite books contains eleven poems, all of which take place during one day, the narrator's thirty-fifth birthday, as he wrestles with the influences of farm, family, and mountain heritage on his present life as a city-dwelling intellectual. A teacher of creative writing and literature at the University of North Carolina at Greensboro since 1964, Chappell had published eight books of poems by 1985, when he was awarded the biennial Bollingen Prize in Poetry.

Robert Morgan, a native of Hendersonville, grew up on the family farm in nearby Zirconia and presently teaches creative writing at Cornell University. His first book, *Zirconia Poems* (1969), deals with the physical and mental landscapes of his home mountains. Tempered by his knowledge of nature and science, he refined the concept of landscape in his subsequent books. Morgan's reputation grew with *Red Owl* (1972), *Land Diving* (1976), *Trunk & Thicket* (1978), *Groundwork* (1979), and *Bronze Age* (1981). Morgan writes from the solid viewpoint of the person who grew up in

Robert Morgan

Jonathan Williams

and loves a natural setting, in contrast to the sometimes effete partisanship of the Johnny-come-lately environmentalist.

Asheville native Jonathan Williams has been touted as the champion of the avant-garde in North Carolina poetry. Combining his talents as graphic designer and poet, Williams serves as executive director of the Jargon Society, a publishing company in Highlands and Winston-Salem. A much-traveled alumnus of the literary colony that gathered in the late 1940s and early 1950s around Black Mountain College, Williams has described his mission as "To keep afloat the Ark of Culture in these dark and tacky times!" Although he is often critical of the American middle class, Williams delights in mountain speech and traditions, frequently quoting hill folk in his poems and essays. Even his book titles ring with audacity and experimentation. Examples are *Four Jargonelles from the Herbalist's Notebook* (1966), *An Ear in Bartram's Tree* (1969), *Untinears & Antennae* (1977), *Elite/Elate Poems* (1979), *Shankum Naggum* (1979), and *Get Hot or Get Out* (1982). His *Blues and Roots: Rue and Bluets* was enlarged and revised in 1985. The noted designer Buckminster Fuller once called Williams "our Johnny Appleseed: we need him more than we know."

Different in many ways from most mountain poets, Williams has a taste for the "odd, difficult, hermetic, and stubborn." *New York Times* critic John Russell in 1983 said "this master of anathema has also a sense of wonder and awe at human quality, at the surviving marvels of landscape on both sides of the Atlantic and at the metaphoric power of both words and music." Williams, one might say, is a busy gadfly who happened somehow to pitch on a slope in western North Carolina. His first volume of essays was *The Magpie's Bagpipe* (1983). A particular joy in reading Williams's work is one's discovery of the interplay of his sometimes outlandish titles with the very lean meat of the text itself. From his chapbook *A Blue Ridge Weather Prophet Makes Twelve Stitches in Time on the Twelfth Day of Christmas* (1977) comes the following short poem, "February," reprinted in *Blues and Roots: Rue and Bluets*:

> if the catbirds chatter
> winter's mite nigh over
>
> and spring is just around the corner but
> we aint seen the corner yet

Martin Duberman's 1972 book *Black Mountain: An Exploration in Community* describes the twenty-three-year existence, from 1933 to 1956, of the experimental community known as Black Mountain College. An aura of originality and flamboyance was associated with the name of the college, Duberman wrote. Both famous and ordinary people gathered there over the years to study and work in the fields of art, music, and literature. Robert Duncan, Charles Olson, and Robert Creeley and their associates became known as the Black Mountain poets, Creeley editing the school's literary magazine for a number of years.

Since 1950, although individual poets both thrive and languish in isolation throughout the state, a number of centers of activity have emerged, and not infrequently they are on or near college campuses. In 1985 an observer could identify clusters of poets in the mountains (concentrated at Boone), the Sandhills (including Laurinburg, Pembroke, and Southern Pines), Charlotte, Greensboro, Chapel Hill, Durham, and Raleigh.

Poetry in the mountain region tends to be somewhat more politicized—because of the area's rapid transition from isolation to mainstream—and is often a vehicle for protest. In addition to Chappell, Morgan, and Williams, many other poets are active although less well known in other parts of the state. Buncombe County native Jim Wayne Miller, a teacher at Western Kentucky University since 1963, writes with sadness of the loss of roots and identity in mountain communities but speaks of the hope for Appalachian rebirth in *The Mountains Have Come Closer* (1980). His character the "Brier," disenchanted with anonymous urbanized life, looks for nourish-

Jim Wayne Miller

ment from family and past to make the future more human. Following his retirement from teaching in New York, Francis Pledger Hulme returned to his home on Beaucatcher Mountain in Asheville and published *Mountain Measure* (1975). Veteran protest poet John Beecher, after a varied career, retired to Burnsville. His *Collected Poems, 1924-1974* was published while he was a North Carolina resident. R. T. Smith, reared and educated in North Carolina, has won a number of writing awards. The most recent of his five volumes of poetry is *From the High Dive* (1983). Smith's poems often employ graphic images, both of beauty and of decay, as in his description of a dead cow in the poem "Find": "She lay in a fence / ditch under ripe persimmons, / wild scuppernong / vines empty, the yellow leaves spinning. . . ." John Foster West of Boone has published three volumes of poems, including *Wry Wine* (1977).

Other promising western poets include part-Indian Hilda Downer of Bandana in Mitchell County, whose *Bandana Creek* was published in 1979; Ann Dunn of Asheville; Kathryn Stripling Byer of Webster; and Grace DiSanto of Morganton (*The Eye Is Single*, 1981). Long the least-populated area of the state, the mountain region in the midst of change and commercial development is beginning to inspire its poets to speak out in defense of the environment and traditional values. A controversial anthology of Appalachian writing, *Voices from the Hills* (1975), which includes the work of many North Carolina authors, was criticized for its "self-conscious regional defensiveness" by University of North Carolina scholar C. Hugh Holman. And Appalachian State University professor W. H. Ward has warned that the rush to create an Appalachian literature may actually inhibit good writing, if politics and promotionalism override art.

Chapel Hill has long been a place where writers gathered, both those native born and those attracted there by teaching or administrative positions at the university. Historically the community has prided itself in having provided an atmosphere of support for creativity. Whatever one might say about municipal pretensions, in recent years there has certainly been no lack of poets in Chapel Hill and adjacent Carrboro.

After Charles Edward Eaton, the best-known Chapel Hill poet at present is probably University of North Carolina English professor William Harmon, a native of Concord. Editor of *The Oxford Book of American Light Verse* (1979) and author of a volume on poet Ezra Pound, Harmon has himself written six books of poetry, most recently *The Intussusception of Miss Mary America* (1975) and *One Long Poem* (1982), plus numerous reviews and essays about poetry Two other English faculty members who are accomplished poets are James Seay, *Let Not Your Hart* (1970) and *Water Tables* (1974), and Christopher Brookhouse, *Scattered Light* (1969) and *If Lost, Return* (1973). Brookhouse, turning more to prose in recent years, has also written two novels, *Running Out* (1970) and *Wintermute* (1978). Other campus-centered poets in Chapel Hill have included Louis Lipsitz, *Cold Water* (1967) and *Reflections on Sampson* (1977), and Salisbury native Harold Grier McCurdy, a more traditional stylist in *The Chasten-*

ing of Narcissus (1970) and *And Then the Sky Turned Blue* (1982).

Narrative poet Richard Kenney, who came to Chapel Hill in the late 1970s, won the 1984 Yale Series of Younger Poets prize for *The Evolution of the Flightless Bird*. Paul Jones has directed the vigorous poetry program at the Art School in Carrboro for several years. Other Chapel Hill poets include Roger Sauls, *Light* (1974); E. T. Malone, Jr., *The Tapestry Maker* (1972) and *The View from Wrightsville Beach* (1986); publisher and poetry promoter Judy Hogan, *Cassandra Speaking* (1977) and *Sun-Blazoned* (1984); environmentalist Wallace Kaufman; and black poet Jaki Shelton Green of nearby Efland, whose powerful book *Dead on Arrival* (1983) confronts her world sensually and directly. Chapel Hill poetry appeared in UNC creative writing teacher Jessie Rehder's *Chapel Hill Carousel* (1967) and in *Womanthology* (1973), edited by six local writers.

Poetry in the Greensboro area in the 1970s and early 1980s was dominated by Fred Chappell, Ann Deagon, and Robert Watson, whose combined achievements perhaps somewhat intimidated their poetic neighbors. Strength in numbers was found by The Greensboro Group, organized in 1976, which published two anthologies of poetry and prose: *More Than Magnolias* (1978), contemporary writings by Guilford County women; and *Writers' Choice* (1981), selected works of fifty-eight North Carolinians. Perhaps the foremost poet of The Greensboro Group is Marie Gilbert, whose most recent works are *From Comfort* (1981) and *The Song and the Seed* (1983). *The Greensboro Reader* (1968), edited by Robert Watson and Gibbons Ruark, was an earlier collection of work by graduates and faculty at the University of North Carolina at Greensboro; the publication celebrates the wealth of creative writing that had originated there during the prior several decades. Preceding *The Greensboro Reader* was an *Alumnae*

Miscellany (1942), edited by Alonzo C. Hall and Nettie S. Tillett. Anthology editors Watson and Ruark are themselves talented writers, Ruark having most recently published *Reeds* (1978).

Watson, who began teaching at UNC-G in 1953, has written five volumes of poems, including more recently *Christmas in Las Vegas* (1971), *Selected Poems*

Robert Watson

(1974), and *Night Blooming Cactus* (1980), which deals with the elusiveness of earthly paradises and attempts to speak with a number of different voices in some of its longer poems. Watson, a playwright and author of two novels, *Three Sides of the Mirror* (1966) and *Lily Lang* (1977), benefited early from the severe criticism of Greensboro colleague Jarrell. His energetic work often deals with life's unavoidable shocks—death, failure, fear, and loss. An unassuming man, Watson once told an interviewer, "It seems today that we have a lot of famous writers, but we don't have a lot of famous books they've written."

Paul Baker Newman of Queens College is the poet of longest reputation in the Charlotte area. This Chicago native, continuing the Wordsworthian tradition of seeing the beauty in ordinary things,

has published six volumes of poetry, including *The House on the Saco* (1977) and more recently *The Light of the Red Horse* (1981). Robert Waters Grey, who teaches English at the University of North Carolina at Charlotte and edits the transplanted *Southern Poetry Review*, has also coedited two anthologies: *Eleven Charlotte Poets* (1971) and *White Trash* (1977).

Charlotte's Julie Suk published poems in a number of magazines before she wrote *The Medicine Woman* (1980). Jean Morgan, a teacher of literature and creative writing at UNC-C, is the author of *The High Priestess of Change* (1983), whose title sounds a similar note. Amon Liner, a highly original young man hampered by a congenital heart defect, died at the age of thirty-six in 1976. By then he had published only one book, *Marstower* (1972). Three volumes of his poetry have been published posthumously by the Carolina Wren Press in Chapel Hill: *Chrome Glass: Poems of Love and Burial* (1976); *Rose, A Color of Darkness* (1980); and *The Far Journey and Final End of Dr. Faustwitz, Spaceman* (1983). At times highly experimental in style, Liner's poetry often speaks bitterly of the hollowness of American culture. Thomas Heffernan, of Irish descent, is a native of Massachusetts who was for two years in charge of the North Carolina Poetry-in-the-Schools program. His book *The Liam Poems* (1981) re-creates from scraps of knowledge the life of an ancestor who was a blind Irish poet. Heffernan's chapbook entitled *City Renewing Itself* (1983) describes Charlotte and Raleigh, and his most recent book is *To the Wreakers of Havoc* (1985). T. J. Reddy, a black poet of Charlotte, has published *Less Than a Score, but a Point* (1974) and *Poems in One Part Harmony* (1980), commentaries on prison experiences and American society.

Literary activity in the Sandhills area increased sharply after Sam Ragan, Norman Macleod, and Ronald H. Bayes moved there in the late 1960s. Ragan

113

turned the *Pilot* of Southern Pines into a forum and a showcase for North Carolina writers. He was one of the leaders of the Friends of Weymouth group that worked with state government officials to raise $700,000 to purchase author James Boyd's plantation and 200 acres of adjoining forest; the resulting Weymouth Center for the Arts and Humanities was dedicated July 20, 1979, in Southern Pines. The following summer the North Carolina Poetry Festival was inaugurated as an annual affair at Weymouth. Since then, more than one hundred poets have appeared every year to read their works at the festival, held the last Saturday in June, and other writers have enjoyed residencies at Weymouth to develop their new work.

Macleod, an important but less-well-known national literary figure from the 1930s and 1940s, came out of retirement to teach at Pembroke State University. An Oregon native, he published his seventh and eighth volumes of poetry, *The Selected Poems of Norman Macleod* (1975) and *The Distance: New and Selected Poems* (1977), while serving on the Pembroke faculty.

Ronald H. Bayes, also born in Oregon, joined the English faculty at St. Andrews Presbyterian College in Laurinburg in 1968 as poet-in-residence and has made North Carolina his home. A lively, spirited individual, Bayes has attracted numerous literary figures—including several from Japan—to the St. Andrews campus. His own poetry, sometimes experimental and highly personal, often draws on his experiences in Asia and elsewhere; his eleven volumes include *Dust and Desire* (1960), *The Casketmaker* (1972), and *A Beast in View* (1985). His four books—*History of the Turtle* (1970), *Porpoise* (1972), *Tokyo Annex* (1977), and *Fram* (1979)—make up the *Umapine Tetralogy*, which is just beginning to receive serious critical notice.

Shelby Stephenson, first at Campbell University in Buies Creek and then at Pembroke State, has been an active critic and promoter of North Carolina poetry. A Johnston County native who grew up on a farm, he depicted rural experiences in his *Middle Creek Poems* (1979).

Grace Gibson of Laurinburg, a Virginia native who has taught both at St. Andrews and Pembroke, has produced two unusually popular books. *Home in Time* (1977) sold five hundred copies in one month and went into a second printing shortly after its original release. *Drake's Branch* (1982) relates valued experiences from the author's childhood in a small town to a present feeling of loss following the recent deaths of persons close to her.

At Sandhills Community College in Southern Pines, Stephen E. Smith has published the valuable anthology *New North Carolina Poetry: The Eighties* (1982). His own poetry includes *The Bushnell Hamp Poems* (1980). Another regional writer is Lew Barton, a Lumbee Indian poet of Pembroke.

The best-known Raleigh poets have been associated with local colleges or the North Carolina Poetry-in-the-Schools program. Ardis Kimzey, a Washington, North Carolina, native, directed that program, edited anthologies of children's poems, and wrote a book entitled *To Defend a Form: The Romance of Administration and Teaching in a Poetry-in-the-*

Ronald H. Bayes

Schools Program (1977). Her own poems were published in *The Illusion of Water* (1978). Campbell Reeves, born in Australia, came to Raleigh in 1946. She has been president of the North Carolina Poetry Society and active in many arts organizations. Her *Bane of Jewels* (1968) was followed by *Coming Out Even* (1973). At North Carolina State University, the black poet Gerald W. Barrax, an Alabama native, has taught creative writing and black studies since 1967. His books are *Another Kind of Rain* (1970) and *An Audience of One* (1980). Barrax speaks with substance, commenting pensively on the world about him.

Betty Adcock

Gerald W. Barrax

Betty Adcock, born in Texas and recently a Kenan writer-in-residence at Meredith College, published her first book, *Walking Out*, in 1975. In *Nettles* (1983), the compelling final poem "The Swan Story" remarks that knowledge at mid-life is "halfway to knowing how." Sally Buckner, teacher of creative writing and English at Peace College, has been an active poet, as has radiologist William H. Sprunt III, whose *A Sacrifice of Dogs* was published in 1976. Thomas N. Walters, a native of Tarboro who taught English at North Carolina State, published *Seeing in the Dark* (1972), a book about motion pictures, and *The Loblolly Excalibur and a Crown of Shagbark*

(1976) before his death at the age of forty-seven in 1983.

In Durham, William Blackburn edited three collections of poetry and prose by Duke University writers: *One and Twenty* (1945), *Under Twenty-five* (1963), and *A Duke Miscellany* (1970). Blackburn, renowned as a teacher of literature and creative writing, had as his students over the years Fred Chappell, Reynolds Price, William Styron, James Applewhite, Mac Hyman (author of the comic novel *No Time for Sergeants*), and many others. At North Carolina Central University, African-born poet Gershon Fiawoo has been a longtime teacher of creative writing.

Wilson County native James Applewhite, a teacher of creative writing at Duke, has published poems in a number of national magazines. His first book, *Statues of the Grass*, was published in 1975. A successful poet of place, he has since written *Following Gravity* (1980) and *Foreseeing the Journey* (1983), all of which draw in various ways on his youthful memories of the sandy tobacco farmland of eastern North Carolina and its undercurrents of depression and restrictive loneliness. These lines are from "My Grandmother's Life" in *Following Gravity*:

Down the lane out of view, past the packhouse
Furred with splinters, ranked with lilies,
Where grasshoppers roosted, chewing tobacco,
To be caught by their cellophane wings,

115

James Applewhite

I recede into time, toward a granite slab
Under the scion pecan of my uncle's planting.

Asheville native Michael McFee, author of *Plain Air* (1983) and also a perceptive critic as well as teacher of creative writing at various area universities, presently makes his home in Durham.

At various other places throughout the state there are poets who have confined their publication efforts primarily to magazines rather than books. Others are better known as novelists, essayists, journalists, or historians and are consequently discussed elsewhere in this book. In the early 1960s Will Inman of Wilmington, concerned for the release of the inner as well as the outer man, published several volumes of poems, including *I Am the Snakehandler* (1960). In Roxboro, Virginia L. Rudder has published *After the Ifaluk* (1976) and *The Gallows Lord* (1978), a poetic perspective on suicide. Georgia native and college teacher Emily Herring Wilson of Winston-Salem wrote *Down Zion's Alley* (1972) and *Balancing on Stones* (1975). Several of her poems deal incisively with the changes brought by aging. A new black poet is Charles Fort, teacher at the University of North Carolina at Wilmington and author of *The Town Clock Burning* (1985). *The Bamboo Harp* (1978), an illustrated collection of haiku, was Ruby P. Shackleford's sixth volume of poems.

The Wilson writer has taught creative writing and English at Atlantic Christian College. Another skillful writer of haiku is the black poet Lenard D. Moore of Raleigh, author of *The Open Eye* (1985). In Fayetteville, Methodist College English professor Walter Blackstock has published nine volumes of poetry, including *Leaves Before the Wind* (1967). The work of Kate Blackburn of Laurinburg, Agnes McDonald of Wilmington, Mary Snotherly of Raleigh, and Shirley Moody of Cary was showcased in *Four North Carolina Women Poets* (1982).

A number of poets who were not native North Carolinians came to the state and contributed to its literature for a time, most typically while teaching in Tar Heel colleges before moving elsewhere. This number includes such people as O. B. Hardison, Jr., Julia Fields, Charles David Wright, and Calvin Atwood. Others who have moved away include Charleen Whisnant Swansea, Adrianne Marcus, Heather Ross Miller, and Juanita Tobin.

In addition to earlier mentioned nationally known figures such as Sandburg and Jarrell, more recent immigrants were Carolyn Kizer, poet-in-residence for several years at Chapel Hill during the 1970s, and Maya Angelou, famous black author of *I Know Why the Caged Bird Sings* (1970), presently residing in Winston-Salem. Critic Donald Vincent Smith called Kizer, author of *Midnight Was My Cry* (1971), "without question the finest woman poet now writing in English." This book dealt strikingly with the anguish of a formerly married woman now single. Kizer was living on the West Coast when her volume *Yin* won a 1985 Pulitzer Prize.

Poetry in the middle 1980s was alive and well in North Carolina, with Poet Laureate Sam Ragan estimating that as many as eighty good poets were active in the state. The "Collards and Culture" challenge issued by Paul Green in 1950, when he called upon North Carolinians to embrace music, art, and literature while still retaining rural values, seemed to have been met.

XVIII

NOVELISTS ONGOING

In May, 1985, Doris Betts took a sabbatical from classroom and administrative duties at Chapel Hill, saying she would "write for a year, finish two novels, I hope, and a textbook, and get reacquainted with fifteen horses, twelve cats, and two dogs. And my husband. Put my husband first—the same one for thirty-three years." And off she went to her farm near Pittsboro. Note that she does not mention short stories. At one time, she defined herself as a short-story writer, not a novelist, but the day came when, she said, "the short story is no longer as aesthetically pleasing to me." It may be, like lyric poetry, "the form of youth, when you still believe in the revelation and the isolated moment . . . that people can change in twenty-four-hour periods."

The settings for most of Betts's early fiction are Statesville, county seat of Iredell County, where she was born, and North Carolina east and west. *The Gentle Insurrection and Other Stories* (1954), her first book, is peopled by lonely old men, a neurotic librarian, a self-assertive mill worker, and others who are troubled, all of them sensing the "difficulty of communication between human beings." *The Astronomer and Other Stories* (1966) again depicts typical characters in the North Carolina piedmont as they pursue their quietly vain search for love and a religious faith to serve as bastions against incomplete lives and certain death. In this collection the eponymous hero in the 112-page novella is one of Betts's most vivid creations. She admits that "The Spies in the Herb House" and "All That Glisters [*sic*] Isn't Gold" are outright autobiography. *Beasts of the Southern*

Wild and Other Stories (1973) moves into one of the mainstreams of southern fiction with components of gothicism, fantasy, and surrealism used to limn the alienated and life-hungry, the malformed and psychotic. On occasions, a redemptive love clears the dark heavens; on others, the choice is between murder and suicide. Stories like "Hitchhiker," in which a typist impulsively drives her car into a river to escape the stagnant small town in which she lives, are among Betts's most impressive productions.

Jim Stratakos, *News and Observer*

Doris Betts

Tall Houses in Winter (1957), her first novel, is a variation on the Paolo-Francesca theme. A college professor returns to his hometown of Stoneville (Statesville) before undergoing a cancer operation, and there he ponders his past and tries to ascertain whether or not he is the father

117

of the ten-year-old son of his brother's wife. Central to *The Scarlet Thread* (1965), a turn-of-the-century episodic family chronicle, is the new cotton mill being built on the Katsewa (Catawba) River in Stone (Iredell) County and the local inhabitants whose lives will be changed because of it. *The River to Pickle Beach* (1972) is set in the summer of 1968 at a rundown resort on the North Carolina coast. To the resort has come a devoted childless couple seeking peace away from a turbulent world. Their plan is disrupted by a young hippie, a retarded mother and son, and an old army acquaintance of the husband. Lusting for the wife, the unbalanced, racially prejudiced, despicable "friend" secretes a cache of arms and ammunition, and in the gruesome climax shoots the two mongoloids on the beach. This novel is a commentary on the violence before and after the assassination of Senator Robert F. Kennedy. In *Heading West* (1981), Betts's first best seller, a spinster, hopelessly trapped in family duties, is kidnapped by a psychopath in the North Carolina mountains. Driving west, they finally arrive at the Grand Canyon, and there the woman allows her captor to fall to his death. Her descent by foot into the canyon and her will to survive is symbolic of her acceptance of responsibility for her own life, not that of others, and her consent to marry the man who loves her. In these four novels, the protagonists feel the need to return to their parental homes in order to reassess themselves before the necessary, salutary process of moving ever forward.

In the 1950s Paul C. Metcalf, great-grandson of Herman Melville, lived near Skyland in a mountain cabin. From his years in North Carolina came *Will West* (1956), in which a Cherokee Indian murders his white mistress, symbolically exacting expiation on behalf of his race for the wrong done it by the white conquerors. During the Cherokee's flight, he follows the westward trail of his ancestors and on the way discovers that he is at ease with a white truck driver. Amity among races, Metcalf would seem to point out, will come only after the cleansing of history's injustices. The author's *Genoa* (1965) is a convoluted work, using difficult avant-garde techniques. In this modern story, a man's immobility juxtaposes the Columbus legend and Melvillian biography and fiction. Metcalf is a poet, too, and "has written historical accounts that read like poetry," according to a critic.

Asheville-born Wilma Dykeman is the author of three novels: *The Tall Woman* (1962) tells of a determined mother's exertions to improve conditions among her primitive people in the mountains; its sequel *The Far Family* (1966) picks up several generations later and shows how long-lasting were her endeavors. *Return the Innocent Earth* (1973) is somewhat based on fact in that Dykeman's husband James R. Stokely, Jr., belonged to the farming family that established the mammoth Stokely canning complex. The book fictionally depicts the internecine contention between those of the family who wish to remain faithful to the soil that brought them good fortune and those who are contemptuous of everything except the money generated by the computer-operated cannery.

Wilma Dykeman Stokely

John Foster West, born near Champion in southwest Wilkes County, wrote *Time Was* (1965), about the hardships and homespun joys of a tenant family in the North Carolina hills. A sequel, *Appalachian Dawn* (1973), obviously a semiautobiographical portrait, resumes this narrative with the birth of a son nine months after the ending of the first novel. West knows the Wilkes County scene like his reflection in a millpond and thus is able to convey to his readers a true-to-life mural of mountain people in the third decade of the century. Besides two slender books of poems, West wrote *The Ballad of Tom Dula* (1970), a biography of North Carolina's beloved folk hero—seducer, murderer, ballad singer, banjo picker—who was hanged in 1868.

Lewis W. Green from Haywood County emulated Thomas Wolfe's style in *And Scatter the Proud* (1969), six earthy novellas showing how "Big Lonesome Mountain" on a snowy night affected variously those who resided on or near it. *The High-Pitched Laugh of a Painted Lady* (1980) is a collection of eight "tough-school" short stories dealing with bobcats and bear dogs, Cherokee Indians and mountain rednecks, plus bums and gypsters in the sordid section of Asheville. In *The Silence of Snakes* (1984), a mountain man, consumed totally with a passion to take revenge on government authorities he believes have wronged him, goes on a killing escapade that results in the death of eight lawmen.

From William Blackburn's writing classes at Duke University, many skillful students were graduated, among them Reynolds Price, who was born in Macon, a village near Warrenton. Price's first and most acclaimed novel was *A Long and Happy Life* (1962), an enchanting story of pastoral Warren County. The heroine, attractive and bighearted, loves a handsome youth more interested in his motorcycle than in a permanent relationship. She succumbs to his masculine entreaties, whereupon he considers it his duty, with considerable indifference, that they be married so that, in accordance with the

Reynolds Price

expected mores of the community, the child she carries may at least have a name. With *A Generous Man* (1966), Price turned back ten years before the time of his first novel to the girl's fifteen-year-old younger brother and his leap into maturity during a three-day "hunting" expedition. This *bildungsroman* is a novel of search: the boy searching for his retarded brother, who is searching for his dog, which is searching for a huge python named Death, which has escaped from a traveling side show. A sheriff's team is searching for the python, too, and also for the boy's grandfather, and for the snake's pretty custodian, with whom the boy has fallen in love. In Price's third novel, *Love and Work* (1968), the central character is an intellectual, thoroughly egotistical professor who believes his academic labors provide him with control over those he loves but learns eventually that his dominance becomes an isolation he had not sought. Price's *The Surface of Earth* (1975) is a lengthy family saga covering four North Carolina generations whose patterns of failure and sorrow are repeated from one generation to the next in a biblical sins-of-the-fathers context. Its sequel, *The Source of Light* (1981), Price insisted, is not autobiographical, but the events in it closely parallel those in the life of the author: the hero's youth and schooling in the bucolic South, his university days at Oxford, his travels in Wales and Italy, his many loves both accepted and rejected, and his return home at the news of his father's illness. The first-person narrator of *Kate Vaiden* (1986) tells of her parents' murder-suicide in Macon when she was eleven, her upbringing by an affectionate aunt and uncle, an affair with the androgynous lover of their son, and her abandonment of a resulting child, whom she does not see for the next forty years. In Price's characterization, Kate is no feckless vagabond, but a woman of courageous independence. In these six novels and two collections of short stories—*The Names and Faces of Heroes* (1963) and *Permanent Errors* (1970)—a principal leitmotif is the complex nature of love: one's surrender to it as well as one's indebtedness to it when it is unrequited. Reynolds Price has been acclaimed by serious critics as a major American writer.

Anne Tyler, brought up in Raleigh, was Reynolds Price's student when he began teaching at Duke after his return from Oxford. At first she had no intention of becoming a writer, but in Montreal during the first half year of her marriage she wrote *If Morning Ever Comes* (1964) because, she said, she "had nothing

© Helen Marcus

Anne Tyler

else to do." Whatever its genesis, the novel was an impressive beginning. In it, the brother of six free-spirited sisters returns home to fictional Sandhill, North Carolina, from law school in the North to straighten out some difficulties brought on by the disclosure that his deceased father had an illegitimate son. The women of the household, not understanding his need to assume authority, have in their quiet individual ways been regulating matters without depending on him, and, when he leaves home to resume his studies, his sense of dismissal and inadequacy is traumatic. *The Tin Can Tree* (1965), which utilizes Tyler's teenage experience working in a tobacco warehouse, tells of the death of a child in a tractor mishap and the effects on the three families occupying the same house beside a tobacco field near "Caraway, North Carolina." Tyler's forte for picturesque details and her ability in delineating various family relationships underscore the plot in this novel. The setting of *A Slipping-Down Life* (1970) is the North Carolina towns of Pulqua and Farinia (Fuquay-Varina, of course) in Wake County. In an impulsive moment an overweight high-school girl inscribes the word "Casey" on her forehead with nail scissors. She does not notice that the letters, from the reverse image in the mirror, spell the word backward. "Drumstrings" Casey is the local, untalented rock singer so idolized by the foolish girl. Complications, naturally, arise upon their marriage, and when they separate after Casey sleeps with the girl's close friend, the girl finally asserts herself by moving out, determined to survive without him. The novel provides the reader with a fictional report on the empty, purposeless existence of young people in the American 1960s.

After these three novels, Tyler left the North Carolina scene, explaining that since she had been away from the South for a decade she was no longer able to ensnare the voices and ways of southerners. Thenceforth her scene was Baltimore, where she and her family took up residence in 1967. But the novels continued uninterrupted: *The Clock Winder* (1972), *Celestial Navigation* (1974), *Searching for Caleb* (1976), *Earthly Possessions* (1977), *Morgan's Passing* (1980), *Dinner at the Homesick Restaurant* (1982), and *The Accidental Tourist* (1985), winner of the 1985 National Book Award. Though *Dinner at the Homesick Restaurant* was her first best-seller, critics had from the mid-1970s been proclaiming her as one of the most astute writers in the United States. Her characters are ordinary people, slightly eccentric, who often run away (usually on a bus) to escape their insularity within the family circle. Her subject is always the family and the everyday tasks they endure, the everyday misunderstandings they create. Unlike the work of so many highly praised southern writers, Tyler's fiction is straightforward, carefully outlined, and unencumbered with symbols or subtle nuances.

A Gothic mist—insanity, degeneration, fantasy, violence, sadism, dreams, arson, murder, hypnotic trances, supernatural intrusions—overlays the first novels of Romulus Linney, Fred Chappell, and Heather Ross Miller. In *Heathen Valley* (1962), Linney, playwright as well as writer of fiction, uses the early history of Valle Crucis for his terror-haunted tale of an Episcopal bishop at a mission church hidden among the high peaks. In the bishop's resolve to convert a clan of savage pagans to Christianity, he is overcome by a malignance that destroys him. The sharp demonology of this book was somewhat modified in *Slowly, by Thy Hand Unfurled* (1965), the diary of a semiliterate woman whose sons and daughters are annihilated when forced to replenish the vacuum in her empty, witless existence. A complete turnabout came with *Jesus Tales* (1980), in which the Master is treated comically in a series of down-to-earth folk yarns. He wanders hither and yon with St. Peter, on whom he plays jokes, meanwhile passing

miracles—but only when it suits Him to do so. The language is that of everyday usage, far from the biblical cadences so familiar to most readers.

Most of Chappell's fiction emanates from his native mountains west of Asheville. *It Is Time, Lord* (1963) concerns a man who, captured in dream and memory, rifles his past—a baleful childhood experience of his sister and himself and some strangers in a barn, his burning of his grandfather's house—to discover some meaning for his present lifelessness and inactivity. In *The Inkling* (1965) Chappell created a circular novel, its opening and conclusion occurring at the same moment. Within a nightmare world of insanity, sex, and murder, the effort of an intellectual, self-reliant young man to arrange his life through the power of his will comes to nothing. The minister in *Dagon* (1968), back at his ancestral home

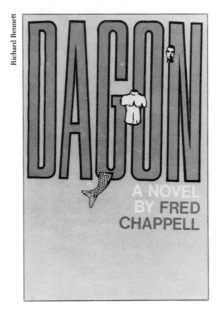

Richard Bennett

in the North Carolina mountains to complete a book to be titled "Remnant Pagan Forces in American Puritanism," is trapped by a young satanic woman who drains him of sexual vigor and lures him toward a knife-red sacrifice to her god Dagon. In these three novels, and the two by Linney, the choice of Gothic paraphernalia is made not so much to shock the reader (though of course it does) as to provide the two novelists with literary devices for psychologically examining those driving impulses, fears, and tensions in the subconscious.

Chappell's fourth novel, *The Gaudy Place* (1973), narrated from the viewpoints of five characters, takes its reader to Asheville to look upon two segments of society: the seamy side with pimps, prostitutes, and petty racketeers, then across town to the professional environment of a history professor and his wayward son. In the eleven short stories of *Moments of Light* (1980), the Gothic elements are muted and Chappell's interest in science fiction predominates. Joseph Haydn, Jesus and Judas, Blackbeard and Benjamin Franklin appear from time to time to illumine the author's theme of the moral quality of justice. Chappell's most endearing novel is *I Am One of You Forever* (1985), fictionalized reminiscences of his boyhood days on a mountain farm. His lovable family circle comes through clear and bright, and the reader is charmed by such frenetic visitors as Uncle Runkin, who sleeps in his handmade coffin. Yet, even in the midst of domestic scenes, Chappell's sunshine realism may amble into Gothic fantasy: Uncle Gurton's long beard that overnight grows and grows until it fills the house and yard, a telegram that reappears on the dining room table even after it has been burned to ashes.

Heather Ross Miller of the Ross "writing family" in Badin—father Fred, uncle James, aunt Eleanor—lost no time in becoming the fourth Ross writer. Her Gothic novel *The Edge of the Woods* (1964) centers on a woman near destruction who delves into her past for a solution and an answer to her present plight, while *Tenants of the House* (1966), which employs dreams and flashbacks and myth, dissects the residents of a row apartment. Miller's third novel, *Gone a Hundred Miles* (1968), is based on the life of an immigrant German doctor who

Clyde Miller

Heather Ross Miller

settles in an isolated area of North Carolina in the early nineteenth century. *A Spiritual Divorce and Other Stories* (1974) analyzes the determinants that result in the alterations in one's personality—for example, a mother's obsessive dreams as they crush her prior naïveté. Though *Confessions of a Champeen Fire-Baton Twirler* (1976) has its usual cast of aberrant characters in Palestine (Badin), at its center is a high-school girl firm in her belief that if she wins the baton-twirling contest she will be rewarded with the love of the wounded soldier she dotes on. In this humorous novel, Miller abrogates the Gothicism of her early books.

After mid-century, Chapel Hill became the home base for three women engaged in writing and teaching: Daphne Athas, Sylvia Wilkinson, and Lee Smith. A Greek-American, Athas set *The Weather of the Heart* (1947) in the Mediterranean country of her forefathers, and *The Fourth World* (1956) drew on her experience in a Massachusetts school for the blind. The semiautobiographical *Entering Ephesus* (1971) is an almost embarrassingly candid narrative of a family's squalid existence in Ephesus (Chapel Hill) during the last years of the Great Depression. While the brilliant father dabbles in unsuccessful schemes, the mother tries to hold things together by such ploys as covering holes in the termite-rotting floors with a Persian rug. Meanwhile, bright and ambitious Urie (Athas herself?) and her two sisters, as one reviewer put it, "connive, cheat, and fox the 'haves' as they grow and learn about sex." In *Cora* (1978) a young American in Greece, seeking a paradigm of the goddess in his fantasies, becomes involved with two women during a brutal political crisis.

In Sylvia Wilkinson's *Moss on the North Side* (1966), with its theme of innocence in the midst of human corruption, an adolescent girl begins her passage into maturity along the fields and country lanes of the sensuous farmlands in central North Carolina. *A Killing Frost* (1967)

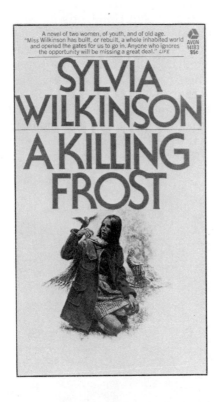

A novel of two women, of youth, and of old age.
"Miss Wilkinson has built, or rebuilt, a whole inhabited world and opened the gates for us to go in. Anyone who ignores the opportunity will be missing a great deal." *LIFE*
AVON 14183 95¢

SYLVIA WILKINSON
A KILLING FROST

dissects the relationship of a thirteen-year-old girl with her dying grandmother during a disturbing autumn. In these two novels, the protagonists are repressed by the customs of their restricted environment, as is the boy in *Cale* (1970), whose mother sees in her son the possibility of

his grasping the happiness in life denied her; but since he cannot accept her chosen role for him, mother and son become estranged. *Shadow of the Mountain* (1977) depicts a genteel girl who leaves college with the ideals and altruism of youth to work among poverty-depressed North Carolina mountain people, but unforeseen events and suspicious, prejudiced natives make her feel despised and rejected. The heroine of *Bone of My Bone* (1982) is a strong-willed girl who refuses to follow her mother's traditional plans for her, choosing instead the life of an artist. For both children and adult readers, Wilkinson has written a number of nonfiction books on automobile racing, most recently *Dirt Tracks to Glory* (1983). It should be noted that in Wilkinson's novels and those of many others in the latter part of the twentieth century, the rural and small-town settings that had served so many of the state's best writers were still being used. In spite of industry and urbanization, North Carolina, at least insofar as its literature was concerned, was a region of farms and woodlands.

Not only is Lee Smith a storyteller, but her characters are storytellers. Three novels written before she moved to North Carolina in 1974 can be called, in view of the major advance exhibited in *Black Mountain Breakdown* (1981), apprenticeship works. The leading character here is a woman, a passive storyteller, symbolic of an inertia that leads to paralysis. The short stories in *Cakewalk* (1981), according to a critic, are "tales shrewdly observant of segments of North Carolina life." Once again Smith's characters are divided into two groups: worthy people who give of themselves and those who are unworthy because they have nothing to give or are determinedly self-indulgent. Near the beginning of *Oral History* (1983) a young mountain man sets out, in the fashion of an old tale straight from folklore, to acquire himself a wife, and he does. She turns out, of course, to be the witch Red Emmy, a half-naked creature with red hair, red mouth, and black eyes.

Lee Smith

She wastes him away till a sorceress convinces the fellow to drive her from his fireside, and he does. But as she leaves, she shouts a curse upon him and his family forevermore. Smith then recounts what tragedies befall the several generations of the young man's descendants. The novel, a work of storytelling without moral implications of any sort, was highly successful. *Family Linen* (1985) was Smith's sixth novel.

Two novelists with backgrounds in North Carolina—John Yount and Gail Godwin—moved north to try their luck, but, as any of their readers will quickly notice, the two writers have voices that have remained distinctly, ineradicably southern.

Yount, born in Boone, wrote *Wolf at the Door* (1967), about an undergraduate at a southern university (Wake Forest?) whose traumas have immobilized him, making him indifferent to his wife, his friends, and even to all commonplace transactions. To those who know him, his dilemma is vastly puzzling. Two ambitious Georgia brothers in *The Trapper's Last Shot* (1973) are frustrated by civil rights activists in accomplishing their goals. For his sympathetic characterizations of the brothers, Yount was much

praised by reviewers. Even more praise was heaped on *Hardcastle* (1980), whose brave, penniless young man during the Great Depression, working for a Kentucky mining company at a time when management and labor were in conflict, concludes that only by unionizing could the oppressive plight of the miners be improved. The hero in *Toots in Solitude* (1984) retreats to a treehouse on the bank of a river to avoid his demeaning wife and the life she represents, but there his solitude, privacy, and tranquillity are thwarted by the intrusion of a drug dealer's runaway girlfriend and the gunmen pursuing her. The conventionality of plot is redeemed by Yount's verbal elegance and the generous understanding of his recluse.

The novels of Gail Godwin, who was brought up in Asheville, are characterized by situations that "hook" the reader immediately. Her stories, mostly about women, turn on the way one's past controls the present. *The Perfectionist* (1970) is based on the author's one-year-long marriage to an aloof, intellectual British psychiatrist and her need to establish her selfness. The wife in *Glass People* (1972)

Gail Godwin

is married to a brilliant district attorney whose only wish is that she remain beautiful. Attempting to escape the cage he has built around her, she visits her mother in a North Carolina mountain city, only to discover from that maternal confrontation and other tests that she is incapable of anything except the exploitation of her beauty. The protagonist in *The Odd Woman* (1975), seeking to modulate her romantic affair with a married man, has no models, no guides to tell her what to do, certainly not her mother or grandmother in western North Carolina, who wish only to be complacent southern ladies. The theme of *Violet Clay* (1978) is the apposition of artist and art. Only when the painter repairs to the mountain cabin of her uncle, an unsuccessful artist and a suicide, does she manage, through her acquaintance with a wise, stout-hearted older woman in the neighborhood, to reach full development as a master of her craft. In *A Mother and Two Daughters* (1982) three women contemplate their uncertain futures while at a family gathering in Asheville for the funeral of a husband and father. In the long chapters that follow, the wife adjusts uneasily into the widows' circle of the town, the older daughter rejects her millionaire suitor, and the younger daughter is wooed by a Winston-Salem podiatrist. The novel ends affirmatively for all three. Most of the action in *The Finishing School* (1985) takes place in a stone hut ("the finishing school") in upper New York State. A fourteen-year-old girl from the South goes there almost daily to visit a middle-aged woman to discuss life and art, music and beauty—illustrating the natural attraction between a young person and a mentor. At the end, a long-ago betrayal of which the woman was guilty is tragically repeated by the girl. This serious "growing-up novel" and its predecessor hit the best-seller lists, assuring the author a success previously denied her. In two collections of short stories, the themes and techniques, though diversified, are signally akin to the novels in the Godwin corpus.

While Yount and Godwin looked down from their northern retreats to North Carolina for literary inspiration, Raleigh's Helen Tucker, after twelve years of wandering and working throughout the United States and in Europe, chose to return home, where she had merely to glance along the streets from her window or ride into the country and adjoining counties to sharpen her imagination.

Helen Tucker

The Sound of Summer Voices (1969) is the tender story of an eleven-year-old boy in a small North Carolina town (Louisburg) who, facing a "conspiracy of silence" from the bachelor uncle and two spinster aunts with whom he lives, turns sleuth to unriddle the secret of his parentage. In its first paragraph, *The Guilt of August Sterling* (1971) cites a plaque on the top of a stone wall: "Brandon College for Men, Brandon, North Carolina, Founded 1834, Pro Humanitate." To this institution (old Wake Forest College) in the 1890s comes an awkward farm boy to study for the ministry. Following his seduction by the wife of his favorite professor, he is so haunted by his guilt that his first pastorate is doomed and he begins even to question his religious faith. At the capital city (Raleigh) in *No Need of Glory* (1972), an exciting

125

gubernatorial race is twisted from its normal political course by the revelation that the favored candidate is a double-dealer with a second wife in a distant city.

Eight novels by Tucker, beginning with *A Strange and Ill-Starred Marriage* (1978), which explores the Regency period (1811-1820) in England, were groomed for the paperback market. Tucker's shift to paperbacks, she explains, was deliberately planned to provide her with more income than the hardbacks had brought in. The plan worked. Her most recent paperback, *Bound by Honor* (1984), is set in Bath Town on the Pamlico River in North Carolina during the Tuscarora War of 1711-1712 and deals with the struggle of Governor Edward Hyde to prevent the usurpation of his office by former Governor Thomas Cary. To Bath Town comes an English girl indentured for four years to a well-favored unmarried colonist living in a one-room cabin. Though their romance is fraught with misunderstandings and perilous ordeals, all of course ends happily.

Patricia Hagan from Goldsboro is another paperback enthusiast. "I do not believe in inspiration," she says, but in "self-discipline." Following a period of concentration on short stories, she wrote two Gothic novels, then turned to historical romances of the Civil War period for *Love and War* (1978) and its sequel, *The Raging Hearts* (1979). The heroine of these novels is an aristocratic young southern woman kidnapped by a Union officer who rapes her and holds her prisoner during a mountain winter. After her escape she returns to her North Carolina ancestral homestead, where later, with the war over, she once again encounters the Yankee officer, whom she has come to love. A reviewer's criticism that the characters in these novels were "too busy making love to make war" did not disturb Hagan, who estimates that her books have sold more than a million copies. When not writing fiction, Hagan covers Grand National stock car racing for the Associated Press.

In Charlotte, Judith H. Simpson (pen names Rosalind Foxx and Sara Logan) also wrote historical romances for paperback fans of the genre. She was particularly drawn to Scottish history, as in *Winds of Fury, Winds of Fire* (1981), which deals with the border wars between England and Scotland in the sixteenth century. *Flame against the Wind* (1983) brings the reader up to the War of 1812, and the action in *Game of Hearts* (1982), which employs Simpson's Sara Logan by-line, takes place at the present-day annual summer gathering of the descendants of Scottish Highlanders on Grandfather Mountain in North Carolina. A Charlotte woman, jilted by her fiancé, flirts with a foreign visitor to make him jealous, her flirtation turning into "true love" when this Scottish laird reveals his aristocratic status. A "romance" (its generic term in current American publishing) like this is a highly remunerative product.

At the zero end of the profit scale is Cleveland P. Robertson of Stoneville in Rockingham County, presently in his

Greensboro News-Record

Cleveland P. Robertson, 1976

nineties. He simply gives his books away at no charge. He hands them out to family, friends, and anyone who asks for a copy. *The Covered Bridge Mystery* (1982), replete with horseless hoofbeats and bloodshed, is based on a Stoneville murder committed a century and a half ago. In his preface Robertson wrote: "This book is not copyrighted, and anyone who will use any part of it will earn the profound gratitude of the author." His next novel, he promised, will be about life two millennia from the present.

On the eve of the 1980s, several writers, after serving their novitiate with short stories, were preparing to launch their first novels. At the head of the line was Candace Flynt of Greensboro. The action

Chuck Flynt

Candace Flynt

in *Chasing Dad* (1980) revolves around the family of an uneducated carpenter in Durham whose only affection is for his elder son. Following the young man's suicide, the kindly, sympathetic younger brother hungers to be a surrogate, chasing his unresponsive dad wherever he goes in hopes that he may receive the love he believes both he and his father are in need of. Though "not a pretty story," opined a reviewer, it is nevertheless an intensely compelling one. Nor was

Flynt's second novel, *Sins of Omission* (1984), a pretty story. In it a crazed, sex-obsessed Greensboro wench resorts to every crafty, unthinkable harassment in order to separate a handsome but rather dull husband from his insipid wife.

When Greensboro native Leo Snow brought out his novel *Southern Dreams and Trojan Women* (1983) at his own expense, he surprised himself and others by managing to sell two thousand copies. A commercial publisher was so impressed that two years later the book was revised and issued in hardcover. In this strong novel of contemporary conflict, two women—a white and a black—arrive in Greensboro to escape the hardships of farm drudgery. Though the two friends, sharing a company millhouse, attract the displeasure of the Ku Klux Klan, their lives and hopes are never diminished.

As Thomas Wolfe and Stanley Olmsted long ago discovered to their dismay, a roman à clef can embitter a community if the characters are portrayed more derogatorily than homefolk think justified. In *Pretty Redwing* (1983), Helen Henslee, born in Hickory, fictionally depicts her own family, especially her affluent mother, in an unfavorable light. It is quite acceptable to describe streets and houses and buildings as they are, but to have the narrator, a "spindly little daughter," reveal, accurately or inaccurately, her mother's passion for her comely, only slightly younger stepson was, according to a Hickory librarian, "an insult to the memory of her mother. Her mother would be horrified. She was such a lovely person."

Three writers of the 1980s—Louise Shivers, Jill McCorkle, and Clyde Edgerton—wrote first novels set in eastern North Carolina. Readers had high praise for the unaffected dialogue, the mellow resonance, and the trim delineation of *Here To Get My Baby Out of Jail* (1983), by Louise Shivers, a native of Stantonsburg and one of ten children. To a small tobacco farm near Tarborough (actually Wilson) in 1937 comes a red-haired, sex-exuding drifter to help in

127

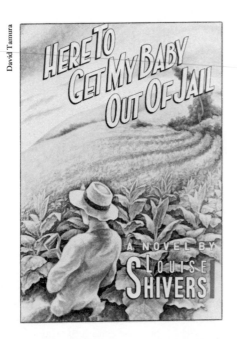

town of Marshboro (Lumberton) during one day in the life of a youthful, disillusioned outsider who happens to alight there after hitchhiking down from New York on a trip back to his native North Carolina. A casual murder opens up the town's underside, the intertwining of relationships among every segment of its social structure. As the hitchhiker becomes involved in the seemingly disjointed contingencies, he finds he must reject his immature conviction that America has a plastic sameness everywhere. This is a New South of rock music and Winn Dixies, of waitresses at a highway truck stop, and of the gradually vanishing social upper crust. In McCorkle's novel the setting, dialect, and characters are unmistakably and ingeniously southern.

It is doubtful that anyone could have foreseen what would happen when Clyde Edgerton, an associate professor of education at Campbell University, published his charming, unpretentious *Raney* in the spring of 1985. A brief novel it was, the warmhearted story of a couple's first two years of marriage, the two having decided to get married mainly because they "made" good country music together. The girl is stubbornly, admirably loyal to her large family of aunts and uncles and cousins and their customs and ways and to the preachings of the Free Will Baptist church, the husband firm in his beliefs in liberal principles and the tenets of the Episcopal church. They differ, too, about language usage, racial matters, and choice of friends. How these two sincere and likable young people work out their disagreements in this often comic, always wistful, story touches the reader's sympathies for both of them.

A few weeks after the novel was published, Edgerton was called before the Campbell University administration. "How does your novel contribute to the purpose of Christian education, to the purpose of this university?" he was asked. Edgerton thought it made a contribution, as did almost all of the professors on the faculty. "The theme of the book,"

planting and harvesting the crop. The electricity between him and the twenty-year-old wife of the farmer leads to adultery, murder, flight, and a sensational trial. At the end of it all, the young woman, narrating her own confessional, realizes that she had "been in a little jail inside my own self ever since I'd been born," and now, after these tragic events, she is at last ready to pursue an unaccustomed freedom. According to a reviewer, "Sights, sounds, smells, textures are so richly described" that one "could feel the tobacco leaves, smell the soil, hear the chickens. . . ."

Jill McCorkle of Lumberton had an unusual, and perhaps unique, publishing experience when her first two novels were issued simultaneously in 1984. *The Cheer Leader*, her curtain raiser, portrays the trauma of a girl from a small North Carolina town (Lumberton) whose accomplishments in high school do not sustain her during her college freshman year. In this "coming-of-age" novel, the girl succumbs to anorexia following a brief affair with an older boy and has only partially recovered by the time the story ends.

The broader canvas of *July 7th* was large enough to encompass the entire

Professor quits at Campbell

BUIES CREEK (AP) — Campbell University professor Clyde C. Edgerton, whose contract was delayed because of a book he wrote, has resigned, saying the school is unwilling to deal with the issue of academic freedom.

"Because the university has not seen fit at any level to deal directly, or openly, with my main concern, the abridgement of academic freedom, I believe I will be happier working elsewhere," Edgerton said in a letter, dated Wednesday, to Norman Wiggins, president of Campbell and the N.C. Baptist State Convention.

In an interview Friday, Edgerton said he had been offered a job as associate professor of teacher education and English at St. Andrew's College, a Presbyterian-affiliated school in Laurinburg. Campbell, in Buies Creek, is affiliated with the Southern Baptist Church.

Wiggins would not comment when reached this morning.

On March 27, Edgerton, associate professor of education at Campbell, disclosed that Campbell officials had withheld his 1985-86 teaching contract because of a book he wrote, "Raney: A Novel." Several days later, he received his contract without a raise.

"Raney" chronicles the first two years of a young couple's marriage. Raney Bell Shephard is a Free Will Baptist from a small North Carolina town, and her husband, Charles, is an Episcopalian from Atlanta. In a series of vignettes, the couple tries to reconcile differing views on race, religion and family relations.

said one of his associates, "is how people of different opinions and beliefs can work through to tolerance, understanding and the grace of God to achieve harmony, love, peace and respect for beliefs and feelings of others." Nevertheless, Edgerton's contract and promised pay raise were withheld, though later restored, and the novelist resigned on the issue of academic freedom to accept a position at St. Andrews Presbyterian College in Laurinburg. Neither then nor thereafter did the Campbell administration retract its statement that the novel satirized the Free Will Baptist church. The controversy was reminiscent of troubles encountered by James M. Shields and Russell Brantley decades earlier.

T. R. Pearson waited only a year after graduating from North Carolina State

T. R. Pearson

University before starting to write his compassionate novel *A Short History of a Small Place* (1985). At that time he was studying at State College, Pennsylvania, but after only one semester left the classroom to devote his entire time to fiction. The "small place" is Neely (Reidsville), as typically Tar Heel as any small place can be. The narrator is a youngster who is continually quoting his sagacious father about the pixilated denizens of the town, among them the spinster who makes a suicidal jump from the water tower, the pleasant old fellow who thinks he is the king of Prussia, and the narrator's mother, who washes dishes when she is unhappy. The book "is more than an impressive debut," wrote a perceptive reviewer; "it is an accomplishment. . . . The world about Neely is mean and nasty and bitter," but "Pearson makes it funny and, at worst, only a little sad." Many of Neely's bizarre folk reappear in Pearson's *Off for the Sweet Hereafter* (1986) along with a group of low-grade riffraff uninhibitedly portrayed. The slow-moving, usually law-abiding Neely inhabitants are terror-shaken by a murder and several hold-ups perpetrated by a "gangly and pointy and carved out and toothsome" local moron who is prodded on by a money-spending live-in hussy with "sweetstraw" hair and skin "pure and milky white." One of the things she would very much like to buy is a small TV set to rest on her stomach while she is lying down. Narrative devices retained from Pearson's first novel are his down-to-earth humor, his details of normally unremarked everyday objects and actions, and the circular verbal redundancies of his style.

Like Pearson, Anderson Ferrell of Black Creek in Wilson County decided while a student at N.C. State that he was going to be a writer. In his first novel, *Where She Was* (1985), the workaday wife of a tenant tobacco farmer searches for a transcendent Being to satisfy her spiritual yearnings. When the local churches prove inadequate, she follows a dark, chimerical Stranger into the pine forests, there to begin an epiphany soon to release her from bewilderment.

Michael Malone, author of the murder mystery *Uncivil Seasons* and several other novels, begins his long, zany, comic *Handling Sin* (1986) at a meeting of the Civitan Club in "Thermopylae, N.C.," whence a trio of scatterbrained fellows set out on a picaresque journey throughout the Southeast. Their outrageous encounters, according to a reviewer, are "capable of making a reader sick with belly laughter."

And so it is that North Carolina's novelists of the mid-1980s, if no Thomas Wolfe appeared among them, were wise and gifted in indefatigably and affirmatively rendering the fictional annals of their state as their predecessors had done during the long, long years before them.

XIX

PUBLISHERS OF BOOKS AND PERIODICALS

The first North Carolina book publishers were printers. James Davis, who established the colony's first press at New Bern (discussed in chapter 2), was followed by only two other active printers before the American Revolution. None of the printers who manufactured North Carolina's first books of sermons, religious reflections, fiction, or poetry in the late eighteenth and early nineteenth centuries was really a publisher in the modern sense of the word, however. George Roulstone, who had printed the *Fayetteville Gazette* in 1789 and the *North Carolina Chronicle* in Fayetteville in 1790, was invited by territorial governor William Blount to migrate to Tennessee in 1791. In September, 1803, Roulstone printed the first book ever published in Tennessee, *The Laws of Tennessee*, which consisted of 320 pages.

Salmon Hall, who came from Connecticut to New Bern in 1800, was active in the book trade there for the next forty years. Although primarily a job printer, he did apparently publish for himself a few books, such as *A New Collection of the Most Approved Hymns and Spiritual Songs, Mostly Original, for the Use of Christians of All Denominations* (1804) and *The English Reader* (1805), by Murray Lindley. Hall's New Bern contemporary Francois-Xavier Martin, of course, was also a publisher (see chapter 3). Joseph Gales, an Englishman, came to Raleigh in 1799 to operate a newspaper. He published, among other items, his wife's novel *Matilda Berkley* (1804) and

a volume of his son-in-law's sermons in 1821.

By 1800 books had been printed at nine locations: Raleigh, New Bern, Wilmington, Edenton, Halifax, Hillsborough, Fayetteville, Salisbury, and Lincolnton. If early printers were sometimes publishers of books, they might also be newspaper editors, bookbinders, booksellers, and merchants of general school, business, and stationery supplies. This continued to be true in North Carolina, where until the middle of the nineteenth century the printing profession had not changed appreciably from that in colonial days. Therefore, the earliest books published in the state were brought out by men who did not consider book publishing their principal business. There were no publishing companies in the present sense until such firms as E. J. Hale & Son of Fayetteville; Sterling, Campbell, and Albright of Greensboro; Edwards & Broughton of Raleigh; Alfred Williams of Raleigh; and the Seeman Printery of Durham were established. And even these firms often played the role of "vanity press." The 1850 census indicates that the percentage of those in North Carolina who could not read was about twice as high as that of neighboring states. The state also lacked a large metropolitan population center capable of supporting a firm devoted solely to traditional publishing.

Possibly the oldest noncommercial publisher in the state is the University of North Carolina Press at Chapel Hill,

Edwards & Broughton Printing Company

PRINTERS, PUBLISHERS AND STATIONERS.
STEEL AND COPPER PLATE ENGRAVINGS.
Manufacturers of
BLANK BOOKS AND LOOSE LEAF SYSTEMS.
Raleigh, N. C.

North Carolina Resources

"One of the most useful series of descriptive books ever published about any State." *Boston Post.*

Hale's Industrial Series.

Two Volumes Now Ready!

1. *The Woods and Timbers of North Carolina.*—Curti's, Emmons', and Kerr's Botanic Reports; supplemented by accurate County Reports of Standing Forests, and illustrated by an excellent Map of the State.

1 *Volume* 12*mo. Cloth,* 273 *pp.,* $1.5.0

II. In the Coal and Iron Counties of North Carolina.—Emmons', Kerr's Laidley's Wilkes', and the Census Reports; supplemented by full and accurate sketches of the Fifty-six Counties, and Map of the State.

1 *Volume* 12*mo. Cloth,* 425 *pp.,* $1.50.

Sold by all Booksellers, or mailed post paid, on receipt of the price, by
E. J. HALE & SON,
Publishers, Booksellers and Stationers,
New York;
OR
P. M. HALE, Publisher, Raleigh, N. C.

ALFRED WILLIAMS & CO.,
LAW PUBLISHERS,
Booksellers & Stationers
119 FAYETTEVILLE STREET AND 8 EXCHANGE PLACE,
RALEIGH, N. C.

The Thompson Publishing Company

Publishers School and College Text-Books

RALEIGH, N. C.

A Home Institution with High Ideals.

ALF. A. THOMPSON, President.
CLARENCE POE, Vice President.
CHARLES J. PARKER, Sec.-Treas.

SUBSCRIBE FOR THE

N. C. Journal of Education,

Address, S. D. POOL, Raleigh, N. C.

TERMS:				
Single Copies,	$1.50 per Annum.		3 Copies,	$4.00 per Annum
Five	" 6.00	"	10	" 10.00 "

The advertisements shown above are typical of those used by North Carolina publishers in the late nineteenth and early twentieth centuries. They represent the following publishers (clockwise, from top): Edwards & Broughton Printing Company, 1913; Alfred Williams & Company, 1882; Thompson Publishing Company, 1913; the *N.C. Journal of Education*, 1875; and E. J. Hale & Son, 1883.

Some North Carolina publishers use distinctive colophons or logos to identify their books. Examples include (clockwise from top left) Algonquin Books, 1986; Duke University Press, ca. 1979; E. J. Hale & Son, 1883; Carolina Wren Press, 1986; Alfred Williams & Co., 1882; and East Woods Press, 1986. Shown at center is logo of St. Andrews Press, 1986.

founded in 1922 with Louis Round Wilson as its first director. (Duke University Press disputes this claim because its own ancestor, Trinity College, began operating earlier.) Devoted, according to its charter, to the "advancement of the arts and sciences and the development of literature," the UNC Press established the earliest regional publishing program by a university press in the United States. The works of sociologist Howard W. Odom were a particular attraction. This publication of books about North Carolina and the South created a pattern that was eventually adopted by many other academic publishers. UNC Press was the first American publisher to establish an ongoing program of books by and about black Americans. Expanding on its traditional fare of history and literary criticism, the press now issues books on

many topics. It does not usually publish novels, however, and has produced only a handful of volumes of short stories and poetry by North Carolina writers. The press has published more than three thousand titles and has sales of over $1 million annually. It presently has more than five hundred books in print.

In Durham, Trinity College history professors William Kenneth Boyd and William T. Laprade were the driving force behind the new Trinity College Press, begun in 1921. Their first book, Randolph G. Adams's *Political Ideas of the American Revolution* (1922), missed winning a Pulitzer Prize by only one vote. When Trinity became Duke University, the press was chartered as Duke University Press in 1926. Duke University Press was a pioneer in the publication of studies of American literature. It took over as publisher of the *South Atlantic Quarterly*, founded in 1901 at Trinity by John Spencer Bassett, a brave and controversial figure in the history of academic freedom. And it was initial publisher of the quarterly *American Literature*, first edited by Jay B. Hubbell in 1929, and of the annual summary volume *American Literary Scholarship*, which celebrated its twenty-fifth anniversary in 1985.

John Fries Blair, a Winston-Salem attorney, realized a longtime dream by creating a regional publishing company in 1954. He was already fifty years old when he began his firm, John F. Blair,

John Fries Blair

Publisher, on a very modest scale in a cluttered office over a downtown bank. Disliking "what New York seems to expect of writers from the South," Blair set out to publish well-designed and printed books on a variety of subjects of regional interest. He believed in the integrity of his homeland and sought to encourage talented writers whose work might not have found a massive commercial market. In the beginning, getting books into the bookstores was not easy, Blair said. "Some towns in the state, particularly in the resort areas, have few, if any, bookstores. I have therefore sold

my books in hotels, motels, gift shops, art galleries, restaurants, grocery stores, a shell museum, a fish market, and a garage. It is sometimes surprising the size of the orders they send in. The fish market . . . had an autograph party for one of my authors." In 1974 Blair erected a new building with editorial offices and a warehouse. By 1984 his firm had published approximately 130 books, a large percentage of them written by North Carolinians or dealing with some aspect of the state.

St. Andrews Presbyterian College at Laurinburg in the 1970s and 1980s was a center of poetic activity, sparked by the vitality of St. Andrews Press, which was receptive to publishing poetry, and of the periodical *St. Andrews Review*. Conceived in 1968, *St. Andrews Review* was launched in 1971 with poet Ronald H. Bayes as its first editor. Institutional cooperation stimulated publication in the western part of the state, where about a dozen colleges, universities, and regional agencies formed the Appalachian Consortium. The consortium established a press at Boone in 1974 to publish books dealing with mountain life and culture.

Algonquin Books of Chapel Hill was a child of the imagination of University of North Carolina literature professor Louis D. Rubin, Jr., who was also dissatisfied with the northeastern big-city idea of what a book ought to be. Since 1982 Algonquin, publishing twenty-two titles in its first three years, has offered a high-quality, diversified list, including fiction but not poetry. The firm's nonfiction books range in subject matter from politics to history to sports to ecology, including works by 1984 Pulitzer Prize winner Vermont Royster.

The Division of Archives and History of the North Carolina Department of Cultural Resources issues books, pamphlets, maps, and periodicals through its Historical Publications Section. Among its publications are governors' papers, county histories, a Civil War troop roster project, a new series of the colonial records of the state, and periodicals such as the *North Carolina Historical Review* and *Carolina Comments*. The *Review*, founded in 1924, is issued quarterly. Its talented editorial staff over the years has included such scholars as Robert Burton House, C. Christopher Crittenden, David Leroy Corbitt, Elizabeth W. Wilborn, Memory F. Mitchell, Marie D. Moore, Jeffrey J. Crow, and Joe A. Mobley.

The North Carolina Historical Review

Moore Publishing Company, established by ophthalmologist and poet Eugene V. Grace, operated in Durham from 1968 to 1981 and produced nearly two hundred titles, providing a non-campus-related outlet for both aspiring and established writers.

F. Roy Johnson, previously mentioned independent publisher in little Murfreesboro, has specialized for several decades in titles dealing with history, Indians, folklore, myth, and legend. His 1985 winter checklist of titles named forty books, twenty-three of which he wrote or edited himself.

Broadfoot Publishing Company of Wilmington is a small firm specializing in reprints and historical titles. It grew out of owner Thomas Broadfoot's thriving Civil War and southern bookshop, located for a number of years near Wendell.

The director and part owner of East Woods Press in Charlotte is the energetic and businesslike Sally Hill McMillan, who in 1977 with two partners resuscitated the East Woods name—the old firm had published but two books—and began to publish outdoor and travel books that deal primarily with the East and the South. Some are published in a special waterproof, tear-resistant format for outdoor use. These so-called "Pak-Books" are the firm's best sellers. One, *Campfire Chillers*, a collection of classic ghost stories, sold more that 15,000 copies in two years.

Another specialty firm, Gallopade Publishing Group in Tryon, began when Carole Marsh Longmeyer, mother of two, decided to have actual children, her own and their friends, solve mysteries at North Carolina historical locations such as Biltmore House, Hope Plantation, and Fort Raleigh on Roanoke Island. Not only were real children used as characters in the books but they also participated in plotting and editing the stories as well as taking part in promotion and sales. At age twelve son Steve Marsh had his own private office in which to work. So successful was the venture that in 1981 husband Bob quit his job and signed on as business manager. Soon Gallopade expanded its list to include books outside the Longmeyer family's pioneer conception.

The Jargon Society, founded at Highlands by Jonathan Williams, has, since the early 1950s, operated as a small, non-profit press specializing in poetry and photography. Many of the artists Williams has chosen to publish have been uniquely talented but little-known or neglected American and European writers.

Magazine publishing probably got an earlier start in North Carolina than can be proved by the surviving publications. The first publication actually to call itself a magazine was the *North Carolina*

Magazine; or Universal Intelligencer, issued in New Bern for four years, 1764-1768. There is some question whether this publication should be classified as newspaper or magazine, but its contents were similar to those of contemporary London magazines. One of its stories concerned a French donkey that was tried and sentenced to hang and be burned after it slipped away from its master on market day, wandered into the village church, and drank up a basin of holy water. In this publication, essays on religious questions, European politics, Roman history, the description of an elephant, and hints on growing hemp accompany notices for vestry elections for Christ Church parish, New Bern; runaway slaves; and printed copies of the colonial acts of assembly for sale. It was the only colonial North Carolina publication to use the word "magazine" in its title.

A later production, also called the *North Carolina Magazine,* published in 1813 in Salisbury, was not strictly literary. Its articles dealt with naval battles, Indian tribes, the plight of Palestinian Jews, and marital relations. As the nineteenth century progressed, numbers of "miscellany" magazines sprang up around the state, often in the most unlikely places. John McLean Harrington, born in upper Cumberland County (now Harnett), was a brilliant but eccentric young man who at age eighteen in 1858 produced a handwritten magazine, *The Young American,* which he laboriously copied and mailed to subscribers. On the title page he declared that it was devoted to prose, poetry, literature, and the news of the day and was "independent in all things, neutral in nothing."

The *North Carolina University Magazine,* begun in Chapel Hill in 1844 and published sporadically over the years, continues today as the *Carolina Quarterly,* its contents metamorphosed into the standard "little magazine" fare—poems, short stories, and reviews—of the 1980s.

North Carolina University Magazine, XXIX (June, 1899)

UNC magazine editors, 1899

Other nineteenth-century magazines included a trio of journals published in the 1850s in Asheboro—the *Southern Index,* edited by Braxton Craven; *Brown's Literary Archive,* edited by R. H. Brown; and *Evergreen,* edited by Craven and Brown. In this period, magazines seemed to spring up everywhere: the *Leisure Hour,* founded in Oxford in 1858; the *Land We Love,* begun in Charlotte in 1866; *At Home and Abroad,* 1881-1883, Charlotte; the *Casket,* ca. 1854, at Chowan Female Collegiate Seminary; the *Raleigh Mercury,* 1864; the *Crescent Monthly,* briefly published in Raleigh, 1866; *Belles Lettres,* 1887, in Whiteville; *Stedman's Salem Magazine,* in the late 1850s; the *South Atlantic,* 1877 and several years thereafter, in Wilmington; and the *People's Literary Casket,* in Wadesboro. Several magazines have originated in Asheville. In its November, 1890, issue, the *Lyceum* contained an article by J. D. Cameron entitled "Southern Fields of Poesy," in which the author noted that the prospects for poetry in North Carolina were not good:

What hope or chance was there that the humble State of North Carolina should twine poetic wreathes around the ornate columns of the Temple of the Muses? From whence were to come her bays, her laurels, her roses? Among a plain unlettered people wedded to tar, pitch and turpentine, delving among the broad leaves of the tobacco field, toiling along in the various avenues of money-winning industries, what time, or interest, or inducement was offered to the enkindling of any latent or transient spark of genius? Was it not rather the temper of our people to quench such spark with ridicule or deprecation, and strengthen the universal verdict that nothing good can come out of Nazareth?

Just before and after the turn of the century, the village of Moravian Falls in Wilkes County was the scene of a surprising amount of publishing activity. R. Don Lawes in 1895 began a vituperatively partisan journal called the *Yellow Jacket*, which claimed a national circulation of 200,000. He also edited the *Rascal-Whipper*. Meanwhile, James Larkin Pearson (later poet laureate of North Carolina) initiated in 1910 the *Fool Killer*, which he edited at various places and under various titles in Wilkes County until 1929.

Although not always of the highest literary quality, the poetry journals of the 1920s and 1930s had a dramatic flair that makes them entertaining reading at the present time in a manner they did not intend. The *Journal of American Poetry* was published in Charlotte for a short time from 1927 to 1929 as the official organ of the Poetry Society of the South; the publication sought to serve a population "sated and disgusted from a literature of revolting realism." *Poetic Thrills*, published for a few years in Wilmington and Salisbury, was another rather odd specimen of poetry journal, with ties to organized labor and the feminist movement. Its editor was Gertrude Perry West, who called herself poet laureate of North Carolina and the author of several versicular "gold mines" that publishers should snap up while they lasted. A stanza on the back page of the first issue revealed the place of this self-proclaimed prodigy's nativity:

Here's to the county where the sun doth shine
Brightest on the sand-hill pine;
Here's to the county of ham and corn;
Progressive Bladen, where I was born!

Father "Dom Placid" Kleppel, a Benedictine monk, was head of the Department of English at Belmont Abbey College and wrote several volumes of poems, including *From the Hid Battlements* (1934) and *The Ballad of Marshal Ney* (1935). He prepared a bibliography of North Carolina poetry in 1934. An enthusiastic member of the North Carolina Poetry Society, he served as associate editor of the organization's journal, the *North Carolina Poetry Review*, which was published monthly from 1933 to 1936 at Gastonia. The *Review*'s editor, Stewart Atkins, appealed to society members to send him five unpublished poems a month, and, if they didn't have any, to write five a month. Seemingly on the same wavelength with these journals was *Scimitar and Song*. Published and edited by Lura Thomas McNair of Jonesboro Heights in Lee County, it endured, amazingly, from 1938 to 1961.

In strong contrast to the conservatism of some of these journals was a magazine called *Contempo*, edited in Chapel Hill by Milton Abernethy and in Durham by Antonio J. Buttitta from 1930 to 1933. This unconventional journal had as contributors a virtual who's who of American writers, including such names as Sinclair Lewis, Charles A. Beard, Lincoln Steffens, Upton Sinclair, Paul de Kruif, Sherwood Anderson, Malcolm Cowley, John Dos Passos, Theodore Dreiser, William Faulkner, Langston Hughes, the Anglo-Irish George Bernard Shaw, and even the Russian Leon Trotsky. One advertiser in *Contempo*, the Intimate Bookshop of Durham, promised to have for sale copies of James Joyce's forbidden novel *Ulysses*, "provided it is cleared by the Court." After finishing English graduate work in Chapel Hill, Buttitta opened a bookshop in Asheville, where his alleged 1935 friendship with novelist F. Scott Fitzgerald is described in his book *After the Good, Gay Times* (1974). The *Reviewer*, published between 1921 and 1925, was edited in Chapel Hill by Paul Green and in Richmond, Virginia, by Emily Tapscott Clark.

Substantial college magazines with nineteenth-century origins were the *Wake Forest Student*, established in 1882, and the *Trinity Archive*, founded in 1887, which became simply the *Archive* at Duke University in 1925.

The North Carolina Folklore Society issues a semiannual journal entitled *North Carolina Folklore*, founded in 1948. For many years it was edited in Chapel Hill by Arthur Palmer Hudson, one of America's leading folklorists. In 1966 the journal's editorial offices were moved to North Carolina State University in Raleigh, and its title was changed to the *North Carolina Folklore Journal*. The publication's second move was to Appalachian State University in 1977.

North Carolina Folklore Journal

Vol. 30, No. 1   Spring-Summer 1982

The *Southern Literary Journal*, published by the Department of English at the University of North Carolina at Chapel Hill, was founded by Louis D. Rubin, Jr., and C. Hugh Holman in 1968. The *Black Mountain Review*, published irregularly between 1954 and 1957 at Black Mountain College, was the best-known Tar Heel literary magazine of its decade, featuring such contributors as Allen Ginsburg, Jack Kerouac, William

Carlos Williams, and Joel Oppenheimer. The *Review* died, however, when financial problems caused the college to close (see chapter 17).

The decade of the sixties marked a tremendous increase in literary magazine activity in the state. The North Carolina Arts Council, created by Governor Terry Sanford and chaired by Sam Ragan, began to provide small monetary grants to publishers and to organize public readings for poets.

In Chapel Hill the *Carolina Quarterly* encountered competition from such publications as Sy Safransky's *Sun*, a magazine of ideas, published since the early 1970s.

Southern Poetry Review, which has enjoyed a reputation for consistent excellence, was created by Guy Owen, who

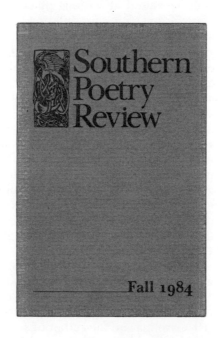

Southern Poetry Review

Fall 1984

had previously edited a small magazine called *Impetus* in Deland, Florida. Since its 1978 removal from the North Carolina State University campus, *Southern Poetry Review* has been located at the University of North Carolina at Charlotte.

The *Greensboro Review*, founded in 1966 as an outlet for graduate students in creative writing at the University of

138

North Carolina at Greensboro, has since grown in national stature. The *Brown Bag*, published in Greensboro irregularly between 1969 and 1971, was edited at various times by poets Fred Chappell, James Applewhite, Tom Kirby-Smith, and others.

Since their beginnings, *St. Andrews Review* at Laurinburg and *Pembroke Magazine* at Pembroke State University in Pembroke have been the strongest literary magazines not located on major college campuses. Norman Macleod was the first editor of *Pembroke Magazine* in 1969. Also published in Pembroke from 1970 to 1972 was *Quetzel*, an Indian-oriented magazine edited by PSU English instructor Randall Ackley for Henry Berry Lowry Community College, a proposed "alternative school" that failed to materialize.

Wilson was the site of *Crucible*, a consistently strong small magazine founded at Atlantic Christian College in 1964, and of a new publication, *Loblolly*, begun in 1984. Other literary magazines of note across the state include the *Above Ground Review*, published first in Durham and then at Arden from 1968 to 1973; *Appalachian Journal*, founded in 1972; and *Cold Mountain Review*, begun in 1974, both at Boone; the *Lyricist*, founded at Campbell College in 1964; *Briarpatch*, published irregularly since 1979 in Davidson; and the *Davidson Miscellany*, founded at Davidson College in 1978. *Tar River Poets*, begun in 1968 in Greenville, became *Tar River Poetry* in 1978. The *Rebel* is the East Carolina University literary magazine, and *Agora* is a commendable small journal published at Belmont Abbey College. *Ex Umbra*, published at North Carolina Central University in Durham, has from time to time produced outstanding issues. *Windhover* is the literary publication at North Carolina State University.

The *International Poetry Review*, an independent magazine, began publishing in Greensboro in spring, 1975. Issued twice yearly, it contains foreign language poetry with facing English translations,

as well as a section of English poetry that often includes works by North Carolina writers. In Winston-Salem, the *Crescent Review*, founded in spring, 1983, specializes in short fiction. At Banner Elk, *Hemlocks and Balsams*, another new magazine, began publication in 1983. The *Uwharrie Review* was begun in 1974 under the sponsorship of the Arts Council of Stanly County. The *Tugboat Review*, now moribund, was published irregularly after 1978 at the University of North Carolina at Wilmington. Langston Hughes was one of the writers who contributed to the sometimes radical magazine *Response*, which operated in the early 1960s in Charlotte. Making more of an impact within the state was the annual *Red Clay Reader*, edited by Charleen Whisnant Swansea from 1964 to 1970.

Of longtime interest to many North Carolinians has been the *State*, started as a weekly magazine in 1933 by Carl Goerch, a "transplanted Yankee." Bill

Jerry Schumacher

Carl Goerch

Sharpe operated it from 1951 until Bill Wright became editor in 1970. Unashamedly homespun in its orientation, the magazine is subtitled "Down Home in North Carolina." Its contents cover everything from commerce to grits, but frequently North Carolina history or literature is treated. A competitor, the

New East, sprang up in Greenville during the early seventies. Changing its name to *Tar Heel*, the magazine flourished for some years but eventually went out of business. Another high-quality magazine that frequently contains articles on North Carolina literature and culture is the quarterly *Southern Exposure*, operated in Durham since the early 1970s and published by the Institute for Southern Studies. The *Spectator* in Raleigh and the *Arts Journal* in Asheville contain reviews of the cultural arts.

Magazines that primarily or occasionally featured the works of North Carolina writers or literature in general were plentiful in the Tar Heel State by the middle 1980s. If the political diversity of the 1960s had waned to some extent, the total number of periodicals was greater than it had ever been before, often with an estimated forty literary magazines operating at any given time.

XX

IN CONCLUSION

Which five North Carolina books have the best chance of still being read a hundred years from now? Of course, no person's guess would be like another's. But simply to serve as a basis for argument, here is a suggested list: John Lawson's *A New Voyage to Carolina* and Thomas Wolfe's *Look Homeward, Angel,* most certainly; W. J. Cash's *The Mind of the South,* quite likely; Robert Ruark's *The Old Man and the Boy* and Manly Wade Wellman's *Who Fears the Devil?* probably. Predicting the longevity of a book, of course, is only a game. Time, and time alone, decides which titles shall last and which shall fade away.

But whatever the future may hold for a book, the production process is alike for the would-be writer of "immortal" poetry and prose and the more or less contented scribbler of potboilers. The requirements are five: paper, pen (or typewriter), thesaurus, dictionary, and an opening sentence. What happens thereafter is in the hands of the gods.

Completed manuscripts, whatever their quality or expectation, do not, even so, tell the full story of a literature. There must be publishers and readers and critics and, heaven help the writer, even literary historians. There must be, if a literature is to be healthy and thriving, editors of magazines, and there must be donors of awards for the best writers and books. There must be others too, especially librarians and proprietors of bookstores.

To the writer, the publisher is the most important of all these supporters and patrons, for without a publisher a book can never make the jump from manuscript to printed page. Pity the nervous publisher, who risks his reputation as a businessman and also money every time a book is put on the market. Since New York has been the publishing center of America for almost a century, most North Carolina writers have to make contacts there, particularly if their books aim at a

Fayetteville Observer-Times, June 23, 1985

Bookmark
—— by Roy Parker Jr.

A SHORT HISTORY OF A SMALL PLACE. A Novel by T.R. Pearson. Linden Press/Simon & Schuster. New York. 381 pages. $16.95.

●

I grew up in an Eastern North Carolina town where there were several certified "conjure women." My great-grandfather was a Confederate deserter, and as a teen-ager my mother "sat with a corpse that rose up at midnight." The police chief's son played the organ for Bank-Night on Wednesday at the Richard Theater. On a summer evening, he climbed the town water tower and jumped.

So I naturally have affinity for Neely, the fictional setting for this diverting first novel by a 29-year-old North Carolinian.

The dust-jacket blurb places Neely on the literary landscape as "east of (Mark) Twain's Mississippi and (William) Faulkner's Yoknapatawpha County."

Geographically, it is in the Blue Ridge foothills somewhere back of Winston-Salem.

In the typography of the heart, it is young and warm and nutty as a fruitcake.

As with several of the new wave of young novelists from Dixie, Pearson speaks his story through the mouth of a babe.

The narrator is teen-ager Louis Benfield, who gets most of his information from "Daddy," a character of prodigious experience and gargantuan appetite for the bizarre.

But then Neely is a place so marked by the zany, the odd, the ineffably eccentric, that state authorities once conjectured there was something in the water.

The story approximately revolves around a spinster lady who emulates my police chief's son, and the funeral of a pet monkey.

But if that sounds strange, you ain't seen nothing yet.

There was the time, for instance, when the visit of Miss Pettigrew (the deceased) to the annual church Christmas pageant causes the Virgin Mary to drop the Baby Jesus, cracking its porcelain head and frightening the goats that were portraying sheep. The Wise Men run away from the goats' horns, and on and on, ending when the Angel of the Lord — suspended from the rafter — unhitches himself and falls through the roof of the stable.

Whew!

There are at least 100 such scenes, antics, vignettes, episodes, and assorted other occurrences in these 381 pages. There are scores of characters.

All interspiced with wisdom passages, folklore, and odds and ends of literary derring-do.

Such as: "In our household we have never kept the seasons by the calendar. Spring commences with the buds on the apricot tree. When Momma lets me go barefoot it is summer. The first chill night after Labor Day means autumn. And I bring winter in myself when I return the rake to the cellar (after raking up under the Mock Orange trees) and meet Momma in the breakfast room where I find her gazing out the back window. 'My, my, Louis,' she always tells me, 'those Mock oranges look a hundred percent better.'"

As you can imagine, this sort of thing makes it very hard to classify this book as a standard novel form. The plot line is barely discernible amid the scenes and characters which tumble so profusely out. But it is there, like a thin stout thread on which are strung a mass of colorful beads.

You would expect to tire of it after a few score pages, once you catch on that this is a literary voyage with a pretty predictable finish, no matter how tempestuous the weather may be before landfall.

But I never did. I savored it to the end.

Part of it is the nostalgic linkage with my own past.

But also for its ring of insane verisimilitude. For its gracious felicity of diction and tone even when caught up in some breathless bit of what otherwise would be slapstick nonsense except that this young writer has positive genius for the discipline of pace.

In it is a curious yet workable mixture of very old and very young, of thin stuff and thick. A fast start for a splendid new talent.

The novel was written 1981-83 while, I presume, the author was a student at N.C. State University. As a matter of fact, it was as if the ghost of that late great soul — Guy Owen — is still haunting those NCSU corridors where he taught and wrote his own unforgettable fiction rooted in the ordinary life of smalltown and rural North Carolina.

Pearson was born near Winston-Salem, and lives now in Fuquay-Varina.

●

national rather than sectional readership. Yet, despite the concentration of publishers in New York, and a few major ones in Boston and Philadelphia and Chicago, North Carolina is better off than one might suspect, just as there are ample periodicals for the writer of poems and short stories.

The best way for a North Carolina book to get the attention of readers and book buyers is a review of it on the book pages of the state newspapers. Betty Hodges of the *Durham Morning Herald*, Sam Ragan of the Southern Pines *Pilot*, Walter Spearman of the *Chapel Hill Newspaper*, Guy Munger of the Raleigh *News and Observer*, Roy Parker, Jr., of the *Fayetteville Observer-Times*, and book-page editors in Greensboro, Winston-Salem, Wilmington, and Asheville are decidedly sympathetic to North Carolina books.

Much later, and long after the book succeeds or fails, the anthologist and literary historian come upon the scene. The anthologist selects the best short pieces and publishes them in a handy one-volume collection. The job of the literary historian is to provide a résumé and a perspective, such as this very *Literary North Carolina*.

Magazine editors and reviewers and publishers do not, however, fill out a writer's world. Like football players and automobile salesmen, a writer wants acclaim for the best of his associates and the best of their efforts. Because of this, supporters and patrons of literature establish literary awards. No North Carolinian is among the six United States citizens who have won the international Nobel Prize in literature. The Pulitzer Prize, top American award, was won by dramatists Hatcher Hughes and Paul Green, but the Pulitzer committee bypassed Thomas Wolfe's *Look Homeward, Angel* and *Of Time and the River* to honor novels long ago forgotten. Thus, if prizewinning is no assurance of literary immortality, it makes glad the heart, even if just temporarily, of the writer who is selected.

Thirteen years before the first Pulitzer Prize was awarded, North Carolina was already acknowledging its own writers. In 1905 President Theodore Roosevelt, on a visit to Raleigh, presented the Patterson Cup to John Charles McNeill for a sheaf of poems later to be published as *Songs, Merry and Sad*. From then on, cups and awards were established to

Patterson Cup

recognize excellence in fiction, nonfiction, children's literature, poetry, history, and many other subgenres, all administered by the state Division of Archives and History through the North Carolina Literary and Historical Association. (See Appendix A.) The most prestigious of all of these trophies is the North Carolina Award, established by the General Assembly and administered by the governor. Each year, at a dinner meeting in Raleigh, the governor, "on behalf of the people of the State of North Carolina," presents four or five awards for achievement in science, public service, fine arts, and literature. Often a North Carolinian living outside the state may be recognized; frequently a recipient in fine arts may also be a writer. A list of all writers, whatever the category cited, who have received the North Carolina Award since it was established, appears in Appendix A.

Winning a literary award does not, even so, ensure the commercial success of a book. It must be bought at bookstores and made available in libraries. The most talked-about books can be

Mayflower Society Cup

North Carolina Award

RICHARD
WALSER
1975

LITERATURE

Sir Walter Raleigh Award

purchased at the small emporiums and the large chain stores throughout the state. There are at least seven bookstores that go out of their way to stock titles by North Carolinians or about North Carolina and keep on their shelves Tar Heel items old, secondhand, and new: The Captain's Bookshelf, Asheville; Carolina Bookshop, Charlotte; The Book Shop (formerly Keith & Martin), Chapel Hill; The Book Room, Raleigh; Stevens's Book Shop, Wake Forest; The Book Trader, Fairmont; and Broadfoot's, Wilmington.

A few large public libraries provide separate sections to shelve their North Carolina books. Among the best known are those at Asheville, Charlotte, Salisbury, Winston-Salem, Greensboro, Fayetteville, Raleigh, Durham, High Point, Wilson,

and Wilmington. Special North Carolina collections can often be found at the state-supported universities. The university library at Chapel Hill has numerically by far the greatest, with its some half million books, pamphlets, pictures, maps, and microfilms dealing with North Carolina. The State Library in Raleigh, primarily a research and extension facility, also specializes in North Carolina books and materials. The largest library in the state is at Duke University with its more than 3 million volumes, but Duke has no separate North Carolina collection.

Roanoke-Chowan Poetry Award

By the time his book is proudly placed on a library shelf, the writer probably is well along into the composition of his next volume. His life, it is said, is a lonely one. He does his best work when he is all

and sheriffs and plumbers meet annually to discuss their mutual interests, and why not writers?

At the instigation of Inglis Fletcher, the first North Carolina Writers Conference was held at Manteo in 1950. At the beginning, it was a loosely organized group, with no dues or bylaws. The only formality was the election of a chairman and a secretary to plan for the next summer's meeting. Requirement for membership was that one must have written at least one book, though even that prerequisite was soon abandoned in order to admit reviewers, publishers, and would-be writers. By 1984 that first small professional group had grown to two hundred assorted members. Routine remained the same. Roundtables and discussion groups were arranged, but the greatest benefit accruing to him who attended was the opportunity to meet his fellow crafts-

Fourth N.C. Writers Conference, Boone, 1953

by himself behind shut doors, with no company but a dictionary and a typewriter. Yet most writers are friendly and sociable people and, like doctors and engineers, they enjoy going to meetings in order to talk with others who are engaged in the same line of work. Paul Green was heard to remark that barbers

man. When the two-day session was over, the writer, regardless of whether he had an established name or was a mere beginner, returned to his desk and typewriter and dictionary, and there he faced the ancient challenge of trying to write a good book.

APPENDIX A:
LITERARY AWARDS

North Carolina Awards for Literature (1964-1985)

SPONSOR: THE STATE OF NORTH CAROLINA

CATEGORY: GENERAL LITERARY EXCELLENCE

1964	Inglis Fletcher; Clarence Poe (fine arts)
1965	Paul Green, Gerald W. Johnson
1966	Bernice Kelly Harris
1967	Jonathan Daniels
1968	Vermont C. Royster, Charles Phillips Russell
1969	Ovid Williams Pierce
1970	Frances Gray Patton
1971	Guy Owen
1972	John Ehle
1973	Helen Smith Bevington, Burke Davis
1974	Thad G. Stem, Jr.
1975	Doris W. Betts
1976	Richard Walser; Foster Fitz-Simons (fine arts)
1977	Reynolds Price; Jonathan Williams (fine arts)
1978	Manly Wade Wellman
1979	Harry Golden
1980	Fred Chappell
1981	Glen Rounds, Tom Wicker
1982	Willie Snow Ethridge
1983	Heather Ross Miller
1984	Lee Smith, Joseph Mitchell
1985	Wilma Dykeman

William Houston Patterson Memorial Cup (1905-1922)

SPONSOR: AWARDED BY THE NORTH CAROLINA LITERARY AND HISTORICAL ASSOCIATION FOR THE PATTERSON FAMILY

CATEGORY: GENERAL LITERARY EXCELLENCE

1905	John Charles McNeill, *Songs, Merry and Sad* (in manuscript)
1906	Edward Mims, *Life of Sidney Lanier*
1907	Kemp Plummer Battle, *History of the University of North Carolina*
1908	Samuel A'Court Ashe, *History of North Carolina*
1909	Clarence Poe, *A Southerner in Europe*
1910	R. D. W. Connor, *Cornelius Harnett: An Essay in North Carolina History*
1911	Archibald Henderson, *George Bernard Shaw: His Life and Works*
1912	Clarence Poe, *Where Half the World Is Waking Up*
1913	Horace Kephart, *Our Southern Highlanders*
1914	J. G. de R. Hamilton, *Reconstruction in North Carolina*
1915	William Louis Poteat, *The New Peace*
1916	No award
1917	Olive Tilford Dargan, *The Cycle's Rim* (poems)
1918	No award
1919	No award
1920	Winifred Kirkland, *The View Vertical and Other Essays*
1921	No award
1922	Josephus Daniels, *Our Navy at War*

The Mayflower Award (1931-1985)

SPONSOR: SOCIETY OF MAYFLOWER DESCENDANTS IN THE STATE OF NORTH CAROLINA

CATEGORY: AT FIRST GIVEN TO A NORTH CAROLINA RESIDENT WITHOUT REGARD TO GENRE; THEN FOR MANY YEARS ALTERNATED BETWEEN FICTION AND NONFICTION; SINCE 1951 HAS BEEN AWARDED ONLY FOR NONFICTION

1931   M. C. S. Noble, *History of the Public Schools in North Carolina*
1932   Archibald Henderson, *Bernard Shaw: Playboy and Prophet*
1933   Rupert B. Vance, *Human Geography of the South*
1934   Erich W. Zimmermann, *World Resources and Industries*
1935   James Boyd, *Roll River*
1936   Mitchell B. Garrett, *The Estates General of 1789*
1937   Richard H. Shryock, *The Development of Modern Medicine*
1938   Jonathan Daniels, *A Southerner Discovers the South*
1939   Bernice Kelly Harris, *Purslane*
1940   David L. Cohn, *The Good Old Days*
1941   Wilbur J. Cash, *The Mind of the South*
1942   Elbert Russell, *The History of Quakerism*
1943   J. Saunders Redding, *No Day of Triumph*
1944   Adelaide L. Fries, *The Road to Salem*
1945   Josephus Daniels, *The Wilson Era: Years of Peace, 1910-1917*
1946   Josephina Niggli, *Mexican Village*
1947   Robert E. Coker, *This Great and Wide Sea*
1948   Charles S. Sydnor, *The Development of Southern Sectionalism, 1819-1848*
1949   Phillips Russell, *The Woman Who Rang the Bell*
1950   Max Steele, *Debby*
1951   Jonathan Daniels, *The Man of Independence*
1952   John McKnight, *The Papacy, A New Appraisal*
1953   Mary T. Martin Sloop and LeGette Blythe, *Miracle in the Hills*
1954   Hugh T. Lefler and Albert Ray Newsome, *North Carolina: The History of a Southern State*
1955   Jay B. Hubbell, *The South in American Literature, 1607-1900*
1956   Glenn Tucker, *Tecumseh, Vision of Glory*
1957   Archibald Henderson, *George Bernard Shaw: Man of the Century*
1958   Ben Dixon MacNeill, *The Hatterasman*
1959   Burke Davis, *To Appomattox: Nine April Days, 1865*
1960   Richard Bardolph, *The Negro Vanguard*
1961   LeGette Blythe, *Thomas Wolfe and His Family*
1962   William P. Sharpe (for Outstanding Literary Achievement over a Period of Years)
1963   Ethel Stephens Arnett, *William Swaim, Fighting Editor*
1964   Glenn Tucker, *Dawn Like Thunder: The Barbary Wars and the Birth of the US Navy*
1965   John Ehle, *The Free Men*
1966   Glenn Tucker, *Zeb Vance: Champion of Personal Freedom*
1967   Joel Colton, *Leon Blum, Humanist in Politics*
1968   George B. Tindall, *The Emergence of the New South, 1913-1945*
1969   John R. Alden, *A History of the American Revolution*
1970   James H. Brewer, *The Confederate Negro, Virginia's Craftsmen and Military Laborers, 1861-1865*
1971   Jonathan Daniels, *Ordeal of Ambition: Jefferson, Hamilton, Burr*
1972   John Bivins, Jr., *The Moravian Potters of North Carolina*
1973   Lionel Stevenson, *The Pre-Raphaelite Poets*
1974   Helen Bevington, *Beautiful Lofty People*
1975   C. Hugh Holman, *The Loneliness at the Core: Studies in Thomas Wolfe*
1976   Eleanor Smith Godfrey, *The Development of English Glassmaking, 1560-1640*
1977   Lawrence Goodwyn, *Democratic Promise: The Populist Moment in America*
1978   Louis D. Rubin, Jr., *The Wary Fugitives: Four Poets and the South*

1979	Paul D. Escott, *Slavery Remembered: A Record of Twentieth-Century Slave Narratives*
1980	William H. Chafe, *Civilities and Civil Rights: Greensboro, North Carolina, and the Black Struggle for Freedom*
1981	Townsend Ludington, *John Dos Passos: A Twentieth Century Odyssey*
1982	Joseph M. Flora, *Hemingway's Nick Adams*
1983	David Reed Goldfield, *Cottonfields and Skyscrapers: Southern City and Region, 1607-1980*
1984	Vermont Royster, *My Own, My Country's Time*
1985	Joel Williamson, *The Crucible of Race*

Sir Walter Raleigh Award (1952-1985)

SPONSOR: HISTORICAL BOOK CLUB OF GREENSBORO

CATEGORY: FICTION

1952	Paul Green (for Outstanding Literary Achievement)
1953	Inglis Fletcher (for Outstanding Literary Achievement)
	Frances Gray Patton, *The Finer Things of Life*
1954	Ovid Williams Pierce, *The Plantation*
1955	Frances Gray Patton, *Good Morning, Miss Dove*
1956	Frances Gray Patton, *A Piece of Luck*
1957	Doris Betts, *Tall Houses in Winter*
1958	Betty Smith, *Maggie-Now*
1959	Ernest Frankel, *Band of Brothers*
1960	Ovid Williams Pierce, *On a Lonesome Porch*
1961	Frank Borden Hanes, *The Fleet Rabble*
1962	Reynolds Price, *A Long and Happy Life*
1963	Richard McKenna, *The Sand Pebbles*
1964	John Ehle, *The Land Breakers*
1965	Doris Betts, *The Scarlet Thread*
1966	Heather Ross Miller, *Tenants of the House*
1967	John Ehle, *The Road*
1968	Sylvia Wilkinson, *A Killing Frost*
1969	Bynum Shaw, *The Nazi Hunter*
1970	Guy Owen, *Journey for Joedel*
1971	John Ehle, *Time of Drums*
1972	Daphne Athas, *Entering Ephesus*
1973	Fred Chappell, *The Gaudy Place*
1974	Doris Betts, *Beasts of the Southern Wild and Other Stories*
1975	John Ehle, *The Changing of the Guard*
1976	Reynolds Price, *The Surface of Earth*
1977	Sylvia Wilkinson, *Shadow of the Mountain*
1978	Mary Sheppard, *All Angels Cry*
1979	Daphne Athas, *Cora*
1980	Guy Owen, *The Flim-Flam Man and Other Stories*
1981	Reynolds Price, *The Source of Light*
1982	Lee Zacharias, *Lessons*
1983	Lee Smith, *Oral History*
1984	Reynolds Price, *Private Contentment*
1985	John Ehle, *Last One Home*

Roanoke-Chowan Award (1953-1985)

SPONSOR: ROANOKE-CHOWAN GROUP OF WRITERS AND ALLIED ARTISTS

CATEGORY: POETRY

1953   Frank Borden Hanes, *Abel Anders*
1954   Thad Stem, Jr., *The Jackknife Horse*
1955   No award
1956   Helen Bevington, *A Change of Sky*
1957   Dorothy Edwards Summerrow, *Ten Angels Swearing*
1958   Paul Bartlett, *Moods and Memories*
1959   Olive Tilford Dargan, *The Spotted Hawk*
1960   Carl Sandburg, (Total of his work)
1961   Carl Sandburg, *Wind Song*
1962   Helen Bevington, *When Found, Make a Verse Of*
1963   Herman Salingar, *A Sigh Is the Sword*
1964   E. S. Gregg, *Reap Silence*
1965   Randell Jarrell, *The Lost World*
1966   Thad Stem, Jr., *Spur Line*
1967   Walter Blackstock, *Leaves Before the Wind*
1968   Paul Baker Newman, *The Cheetah and the Fountain*
1969   Guy Owen, *The White Stallion, and Other Poems*
1970   Charles Edward Eaton, *On the Edge of the Knife*
1971   Paul Baker Newman, *The Ladder of Love*
1972   Fred Chappell, *The World Between the Eyes*
1973   Ronald H. Bayes, *The Casketmaker*
1974   Campbell Reeves, *Coming Out Even*
1975   Marian Cannon, *Another Light*
1976   Fred Chappell, *River: A Poem*
1977   Norman W. Macleod, *The Distance*
1978   Mary Louise Medley, *Seasons and Days*
1979   Fred Chappell, *Bloodfire: A Poem*
1980   Fred Chappell, *Wind Mountain, a Poem*
1981   James Applewhite, *Following Gravity*
1982   Thomas Heffernan, *The Liam Poems*
1983   Reynolds Price, *Vital Provisions*
1984   Betty Adcock, *Nettles*
1985   Fred Chappell, *Castle Tzingal*

AAUW Award (1953-1985)

SPONSOR: AMERICAN ASSOCIATION OF UNIVERSITY WOMEN

CATEGORY: JUVENILE BOOKS

1953   Ruth and Latrobe Carroll, *Peanut*
1954   Mebane Holoman Burgwyn, *Penny Rose*
1955   Ruth and Latrobe Carroll, *Digby, the Only Dog*
1956   Julia Montgomery Street, *Fiddler's Fancy*
1957   Nell Wise Wechter, *Taffy of Torpedo Junction*
1958   Ina B. Forbus, *The Secret Circle*
1959   Thelma Harrington Bell, *Captain Ghost*
1960   Jonathan Daniels, *Stonewall Jackson*
1961   Glen Rounds, *Beaver Business*
1962   Manley Wade Wellman, *Rifles at Ramsour's Mill*
1963   Julia Montgomery Street, *Dulcie's Whale*
1964   Randall Jarrell, *The Bat-Poet*
1965   Alexander Key, *The Forgotten Door*

148

1966	Richard Walser and Julia Montgomery Street, *North Carolina Parade, Stories of History and People*
1967	Glen Rounds, *The Snake Tree*
1968	Neal F. Austin, *A Biography of Thomas Wolfe*
1969	Mary Lina Bledsoe Gillett, *Bugles at the Border*
1970	Mebane Holoman Burgwyn, *The Crackajack Pony*
1971	Suzanne Newton, *Purro and the Prattleberries*
1972	No award
1973	Barbara M. Parramore, *The People of North Carolina*
1974	Suzanne Newton, *C/O Arnold's Corners*
1975	Alexander Key, *The Magic Meadow*
1976	Glen Rounds, *Mr. Yowder and the Lion Roar Capsules*
1977	Ruth White Miller, *The City Rose*
1978	Suzanne Newton, *What Are You up to, William Thomas?*
1979	Suzanne Newton, *Reubella and the Old Focus Home*
1980	Caroline B. Cooney, *Safe As the Grave*
1981	No award
1982	Suzanne Newton, *M. V. Sexton Speaking*
1983	Glen Rounds, *Wild Appaloosa*
1984	Belinda Hurmence, *Tancy*
1985	Catherine Petroski, *The Summer That Lasted Forever*

APPENDIX B:

SELECTED ANTHOLOGIES AND GENERAL WORKS ON NORTH CAROLINA LITERATURE

GENERAL

Bain, Robert, Joseph M. Flora, and Louis D. Rubin, Jr., editors. *Southern Writers: A Biographical Dictionary*. Baton Rouge: Louisiana State University Press, 1979.

Binding, Paul. *Separate Country: A Literary Journey Through the American South*. New York & London: Paddington Press, 1979.

Blackburn, William, editor. *A Duke Miscellany: Narrative and Verse of the Sixties*. Durham: Duke University Press, 1970.

_____, editor. *One and Twenty: Duke Narrative and Verse, 1924-1945*. Durham: Duke University Press, 1945.

_____, editor. *Under Twenty-five: Duke Narrative and Verse, 1945-1962*. Durham: Duke University Press, 1963.

Branson, Levi. *Branson's Hand Book of North Carolina Authors*. Raleigh: Levi Branson, 1900.

Carr, John, editor. *Kite-Flying and Other Irrational Acts: Conversations with Twelve Southern Writers*. Baton Rouge: Louisiana State University Press, 1972.

Greensboro Group, editors. *Writers' Choice: Selected Poetry and Fiction by 58 North Carolina Writers*. [Greensboro]: TransVerse Press, 1981.

Henderson, Archibald. *North Carolina: The Old North State and the New*. Chicago: Lewis Publishing Company, 1941. 2 volumes. Vol. I, 546-654; Vol. II, 644-833.

Higgs, Robert J., and Ambrose N. Manning, editors. *Voices from the Hills: Selected Readings of Southern Appalachia*. New York: Frederick Unger; Boone: Appalachian Consortium Press, 1975.

Hoyle, Bernadette. *Tar Heel Writers I Know*. Winston-Salem: John F. Blair, 1956.

Library of Southern Literature. Atlanta: Martin and Hoyt, 1907-1923. 17 volumes.

North Carolina Authors. Chapel Hill: University of North Carolina Library, 1952.

Obrist, Cynthia Louise Walters. "North Carolina Little Magazines, 1950-1980: An Annotated Bibliography." Library Science Master's Paper, University of North Carolina at Chapel Hill, 1983.

Paschal, George Washington. *A History of Printing in North Carolina*. Raleigh: Edwards & Broughton, 1946.

Pool, Bettie Freshwater, editor. *Literature in the Albemarle*. Baltimore: Published for the author by the Baltimore (Md.) City Printing and Binding Company, 1915.

Powell, William S., editor. *North Carolina Lives: The Tar Heel's Who's Who*. Hopkinsville, Ky.; Historical Records Association, 1962.

Rehder, Jessie, editor. *Chapel Hill Carousel*. Chapel Hill: University of North Carolina Press, 1967.

Rubin, Louis D., Jr., et al., editors. *The History of Southern Literature*. Baton Rouge: Louisiana State University Press, 1985.

Stem, Thad, Jr. *The Tar Heel Press*. Charlotte: Heritage Printers, Inc., for the North Carolina Press Association, Inc., 1973.

Thornton, Mary Lindsay, compiler. *A Bibliography of North Carolina, 1589-1956*. Chapel Hill: University of North Carolina Press, 1958.

Walser, Richard, assisted by E. T. Malone, Jr. *Literary North Carolina: A Brief Historical Survey*. Rev. ed. Raleigh: Division of Archives and History, North Carolina Department of Cultural Resources, 1986.

Walser, Richard, and Mary Reynolds Peacock. *Young Readers' Picturebook of Tar Heel Authors*. Rev. fifth ed. Raleigh: Division of Archives and History, North Carolina Department of Cultural Resources, 1981.

Watson, Robert, compiler. *The Greensboro Reader.* Edited by Robert Watson and Gibbons Ruark. Chapel Hill: University of North Carolina Press, 1968.

DRAMA

Green, Paul. *Out of the South.* New York: Harper & Brothers, 1939.
Harris, Bernice Kelly. *Folk Plays of Eastern Carolina.* Edited by Frederick H. Koch. Chapel Hill: University of North Carolina Press, 1940.
Koch, Frederick H., editor. *Carolina Folk Comedies.* New York: Samuel French, 1931.
_____. *Carolina Folk-Plays.* New York: H. Holt, 1928.
Nordstrom, Mary. *Outdoor Drama.* Winston-Salem: Hunter Publishing Company, 1985.
Parker, John W., editor. *Adventures in Playmaking.* Chapel Hill: University of North Carolina Press, 1968.
Selden, Samuel, and Mary Tom Sphangos. *Frederick Henry Koch, Pioneer Playmaker: A Brief Biography.* Chapel Hill: University of North Carolina Library, 1954.
Spearman, Walter, assisted by Samuel Selden. *The Carolina Playmakers: The First Fifty Years.* Chapel Hill: University of North Carolina Press, 1970.
Walser, Richard, editor. *North Carolina Drama.* Richmond: Garrett and Massie, 1956.

FICTION

Broadfoot, Thomas W., editor. *North Carolina Fiction, 1958-1971: An Annotated Bibliography.* Wendell: Broadfoot's Bookmark, 1972.
Corrington, John William, and Miller Williams, editors. *Southern Writing in the Sixties: Fiction.* Baton Rouge: Louisiana State University Press, 1966.
Powell, William S., editor. *North Carolina Fiction, 1734-1957: An Annotated Bibliography.* Chapel Hill: University of North Carolina Library, 1958.
Walser, Richard, editor. *Short Stories from the Old North State.* Chapel Hill: University of North Carolina Press, 1959.

POETRY

Albright, Alex, and Luke Whisnant, editors. *Leaves of Greens: The Collard Poems.* Ayden, N.C.: Ayden Collard Festival, Inc., in cooperation with the Pitt County Community Schools, 1984.
Brooks, Eugene Clyde, editor. *North Carolina Poems.* Raleigh: North Carolina Education, 1912.
Clarke, Mary Bayard [Tenella, pseud.], compiler. *Wood-Notes; or, Carolina Carols: A Collection of North Carolina Poetry.* 2 vols. Raleigh: Warren L. Pomeroy, 1854.
Kleppel, Placid, editor. *A Bibliography of North Carolina Poetry.* Belmont: Abbey Press, 1934.
Moore, Hight C., compiler. *Select Poetry of North Carolina.* Raleigh: Edwards & Broughton, 1894.
North Carolina Poetry Society. *A Time for Poetry: An Anthology of the North Carolina Poetry Society.* Winston-Salem: John F. Blair, 1966.
Owen, Guy, editor. *North Carolina Poetry/1970* (special issue of *Southern Poetry Review*). Raleigh: Southern Poetry Review, 1970.
Owen, Guy, and Mary C. Williams, editors. *Contemporary North Carolina Poetry.* Winston-Salem: John F. Blair, 1977.
_____, editors. *North Carolina Poetry: The Seventies* (special issue of *Southern Poetry Review*). Raleigh: Southern Poetry Review, 1975.
Shuman, R. Baird, editor. *Nine Black Poets.* Durham: Moore Publishing Company, 1968.
Smith, Stephen E., editor. *New North Carolina Poetry: The Eighties.* University Center, Mich.: Green River Press, 1982 (c. 1983).
Walser, Richard, editor. *North Carolina Poetry.* Rev. ed. Richmond: Garrett and Massie, 1951.
_____. *Poets of North Carolina.* Richmond: Garrett and Massie, 1963.
Ward, Vernon, and Frank W. Motley, editors. *Sixty North Carolina Poets* (special North Carolina poetry issue of *Tar River Poets* featuring Robert Waters Grey). Greenville: East Carolina University Poetry Forum Press, 1974.
Watterson, William B., editor. *Carolina Voices.* Banner Elk, N.C.: Janeric Press, 1983.

Index

A

160

Fuller, Edwin Wiley, 28; illus., 28
Fuquay-Varina, 120

G

Gaelic language, 7
Gales, Joseph, 131
Gales, Mrs. Joseph (Winifred Marshall), 9, 16
Gallopade Publishing Group, 135
Gallows Lord, The, by Virginia L. Rudder, 116
Game of Hearts, by Sara Logan, 126
Gameplayers of Zan, The, by M. A. Foster, 95
Gardner, Martin, 95
Garrett and Massie (publishing company), 151
Garrett, Mitchell B., 146
Gaston, William, 15, 16, 19
Gastonia, 80, 81, 104, 137
Gaudy Place, The, by Fred Chappell, 122, 147
Gauntlet, The, by James Street, 84
Gay, James, 8
Generous Man, A, by Reynolds Price, 119
Genoa, by Paul C. Metcalf, 118
Gentle Insurrection and Other Stories, The, by
    Doris Betts, 117
Gentleman of Elvas, 2
*Geographical Catechism, To Assist Those Who
    Have Neither Maps nor Gazetteers, A*, by
    Henry Pattillo, 14, illus., 14
Geographical Reader for the Dixie Children, by
    Marinda B. Moore, 18
George Bernard Shaw: His Life and Works, by
    Archibald Henderson, 145
George Bernard Shaw: Man of the Century, by
    Archibald Henderson, 146
Georgetown (S.C.), 2
Georgia, 80, 116, 124
German language, 12
Germany, 54, 56
Get Hot or Get Out, by Jonathan Williams, 110
Get Out of Town, by Paul Connolly, 89
Ghost Tales of the Uwharries, by Fred T.
    Morgan, 49
Gibson, Grace, 114
"Gift of the Magi, The," by O. Henry, 99
Gilbert, Marie, 112
Gillett, Mary Lina Bledsoe, 149
Ginsburg, Allen, 138
Girl Called Boy, A, by Belinda Hurmence, 71
Girl from Ipanema, The, by Charles Edward
    Eaton, 108
Glass People, by Gail Godwin, 124
Go and Hush the Baby, by Betsy Byars, 69
Godfrey, Eleanor Smith, 146
Godfrey, Thomas, 6, 8, 51; illus. of tombstone, 7
Godwin, Gail, 124-125; illus., 124
Goerch, Carl, 34, 139; illus., 139
Gold Star, by Zach Hughes, 96
Golden Enemy, The, by Alexander Key, 68
Golden, Harry, 34, 44, 104, 145
Goldfield, David Reed, 147
Goldsboro, 13, 106, 126

Gone a Hundred Miles, by Heather Ross Miller,
    122
Gone with the Wind, by Margaret Mitchell, 34
Good Morning, Miss Dove, by Frances Gray
    Patton, 101, 147
Good Old Days, The, by David L. Cohn, 146
Goodwyn, Lawrence, 146
Goose Elk (fictional place), 69
Gordon, Ian, 89
Gotschalk, Felix C., 95
Grace, Eugene V., 135
Graham, Billy, 45
Graham, Frank Porter, 78-79
Grand Canyon, 118
*Grand Old Ladies: North Carolina Architecture
    during the Victorian Era*, by Marguerite
    Schumann, 40
Grandfather Mountain, 13, 126
Grandfather Tales, by Richard Chase, 48
Grandfather's Tales of North Carolina History,
    by Richard Benbury Creecy, 63; illus., 63
Granville County, 14, 105
*Grave Humor: A Collection of Humorous
    Epitaphs*, by Alonzo C. Hall, 35
Graveyard of the Atlantic, by David Stick, 40;
    illus., 41
Gray, Elizabeth Janet, 63
Great Saturday Night Swindle, The, by Stephen
    E. Smith, 102
Great Smoky Mountains, 39, 65, 66, 100
Greece, 123
Green, Jaki Shelton, 112
Green, Lewis W., 119
Green, Paul, 46, 47, 51, 52, 53, 54, 55, 100, 116,
    137, 142, 144, 145, 147, 151; illus., 53
Green Pond, by Evan Brandon, 81
Green River Press, 151
Greene, Nathanael, 77
Greensboro, 9, 18, 24, 33, 35, 49, 84, 90, 95, 98,
    99, 104, 111, 112, 113, 127, 131, 139, 142, 143,
    150
Greensboro Group, The, 112, 150
Greensboro News and Record, 39
Greensboro Reader, The, edited by Robert
    Watson and Gibbons Ruark, 112, 151
Greensboro Review, 138
Greenville, 30, 48, 139, 140, 151
Gregg, E. S., 148
Grenadine Etching, by Robert Ruark, 34
Grenadine's Spawn, by Robert Ruark, 34
Grey, Robert Waters, 113, 151
Grosscup, Ben S., 39
Groundwork, by Robert Morgan, 109
Growing Up in Tier 3000, by Felix C. Gotschalk,
    95
Growth of North Carolina, The, by Albert R.
    Newsome and Hugh T. Lefler, 38
Grube, Adam, 6
Gualdape River, 2
Guaxule, 2

162

S

178